The Roosevelts

The Roosevelts

An Intimate History

Geoffrey C. Ward

Based on a documentary film by Ken Burns
With a preface by Ken Burns

Picture research by Susanna Steisel · Design by Maggie Hinders

 ALFRED A. KNOPF · NEW YORK · 2014

THIS IS A BORZOI BOOK
PUBLISHED BY ALFRED A. KNOPF

Copyright © 2014 by Geoffrey C. Ward and Ken Burns
All rights reserved. Published in the United States
by Alfred A. Knopf, a division of Random House LLC, New York,
and in Canada by Random House of Canada Limited, Toronto,
Penguin Random House companies.

www.aaknopf.com

Knopf, Borzoi Books, and the colophon
are registered trademarks of Random House LLC.

ISBN: 978-0-307-70023-0 (hardcover) ISBN: 978-0-385-35306-9 (eBook)

Front-of-jacket photographs (left): Theodore Roosevelt Collection, Houghton Library, Harvard University;
(center and right) Franklin D. Roosevelt Presidential Library. Photo arrangement by Evan Barlow.
Jacket design by Kelly Blair

Manufactured in the United States of America
First Edition

For the late Arthur M. Schlesinger, Jr.,

who helped us at the beginning,

and for William E. Leuchtenburg,

who has been helping us ever since

Contents

Hip! Hip! Hurrah!

In the spring of 1869, the Roosevelts began a yearlong trip to Europe, hoping that travel abroad might somehow improve ten-year-old Theodore's health. He kept a journal in which he displayed characteristics that would stay with him all his life: strong opinions and insatiable curiosity; a highly developed sense of drama; a craving always to be at the center of things; and a love of the outdoors that helped him in his struggle to breathe.

MAY 12TH. We sail in the English steamship, Scotia. . . . We three jumped around the deck and played. . . . I was a little seasick . . .

JUNE 18TH. EDINBURGH. We saw the Melrose Abbey (a mere ruin) and then crossed the Tweed (quite a decent brook) to Dryburg Abbey where there was the tomb of Sir Walter Scott.

JULY 10. We all went to the Tower of London . . . and I put my head on the block where so many had been beheaded.

AUGUST 21. SWITZERLAND. We went through the Grimsel Pass and I, Papa and a Scotch gentleman walked far ahead and had fresh cream and raspberries. I walked 20 miles and Papa 22 miles.

AUGUST 23. SWITZERLAND. In the afternoon we . . . threw paper balls at [the] waiter and chambermaid and rushed around upstairs and downstairs to dodge them.

SEPTEMBER 24. VENICE. I was sick with asthma and did not sleep at all.

SEPTEMBER 26. TRIESTE. I was sick of the asthma. I sat up for four successive hours [and Papa made me smoke a cigar {to help me breathe}].

SEPTEMBER 30. VIENNA. Father and I went to a Natural History Museum. In the department of nests I recognized two with birds which I had seen wild at home. Their names: "Baltimore Oriole" and "Waxen Chatterer."

OCTOBER 27. COLOGNE. It is my [eleventh] birthday and the first of my birthdays that it snowed on. . . . Papa played tag with us [and] told us a story of a runaway slave and at five we had dinner, and afterwards I received my presents. . . . Splendid!

NOVEMBER 22. PARIS. Mama showed me the portrait of Edith Carow and her face stirred in me homesickness and longing for the past which will come again never, alack, never.

DECEMBER 8. NICE. [We] tossed bread on the heads of waiters and ran about generally. I read till Mama came in and then she lay down and I stroked her head and she felt my hands and nearly cried because they were feverish. We had a fine sociable time . . .

DECEMBER 14TH. SAN REMO. The beggars came round. . . . Papa bought two baskets of doughy cakes. A great crowd of boys and girls and women. We tossed the cakes to them and I fed them like chickens with small pieces of cake and like chickens they ate it. . . . We made [them] give three cheers for the U.S.A. before we gave them cakes.

DECEMBER 31, 1869. MT. VESUVIUS. I began the ascent of the snow-covered [slope and] soon passed the rest far behind.

JANUARY 31, 1870. ROME. We saw the Pope and we walked along and he extended his hand to me and I kissed it!! Hem!! Hem!!

SUNDAY, APRIL 17. FONTAINEBLEAU. Today was the happiest Easter I ever spent. Mama, Papa and all we children went in the woods to hunt for violets and see if the bunnies had [laid] any eggs. [We] had Sunday school in the woods and picked cowslips and heard the cuckoo sing. We had such a happy time.

MAY 25. This morning we saw land of America . . . New York!! Hip! Hip! Hurrah!

Seeing this portrait of his seven-year-old playmate Edith Carow made Theodore long for home; leaving her behind, he wrote as his voyage began, had been "verry hard."

You Must Make Your Body

Happy to be home, Theodore returned to the activities he enjoyed most—reading books of history and science and adventure and running what he grandly called the "Roosevelt Museum," a constantly expanding collection of "curiosities and living things." He kept live mice in his shirt drawer and dead ones in the icebox, tied turtles to the laundry tubs, and took lessons in taxidermy, a noisome hobby that made family maids reluctant to enter his bedroom.

"My triumphs," he recalled, "consisted in such things as bringing home and raising—by the aid of milk and a syringe—a family of very young gray squirrels, in fruitlessly endeavoring to tame an excessively unamiable woodchuck, and in making friends with a gentle, pretty, trustful white-footed mouse which reared her family in an empty flower pot."

Unable to win his rightful place in his loving but fiercely competitive family through size and strength, he learned the power of words and charm and book learning to call attention to himself. He talked incessantly, his thoughts sometimes tumbling so far ahead of his words that some visitors thought he suffered from an impediment.

There was nothing wrong with Theodore's mind, his father told him in 1872, but sickness, his father said, was "always a shame and often a sin." To overcome asthma, he told his fragile son, "[y]ou must make your body." Theodore did his best to comply, spending hour after hour on rings and parallel bars set up on the third-floor piazza of the family home. He took boxing lessons from an ex-prizefighter, too, so that his younger brother, Elliott, wouldn't have to shield him from bullies anymore.

When he was fourteen, his father presented him with a gun; when he couldn't manage to hit anything with it, Theodore Sr. bought him spectacles that opened up the world still further. He began to think of pursuing a career in science.

The Roosevelts went to Africa in 1873 and spent several months sailing on the Nile, while work was finished on a new family house on West Fifty-seventh Street. By then, Theodore was fit enough to spend whole days in the saddle, shooting some two hundred birds for his collection.

He would never fully conquer asthma, but his struggle against it reinforced his belief that life itself was an ongoing battle. His father gave him the credo by which he would continue that struggle: "Do things. Be sane. Don't fritter away your time; create, act, take a place wherever you are and be somebody; get action."

ABOVE Theodore at eleven

ABOVE The freshly completed American Museum of Natural History dominates the still largely unbuilt Upper West Side of Manhattan, 1880. Over the years, the museum became a sort of Roosevelt family project. Theodore Sr. was one of its founders; the documents of incorporation were signed in his parlor. Both his son Theodore and his distant cousin Franklin Roosevelt would contribute specimens to its collections.

LEFT Theodore's rendering of a pet mouse, one of the prize exhibits in his personal "Roosevelt Museum"

A Superabundance of Energy

I n the summer of 1875, the United States was in the third year of a depression. Factories were shuttered. Banks had failed. A million workers had lost their jobs, and most of those who continued to work saw their wages cut by a quarter. Striking coal miners and railroad workers battled state militias.

None of it affected the Roosevelts, now enjoying their second season in the rented house they called "Tranquility" at Oyster Bay. "These Roosevelts were without inhibitions to an unusual degree," a summer playmate remembered, and "so rarely gifted that [they] seemed touched by the flame of divine fire."

All five Roosevelt children were photographed that summer. Each had a distinct personality.

LEFT Bamie, shown here with the father she adored, was nineteen in 1875 but old beyond her years. She suffered from a deformation of the spine, and had become an adviser rather than a playmate to her younger siblings, who always saw her as one of "the big people."

OPPOSITE The rest of the Roosevelt children: Elliott, at the right, was fourteen that summer—handsome, athletic, and charming, but already persuaded that he could never match the achievements of his older brother. Twelve-year-old Corinne, her back to the tree, was the baby of the family, witty, sensitive, and worshipful of her brothers. But the focus of everyone's attention was fifteen-year-old Theodore, at the left. He seemed infatuated with everything—so long as it provided him with the opportunity to excel. As a cousin later remembered, "He always thought he could do things better than anyone else." He was rugged, exuberant, aggressive, and in almost perpetual motion: riding, swimming, shooting, competing in the long jump and hundred-yard dash against his brother and his cousins. He rarely won; he always tried. "His energy seems so superabundant," his father wrote, "that I feel it may get the better of him in one way or another." The young woman seated on the grass is Theodore's sometime sweetheart, Edith Carow.

See Here, Roosevelt

In the fall of 1876, Theodore Roosevelt descended on Harvard. His sister Bamie had picked out and furnished his Cambridge rooms. A manservant was hired to black his boots and keep things tidy. "If you asked me to define in one word the 'temper' of the Harvard I knew," one of Roosevelt's Harvard contemporaries recalled, "I should say it was patrician, strange as that word may sound to American ears." Roosevelt fit right in, choosing his friends exclusively from classmates he called "the gentleman sort," concerned that he not become "very intimate" with anyone whose "antecedents" he didn't know.

But he was also uniquely himself. A young Cambridge woman who met him during his freshman year remembered him as freakish, "with stuffed snakes and lizards in his room, with a peculiar violent vehemence of speech and manner, and an overriding interest in everything." He quickly wearied of the dry kind of science being taught and spoke up so often in his geology class that the professor snapped, "See here, Roosevelt, let me talk."

ABOVE Mrs. Richardson's boardinghouse at 16 Winthrop Street in Cambridge, where Theodore lived throughout his time at Harvard, and a flyer providing the first-known opportunity to hear him hold forth

RIGHT An undergraduate makes his way across Harvard Yard during Theodore's sophomore year: "When it was not considered good form to move at more than a walk," a classmate remembered, "Roosevelt was always running."

OPPOSITE Theodore, ready for rowing. He hurled himself into sports at Harvard: rowing, wrestling, boxing. A classmate was initially amused to watch him work out in the gymnasium: Roosevelt must be a "humble-minded chap," he wrote, "to be willing to give such a lady-like exhibition in a public place." But he changed his mind when he watched him ice-skate on Fresh Pond for three hours in the face of a freezing wind that drove everyone else off the ice.

He Was Everything to Me

Corruption had been a central issue in the presidential election of 1876. Republicans abandoned the struggle over the status of freedmen in the South in the interests of a more lucrative ongoing battle with the Democrats over the spoils of office. Everything seemed to be for sale, and bosses in both parties were determined that it stay that way.

In 1877, Theodore Roosevelt Sr. allowed the new Republican president, Rutherford B. Hayes, to nominate him as collector of customs as a symbol of his administration's commitment to civil service reform. But in the end, the old, corrupt machine crushed his nomination. He said he was relieved. "To purify our Customhouse would have been a terrible undertaking," he told his son. But he did feel "sorry for the country as it shows the power of partisan politicians who think of nothing higher than their own interests. We cannot stand so corrupt a government for any great length of time."

Two days after his appointment fell through, Theodore Roosevelt Sr. collapsed. On February 9, 1878, he died of cancer of the bowel. He was only forty-six. His eldest son rushed home from Harvard too late to say goodbye. Theodore was shattered. "Sometimes when I realize my loss I feel as if I should go wild," he wrote. "He was everything to me. . . . I have lost the only human being to whom I told everything. . . . With the help of my God I will try to lead such a life as he would have wished." His father's example would be a touchstone for Theodore Roosevelt to the end of his life.

Still mourning at Oyster Bay that summer, Theodore suffered a second blow. He and his childhood friend Edith Carow had always been close and may have had an understanding that they would marry. But in the summer house one afternoon they quarreled and ended their relationship. Neither ever told anyone what had come between them. Theodore later admitted to Bamie only that "we both of us had . . . tempers that were far from the best." Afterward, he tried to outpace his anger and his grief—rowing furiously back and forth across Long Island Sound, galloping so hard he injured his horse, shooting a neighbor's dog when it dared bark at him.

Finally, he fled to the Maine woods to hike and hunt, finding there what he would always find in wildness—a world in which to restore himself.

ABOVE This portrait of Theodore Roosevelt Sr., painted by Daniel Huntington from a photograph, is one of four commissioned by his children after his death. Without him, Bamie recalled, "we all had to work out our own salvation."

OPPOSITE Nineteen-year-old Theodore Roosevelt, still grieving three months after the loss of his father. "I often feel badly that such a wonderful man as Father would have had a son of so little worth as I," he noted in his diary. "I realize more and more every day that I am as much inferior to Father morally and mentally as physically."

The Sunny-Faced Queen

Theodore Roosevelt now had a sizable inheritance—so large, he remembered, it allowed him to live "like a prince" in Cambridge. "Funnily enough, I have enjoyed quite a burst of popularity since I came back," he wrote his mother after returning to Harvard. "Please send my silk hat at once. Why has it not come before?"

Everything seemed to go his way. "I stand 19th in the class, which began with 230 fellows," he boasted to his sister Bamie, and "only one gentleman stands ahead of me." He edited a newspaper, won election to Phi Beta Kappa, and was asked to join three of the college's most prestigious organizations, the Dickie, Hasty Pudding, and the Porcellian Club. And somehow he found the time—as an undergraduate—to begin writing a 498-page history, *The Naval War of 1812*, that would eventually influence a generation of naval planners.

He also fell in love. Alice Lee was seventeen when he first met her at a classmate's home. She was tall, blond, full of life. "See that girl?" Theodore said. "I am going to marry her, she won't have me, but I am going to have her!" It took him a year to win her. She was his "sunny-faced Queen," his "bright bewitching darling." "So pure and holy," he wrote, "that it almost seems profanation to touch her." She called him "Teddy" and "Teddykins."

They were married in Brookline, Massachusetts, on October 27, 1880. "Alice looked perfectly lovely," a guest remembered, "and Theodore was so happy, and responded in the most determined Theodore-like tones." Edith Carow was among the guests and made a point of outdancing everyone else.

"Our intense happiness," Theodore noted in his diary a few days after the wedding, "is too sacred to be written about." Together, he and Alice began planning a big hilltop house of their own at Oyster Bay—a fourteen-bedroom "cottage" to be called "Leeholm" in her honor.

ABOVE, LEFT Alice Hathaway Lee. Theodore's pursuit of her was so intense that he once ordered a pair of dueling pistols, intending to challenge another suitor to a duel. A cousin hurried to Cambridge to calm him down.

LEFT Theodore (middle row, third from the left) with fellow members of Harvard's oldest and most exalted final club, Porcellian. "I am delighted to be in [the club]," he told Bamie. "There is a billiard table, magnificent library, punch room &c, and my best friends are in it." On Sundays, the boys enjoyed champagne breakfasts.

OPPOSITE In a formal group photograph in the summer of 1880, Theodore (front row, second from right) seems unable to tear his gaze away from the fiancée he was to marry on his twenty-second birthday in October. "I worship you so that it seems almost desecration to touch you," he told her, "and yet when I am with you I can hardly let you out of my arms."

So Much Enjoyment in the Country

ABOVE Sara Delano Roosevelt in 1878, two years before Bamie Roosevelt introduced her to James Roosevelt. The most beautiful of five sisters, at home in French and German, she had been courted on three continents by then; her most ardent suitor had been the future architect Stanford White, whom her protective father had dismissed as "the red-headed trial."

ABOVE Sara Delano Roosevelt in 1878, two years before Bamie Roosevelt introduced her to James Roosevelt. The most beautiful of five sisters, at home in French and German, she had been courted on three continents by then; her most ardent suitor had been the future architect Stanford White, whom her protective father had dismissed as "the red-headed trial."

OPPOSITE James Roosevelt at home in Hyde Park. A reform-minded Democrat widely admired by his Republican neighbors, he served a single term as town supervisor but refused ever to run for any other public office. To him, the sweaty world of electoral politics was not for gentlemen.

That same fall of 1880, there was another marriage in the extended Roosevelt clan.

Fifty-six-year-old James Roosevelt belonged to the Hudson River branch. His summer home was "Springwood," a sprawling estate high above the river's eastern shore, near the village of Hyde Park. There he lived the life of an English country gentleman, his money made in coal and railroads and investments. Springwood delighted him. "I often wonder," he once wrote, "why men are satisfied to live all their lives between brick walls and thinking of nothing but money and the so-called recreations of so-called society when there is so much enjoyment in the country."

His servants and tenant farmers all called him "Mr. James." He was an Episcopalian and a Democrat who took both his religious and civic duties seriously. But he had been a widower for four years. His late wife, a distant cousin, had died of heart disease. Their only child, a son, James Roosevelt Roosevelt, nicknamed "Rosy," had married an heiress to the Astor fortune and moved away.

In his loneliness, Mr. James had once suggested marriage to Theodore Roosevelt's sister Bamie. Although she thought him the "most absolutely upright gentleman" she ever knew, she gently turned him away—he was older than her late father would have been had he lived—and then invited him to dinner to meet a friend of hers, Miss Sara Delano. "He talked to her the whole time," Theodore's mother, Mittie, remembered. "He never took his eyes off her."

Sara Delano was twenty-five, less than half James's age, tall and regal, a member of a French Huguenot clan that had flourished in America even longer than the Roosevelts had. Her father, Warren Delano, who had made himself a millionaire selling tea and opium in the China trade, had "the true patriarchal spirit," Sara remembered, and supervised every detail of family life within the big walled estate he'd built at Newburgh, twenty-five miles downriver from Hyde Park. No Democrat could ever work for him, Warren Delano once explained, because, while not all Democrats were horse thieves, it had been his experience that all horse thieves were Democrats.

His five daughters attracted what he called an "avalanche of suitors," but he was startled when Mr. James asked for Sara's hand. James was a business associate and Mr. Delano's rough contemporary, after all, and he was a Democrat. Before he gave his approval, Mr. Delano had to be convinced that Sara was, as he said, "earnestly, seriously, entirely" in love.

She was. James Roosevelt and Sara Delano were married on October 7, 1880, just six months after they met. A guest remembered that several women wept at the thought that "such a lovely girl should marry an old man."

On January 30, 1882, at Springwood, they had a son. Sara and her baby very nearly did not make it. Labor had stretched on for more than twenty-four hours. Sara was given too much chloroform. The doctor had to breathe life into her boy.

Seven weeks later, at St. James' Episcopal chapel in Hyde Park, the baby was christened Franklin Delano Roosevelt. Sara asked Elliott Roosevelt, Theodore's younger brother, to be his godfather. Mittie Roosevelt came to visit and wrote that the child was "such a fair, sweet, cunning, little bright . . . darling baby. Sara looks so very lovely with him like a Murillo Madonna and infant."

ABOVE This splendid enameled watch from Cartier was presented to Sara when Mr. James learned his new wife was pregnant. Its face is ringed with pearls; diamonds decorate the reverse side.

OPPOSITE Franklin and his mother, 1882. "At the very outset he was plump, pink and nice," she remembered. "I used to love to bathe and dress him." For the first nine years of his life, a Scottish nurse saw to his needs, but his mother was rarely more than a few steps away.

Who's the Dude?

Six days before Franklin Delano Roosevelt was born, Theodore Roosevelt made his first headlines—as the brand-new Republican assemblyman from Manhattan's 21st District and, at twenty-three, the youngest man ever elected to the New York Assembly. Albany had never seen anyone quite like him. A fellow assemblyman remembered his first glimpse of the newcomer: "Suddenly our eyes . . . became glued on a young man who was coming in through the door. His hair was parted in the center, and he had sideburns. He wore a single eye-glass. . . . He carried a gold-headed cane in one hand, a silk hat in the other, and he walked in the bent-over fashion that was the style with the young men of the day. . . . 'Who's the dude?' I asked another member. . . . 'That's Theodore Roosevelt of New York.'"

He had dropped plans to become a scientist while still at Harvard, then dropped out of Columbia Law School, refused to go into the family business, and finally surprised everyone by deciding to try his hand at Republican politics and run for the assembly.

Some of his friends had advised him against it. Politics in either party was no place for a gentleman, they told him. It was a "low" business, run by "saloon-keepers, horse-car conductors and the like." "That merely means that the people I know do not belong to the governing class," he answered, "and I intend to be one of the governing class."

He took to the floor again and again, denouncing both Democratic and Republican machines, pushing for municipal reform bills sometimes even when they were opposed by his own party's leaders, forcing an investigation of a state supreme court justice for accepting bribes, and denouncing Jay Gould, the powerful Wall Street manipulator, for offering them. "I . . . mean to act up here [in Albany] on all questions as nearly as possible as I think Father would have done. . . . I thoroughly believe in the Republican Party when it acts up to its principles—but if I can prevent it I never shall let party zeal obscure my sense of right and decency."

When the courts overturned his bill meant to relieve the terrible conditions under which tenement dwellers were forced to manufacture cigars, he angrily denounced the judiciary. "It was this case," he remembered, "which first waked me to a dim and partial understanding of the fact that the courts were not necessarily the best judges of what should be done to better social and industrial conditions. They knew legalism, but not life."

Always, he would seek a middle course between change and stability: he had a deep lifelong fear of what he called "the mob." He saw everything in terms of right and wrong, and seemed, one critic wrote, "to have been born with his mind made up." Those who dared oppose him were by definition self-interested and dishonest. "The average Democratic Catholic Irishman . . . as represented in this Assembly," he confided to his diary, "is a low, venal, corrupt and unintelligent brute."

They didn't like him, either. When a hulking assemblyman known as "the McManus," a representative of the Democratic Tammany machine, was overheard planning to toss the freshman assemblyman in a blanket, Roosevelt tracked him down. "By God!" he told him. "If you try anything like that I'll kick you, I'll bite you. I'll kick you in the balls. I'll do anything to you—you'd better leave me alone." The McManus backed off.

Democratic newspapers lampooned him as "His Lordship" and "Jane-Dandy." Republican papers praised his courage and independence. But all the newspapers loved him for the colorful copy he provided. He was reelected twice, served a term as minority leader, and made himself the best-known Republican in New York State—all before he was twenty-six.

ABOVE Assemblyman Theodore Roosevelt in 1884. To a good many Albany veterans he seemed at first a representative of what one called the "kid glove, scented, silk-stocking, poodle-headed, degenerate aristocracy." But as the months went by he began to make friends outside his own circle, he remembered, men able to "grapple with real men in real life . . . bankers and bricklayers, . . . merchants and mechanics, . . . lawyers, farmers, day-laborers, saloon-keepers, clergymen and prize-fighters."

OPPOSITE Roosevelt's greatest triumph as a New York legislator, heralded by a cartoonist for *Puck*. His bill changed the New York City charter to empower New York mayors to hire and fire personnel without having to consult the Tammany-dominated board of aldermen. The cartoon was published on February 20, 1884, just one week after Roosevelt suffered the worst tragedy of his life.

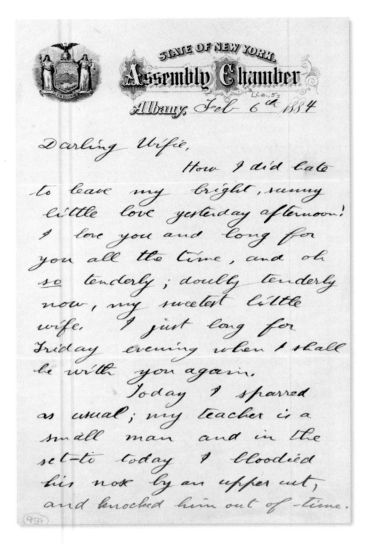

The Light Has Gone Out of My Life

February of 1884 looked to be a momentous month for the Roosevelts. Alice was nine months pregnant and under the care of her mother-in-law in Manhattan. Theodore was engaged in a fierce struggle in Albany over his measure to reform the New York City charter—and delighting in the fact that the newspapers were calling it the "Roosevelt Bill."

The baby was due on Thursday, February 14—Valentine's Day. Theodore had come home the previous weekend but on Tuesday decided to make a quick trip back to Albany to see how his bill was faring. He was in the legislative chamber on Wednesday morning the 13th when he was handed a telegram: his wife had given birth to a healthy girl the night before. She would be named for her mother—Alice. His fellow assemblymen crowded around to offer congratulations. He was "full of life and happiness," one remembered.

Then a second telegram arrived. He rushed for the railroad station. Dense winter fog shrouded the tracks. It took more than five hours to reach New York. He did not get to 6 West Fifty-seventh Street until midnight. His brother, Elliott, opened the door. "There is a curse on this house," he said. "Mother is dying, and Alice is dying, too."

Mittie Roosevelt had typhoid fever. Alice was barely conscious, weakened by childbirth, and suffering from Bright's disease—kidney failure. Helpless, Theodore went back and forth between their bedsides. His mother died at three o'clock in the morning of February 14. Alice died at two o'clock that afternoon. Only the baby survived.

Two hearses waited outside the double funeral service outside the Fifth Avenue Presbyterian Church. Many in the congregation wept at the sight of two rosewood coffins side by side.

Afterward, Theodore gave his favorite photograph of Alice to his aunt, saw to it that his newborn daughter was christened, handed her off to his sister Bamie to raise as if she were her own, and asked her to help close up the Roosevelt house; he could not bear to enter it again.

Then, just three days after the funeral, he hurried back to Albany and the legislative struggle. "From that time on there was a sadness about his face that he never had before," a fellow assemblyman recalled. "You could not talk to him about it. He did not want anybody to sympathize with him. It was a grief that he had in his soul."

He could only rarely bring himself to speak of Alice again, not even when speaking with the troubled daughter who would grow up bearing her name.

ABOVE In Theodore's last letter to his wife, written from Albany a week before her death, he wanted her to know both how much he missed her and how well he'd done in his daily sparring match with the prizefighter he'd hired to teach him how to box.

In the diary image:

FEBRUARY, THURSDAY 14. 1884.

X

The light has gone out of my life

ABOVE Alice Roosevelt was just twenty-two years old when her husband marked her passing in his diary. "She was beautiful in face and form, and lovelier still in spirit," he would write in a formal tribute a few weeks later. "As a flower she grew, and as a fair young flower she died."

RIGHT Two-year-old Alice Lee Roosevelt and Bamie Roosevelt, whom she called "Auntie Bye," 1886. Bamie was "the single most important influence in my childhood," Alice remembered, "the only one I really cared about when I was a child."

The Party Is Most of All

Roosevelt hurled himself back into committee work, reporting out as many as twenty-one bills on a single day. If he weren't working so hard, he admitted to a friend, "I think I should go mad." But he refused the nomination for a fourth assembly term. He needed to get away, he said, to the West, where he had spent a summer as a would-be rancher the year before.

But first, he had one more duty to perform. The Republican Party was gathering in Chicago to pick its presidential nominee. Roosevelt was a member of the New York delegation. The front-runner was Senator James G. Blaine of Maine—handsome, magnetic, and so corrupt, one editor wrote, that "he wallows in spoils like a rhinoceros in an African pool." To Theodore, it was a vivid echo of the situation that had lured his late father into politics eight years earlier, and he determined to act so far as possible as he believed his father would have acted.

He helped lead a band of reform-minded delegates pledged to stop Blaine. One of his closest allies was a member of the Massachusetts House of Representatives and fellow Porcellian, Henry Cabot Lodge. So elegant and aristocratic his enemies called him "La-de-da Lodge," he was as high-minded as Roosevelt and even better read. They would be intimate friends and allies almost all their lives.

Their candidate—George F. Edmunds, a clean but colorless senator from Vermont—never stood a chance. The best Roosevelt and his allies could manage to do was delay the vote, embarrass the eventual nominee—and anger party veterans, one of whom denounced Theodore as a "schoolboy" with an "inexhaustible supply of insufferable dudism and conceit."

The battle was so bitter that when it ended many of Roosevelt's allies bolted the Republican Party and voted Democratic rather than support its nominee. They expected him to do the same.

He did not. "The man is not everything," he said; "the party is most of all." Old friends accused him of abandoning principle, betraying the memory of his father. But Roosevelt had learned from his time in Albany. He'd chosen to go it alone at first, he remembered, and most of the bills he cared about had been blocked by resentful colleagues. "I suppose that my head was swelled," he wrote. "That was my first lesson in real politics. It is just this: if you are cast on a desert island with only a screw-driver, a hatchet, and a chisel to make a boat with, why, go make the best one you can. It would be better if you had a saw, but you haven't. So [it is] with men." Unless he could find a better way to work with other politicians, he would never be able to do the things he wanted done or wield the power he already wished to wield; only by remaining a Republican, he now argued, would he ever have the chance to do good. Some old friends remained unconvinced. "The great good, of course," one said, "was Teddy."

ABOVE Theodore Roosevelt, New York delegate to the 1884 Republican convention. "I found Mr. Roosevelt to be a young man of rather peculiar qualities," an Ohio delegate wrote. "He is a little bit young, and on that account has not quite so much discretion as he will have after a while."

OPPOSITE One of a series of savage *Puck* cartoons by Bernhard Gillam that depicted Republican presidential nominee James G. Blaine indelibly tattooed with alleged sins and indiscretions that helped bring about a Democratic victory for Chester A. Arthur that November.

PUCK.

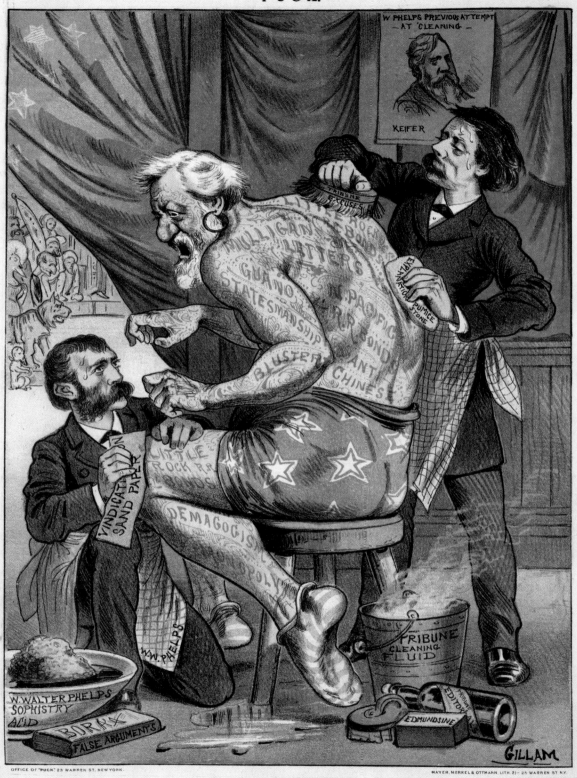

"LOVE'S LABOR 'S LOST."

Black Care Rarely Sits Behind a Rider Whose Pace Is Fast Enough

Back in 1883, Theodore Roosevelt had begun to build himself a ranch house at Chimney Butte on the Little Missouri in the badlands of North Dakota. It had been an investment at first, and he would eventually sink half his fortune in it. But now, in the summer of 1884, the badlands became a refuge, a place to rebuild his broken spirit.

When he arrived he was brooding, uncharacteristically silent, unable to sleep. "Nowhere," he wrote, "not even at sea, does a man feel more lonely than when riding over the far-reaching, seemingly never-ending plains; and after a man has lived a little while on or near them, their very vastness and loneliness and their melancholy monotony have a strong fascination for him. . . . Nowhere else does one seem so far off from all mankind."

Ranching, Roosevelt believed, was "the pleasantest and healthiest and most exciting phase of American existence." He was not alone. Hundreds of easterners were flocking to the plains that summer, eager to cash in on what was being called the "beef bonanza."

Roosevelt was an exotic presence at first, once overheard urging his cowboys to "Hasten forward quickly there!" His men called him "Old Four-Eyes" behind his back; when one drunken cowboy dared say it to his face and threatened him with two revolvers, Roosevelt knocked him senseless.

But he eventually won respect, helping to build a second ranch house, called Elkhorn, with his own hands, enduring a monthlong roundup that covered almost a thousand miles, hunting down three thieves who had stolen his boat and marching them forty-five miles to the nearest sheriff's office—and then carefully staging the capture again for the camera.

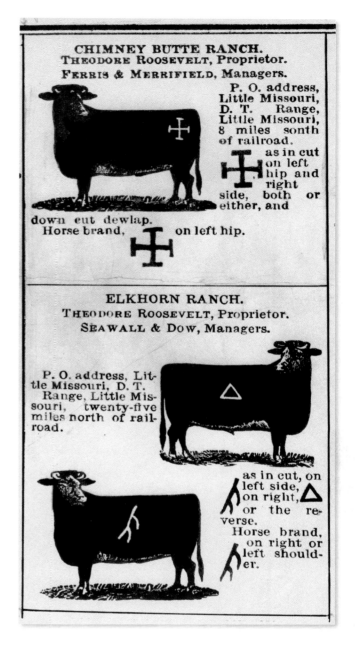

OPPOSITE Studio portrait of Theodore Roosevelt intended for the frontispiece of *Hunting Trips of a Ranchman*, the first of two books he wrote about his time in the West. He had designed his own fringed buckskin costume; his silver-mounted Bowie knife came from Tiffany's. "I now look like a regular cowboy dandy," he wrote Bamie, "with all my equipment finished in the most expensive style."

ABOVE Theodore Roosevelt's cattle brands, depicted in the *Stockgrowers' Journal*, published in Miles City, Montana. The Chimney Butte Ranch—also called the Maltese Cross—was forty miles from the Elkhorn; to get from one ranch to the other required a rider to cross the Little Missouri more than twenty times.

He spent weeks on the hunting trail, too, shooting 170 birds and animals on one camping trip through the Bighorns—including a grizzly bear felled at twenty paces, Roosevelt reported, with a bullet placed so "exactly between his eyes as if I had measured the distance with a carpenter's rule." All of it eased his burdens. "I have had . . . enough excitement and fatigue to prevent overmuch thought," he wrote to Bamie, "and moreover I have been at last able to sleep well at night."

The eleven months or so that Theodore Roosevelt spent off and on in the West between 1883 and 1887 changed him. Everyone could see it. His voice grew deeper, less shrill. "He weighed one hundred and fifty pounds," a friend remembered, "and was clear bone, muscle and grit." He had also proved he could hold his own among men of every class, and he had demonstrated to himself once again that action enabled him to conquer the grief that had threatened to destroy him. "Black care," he wrote, "rarely sits behind a rider whose pace is fast enough."

"There were all kinds of things of which I was afraid at first," Theodore Roosevelt remembered, "ranging from grizzly bears to 'mean' horses and gun-fighters; but by acting as if I was not afraid I gradually ceased to be afraid. Most men can have the same experience if they choose."

"If it had not been for my years in North Dakota," he wrote, "I never would have become President of the United States."

ABOVE Theodore and his favorite horse, Manitou. "Perfectly sure-footed . . . willing and spirited," Manitou carried him for miles across the badlands—and away from his demons.

OPPOSITE, TOP Roosevelt stands guard over his supposed captives on the bank of the Little Missouri. He really did hunt down and arrest three thieves, but the two men whose faces are mostly hidden here were actually employees who helped with the capture, while the identity of the third man is unknown.

OPPOSITE, BOTTOM A thicket of antlers marked the eight-room Elkhorn Ranch house. In the evenings, a friend remembered, Roosevelt liked to sit in one of the rockers on the porch, reading poetry.

ABOVE Etching of St. George's Church, by F. Hopkinson Smith, and a page from the church register recording the marriage of Edith Kermit Carow, "Spinster," to Theodore Roosevelt, "Ranchman"

OPPOSITE Edith Carow, photographed shortly before her marriage. She was refined, self-assured, and disciplined—"born mature," as her friends liked to say—and she had been devoted to Theodore since childhood. But she was proud, too, and never quite got over the fact that she had been his second choice.

Edith

On August 29, 1886, the *New York Times* reported, "The engagement was announced during the week of ex-Assemblyman Theodore Roosevelt and Miss [Edith] Carow of New York. Mr. Roosevelt is a widower, his first wife, formerly Miss [Lee] of Boston, died [two] years ago."

When Bamie Roosevelt opened the paper and read of her brother's supposed engagement, she demanded an immediate retraction. It was unthinkable that her brother, who had so recently lost his wife, would be planning to remarry so soon—and still more unthinkable that he could have become engaged to one of their closest childhood friends without her knowledge.

She was wrong. A letter arrived from Theodore a day or two later, begging her forgiveness. He and Edith had been secretly engaged for a year, it said. He planned to marry her in London before Christmas. "You could not reproach me one-half as bitterly for my inconstancy and unfaithfulness as I reproach myself for my inconstancy and unfaithfulness," he told his sister. "Were I sure there were a heaven my one prayer would be I might never go there, lest I should meet those I loved on earth."

He had believed so deeply that a second marriage would represent a betrayal of the departed that he had deliberately avoided coming in contact with Edith Carow for months after Alice's death. But they had encountered one another by accident and began to see one another in secret, Theodore confining his diary entries to the single letter "E" to keep their courtship from prying eyes.

To his surprise, the Republican Party asked him to run for mayor that fall. He made a spirited run but came in a poor third, behind the Democratic winner and a Labor candidate, Henry George.

The next day, he boarded a ship bound for England using an assumed name to keep from drawing attention to the coming wedding. On December 2, 1886, a day when all of London was hung with fog, he and Edith were quietly married at St. George's Church on Hanover Square.

Sagamore

After the newlyweds returned to the United States in the spring of 1887, they moved into the newly completed house at Oyster Bay that Theodore and Alice Lee had planned together. It was no longer Leeholm; there was to be no reference made to Theodore's first wife. Now it was Sagamore Hill—"Sagamore" being the Algonquin word for "chieftain."

Edith asked to be allowed to raise Theodore's daughter, Alice, as if she were her own. "It almost broke my heart to give her up," Bamie remembered, and nothing Alice's father or her stepmother could do ever made her feel wholly part of the family.

At Sagamore in September of 1887, Edith gave birth to a child of her own, Theodore Roosevelt Jr. Five more children would follow.

ABOVE, TOP AND RIGHT A family snapshot of Sagamore's proud builder, in front of the dining-room fireplace, taken in 1894; and the house in winter, surrounded by the snowy slopes on which Roosevelt and his children skied and tobogganed

OPPOSITE Alice sits at the center of this 1899 photograph, encircled by family pets and all her half siblings. Clockwise from left: Ted Jr., Ethel, Quentin, Kermit, and Archie

For the next thirty-two years, no matter what official role Theodore Roosevelt was called upon to play, no matter where his duties took him, his real home and headquarters would always be Sagamore Hill. "At Sagamore Hill," he wrote, "we love a great many beautiful things—birds and trees and books, and all things beautiful, and horses and rifles and children and hard work and the joy of life. We have great fireplaces and in them the logs roar and crackle during the long winter evenings. The big piazza is for the hot-still afternoons of summer. . . . There could be no healthier and pleasanter place in which to bring up children than in that nook of old-time America around Sagamore Hill."

OPPOSITE, LEFT AND RIGHT Edith leads Ethel down the driveway, and Alice and Ted Jr. watch their father teach football to an exuberant scrum of Roosevelt cousins.

ABOVE Theodore Roosevelt times a footrace between young Roosevelts in front of the barn at Sagamore Hill. "I love all these children and have great fun with them," he told his sister-in-law, "and I am touched by the way they feel I am their special friend, champion and companion." Both young Franklin and Eleanor Roosevelt would prize every chance they had to join their cousins at Sagamore Hill.

LEFT Edith and Alice frolic with three family dogs on the lawn.

VOL. XXV.—No. 644.   NEW YORK, JULY 10, 1889.   PRICE, TEN CENTS.

KEPPLER & SCHWARZMANN, Publishers.   COPYRIGHT, 1889, BY KEPPLER & SCHWARZMANN.   PUCK BUILDING, Cor. Houston & Mulberry Sts.

ENTERED AT THE POST OFFICE AT NEW YORK, AND ADMITTED FOR TRANSMISSION THROUGH THE MAILS AT SECOND CLASS RATES.

THE BRAVE LITTLE GIANT-KILLER.

SPOILS SYSTEM GIANT.— Calm yourself, Theodore — if you go too far, you 'll find yourself jerked back mighty sudden !

A Thorn in Our Side

Roosevelt's ranching adventure had ended in financial disaster. The coldest winter in recorded history swept across the plains in the winter of 1886–1887. Hundreds of thousands of cattle froze to death—including most of Theodore's herd. "The losses are crippling," he admitted to Bamie, and in the coming years he would often have to fall back on his writing simply to meet expenses. Before he was through he would publish some thirty-five volumes, on everything from bear hunting to Oliver Cromwell to what he believed to be the principles of Americanism.

In early 1888, he was hard at work on the first volume of what would become a best-selling four-volume history, *The Winning of the West*. "I'm a literary feller, not a politician these days," he told a friend.

But he didn't mean it. He was still only thirty, too young to abandon the political field, too eager for action to settle for life behind a desk. He campaigned hard that fall for General Benjamin Harrison, the successful Republican candidate for president, even though he privately thought him just "a genial little runt," and was rewarded with appointment as one of three federal civil service commissioners in Washington. He made the most of it, battling publicly with the postmaster general, who had dismissed thousands of workers merely because they were Democrats. "That young man," Harrison muttered, "wants to put the whole world right between sunrise and sunset."

He also conducted probes of political appointees who tried to get around the law that made it illegal to demand campaign funds from federal employees.

"How do you do your cheating?" he asked one.

"Well," the man answered, "we do our cheating honorably."

"I have made this Commission a living force," Roosevelt boasted, "and in consequence the outcry among the spoilsmen has become furious." He proved so evenhanded that Grover Cleveland, Harrison's Democratic successor, eventually asked him to stay on. "Well, my boy," said a departing member of Harrison's cabinet, "you have been a thorn in our side during four years. I earnestly hope that you will remain to be a thorn in the side of the next administration."

Roosevelt learned the ways of Washington during his six years in the nation's capital and he made friends who would prove useful to him later in his career. "There was a vital radiance about the man," one Washingtonian remembered, "a glowing unfeigned cordiality toward those he liked that was irresistible." But rooting out unqualified postmasters did not command the sustained national attention he craved. "I used to walk past the White House," he remembered, "and my heart would beat a little faster as the thought came to me that possibly—possibly—I would some day occupy it as President."

OPPOSITE An 1889 *Puck* cartoon by Louis Dalrymple suggests that President Benjamin Harrison—wearing the too-large hat of his grandfather, President William Henry Harrison—will keep the impetuous Roosevelt from doing any real damage to the spoils system. But Roosevelt was soon "battling with everybody," he wrote, "the little gray man in the White House looking on with cold and hesitating disapproval."

ABOVE TR's friend Henry Cabot Lodge, now a Massachusetts congressman, was instrumental in persuading Harrison to offer Roosevelt a job in his administration, even though the president "was by no means eager" to do so.

The Moral Maniac
and Little Nell

On August 17, 1891, Theodore Roosevelt opened the *New York Sun* and read a headline he had feared was coming but had hoped never to see: ELLIOTT ROOSEVELT INSANE. There had been potential scandal in the Roosevelt family at least once before: Theodore's uncle Robert had fathered two sets of children, one legitimate, one with a longtime mistress whom he married after his first wife died. But that story had never reached the newspapers. This was different.

The story of Elliott Roosevelt's sad decline embarrassed Theodore and wounded his sisters, but its impact on Elliott's daughter, Eleanor, would shape the way she saw the world and her role within it.

At first, Elliott had seemed the more promising of the Roosevelt boys. But in his teens he had begun to fall behind. Crushing headaches, inexplicable seizures, and an opaque diagnosis of "congestion of the brain" ended his schooling. He couldn't seem to find a focus or hold a job even in businesses run by understanding relatives, and spent his time yachting, hunting big game, playing polo, riding to the hounds—and drinking.

Theodore had hoped Elliott's marriage to Anna Hall would "give the dear old boy . . . something to work for," and when Elliott's first child, Anna Eleanor Roosevelt, was born on October 11, 1884, Theodore was her proud godfather. Elliott was delighted at her birth, and called her "Little Nell" after the relentlessly virtuous orphaned heroine of Dickens's *The Old Curiosity Shop*. But her mother seems to have been disappointed in her almost from the first. Anna was herself a celebrated beauty while Eleanor was plain, grave, shy. She called her daughter "granny" and once explained to her that since she had "no looks" she would need to have especially good manners.

Anna would bear two more children, Elliott Jr. and Gracie Hall, but she was a distracted mother, hurt and baffled by her husband's increasingly strange behavior, soon worsened by fresh addictions to drugs as well as drink. "It is all horrible beyond belief," Theodore told Bamie. "He is a maniac morally as well as mentally . . . a flagrant male swine." Elliott took at least two mistresses; threatened his wife, then begged for forgiveness, then threatened her again; vowed to kill himself; finally got a family maid pregnant. To keep that scandal out of the newspapers, the Roosevelts had to pay thousands of dollars to the woman's family, had Elliott committed to a French asylum for a time, and afterward insisted he stay away from his wife and children unless he changed his ways. He could not do it.

OPPOSITE Five-year-old Eleanor Roosevelt and her father, Elliott Roosevelt, 1889. Elliott was erratic, unfaithful to his wife, and alcoholic, but to his daughter he would remain always "the love of my life."

ABOVE Anna Hall Roosevelt, Eleanor's mother, was thought so beautiful that one summer when she and her husband were in Europe Robert Browning begged just to be permitted to read aloud to her while she was having her portrait painted. "She never entered a room as others did," a woman friend recalled, "she seemed almost to float forward."

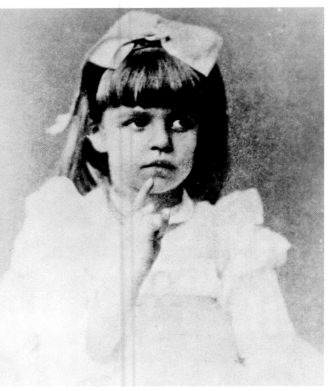

Meanwhile, migraines forced his anguished wife to spend days in her darkened bedroom, where seven-year-old Eleanor was allowed to sit with her and stroke her head for hours at a time. "The feeling that I was useful was perhaps the greatest joy I experienced," she remembered. That would be true all her life. To be useful was to feel that she belonged to someone; if she could not be loved, she could at least be needed.

In December 1892, at the age of twenty-nine, Anna Hall Roosevelt died of diphtheria, and Eleanor and her brothers were sent off to live with their maternal grandmother—pious, grim, dutiful. An unstable aunt lived at home. So did two drunken uncles. None of them was much interested in Eleanor. Within six months, three-year-old Elliott Jr. would die of the same disease that had taken his mother. Eleanor was a lonely girl, she remembered, timid, withdrawn, and "frightened of practically everything"—mice, the dark, other children, "displeasing the people I lived with." Her only solace was dreams of her banished father, who sent her letters full of promises he could never keep: she would come and care for him someday; they would travel the world together; he would show her the Taj Mahal by moonlight. "Somehow," she remembered, "it was always he and I."

Elliott was now drinking half a dozen bottles of brandy and champagne a day. "He can't be helped," Theodore wrote, "and he must simply be let go his own gait." On August 13, 1894, suffering from delirium tremens, he tried to climb out a second-floor Manhattan window, raced hysterically up and down the stairs, collapsed with a seizure, and died the following day. He was only thirty-four. When Theodore went to see his brother's body, his sister Corinne recalled, "he was more overcome than I have ever seen him—cried like a little child."

Eleanor's memories of her parents left her with a mixed legacy. She remembered most her preoccupied mother's severity and distance that ill-equipped her to be a nurturing mother when the time came. She worked hard to embody the qualities her father had encouraged—"unselfishness, generosity, loving tenderness and cheerfulness"—but his example also helped distort her perceptions of people; she tended to exaggerate their virtues at first, and then was inordinately disappointed later on when, inevitably, they failed to act as she had dreamed they would. From the sad lives of both her parents she also learned that no one's love for her was likely to last, that those upon whom she counted most were sure to let her down.

During her infrequent visits to Sagamore Hill, Theodore Roosevelt was always warm toward his late brother's daughter: he once hugged her so hard he tore the buttonholes out of her petticoat. But he was also fearsome: when he learned she could not swim, he ordered her to jump into Oyster Bay anyway. She plunged to the bottom, came up gasping for air, and was left with a lifelong fear of water. "Poor little soul, she is very plain," Edith Roosevelt told Bamie after one of Eleanor's visits. "Her mouth and teeth seem to have no future." It seems to have occurred to no one in the family to see to it that her crooked teeth were straightened.

Bamie would indirectly prove Eleanor's salvation. She had spent a season overseas in a girl's school run by an extraordinary woman named Marie Sou-

OPPOSITE, TOP Eleanor at two and a half in 1887. Her parents had left her with relatives for six months that year, hoping a long vacation would calm her father's unpredictable behavior. She felt abandoned and asked her aunt, "Where is baby's home now?"

OPPOSITE, BOTTOM "Little Nell Scolding Elliott," Elliott Roosevelt's favorite photograph of his daughter. She herself remembered that she had been "very solemn" even as a small child, "entirely lacking in the spontaneous joy and mirth of youth."

ABOVE Eleanor and her father at the home he built in Hempstead, Long Island, in the late autumn of 1889. In constant pain from a shattered ankle, he was now addicted to morphine and laudanum as well as alcohol.

LEFT Eleanor and her brothers, Elliott Jr. and Gracie Hall Roosevelt, 1891. They were now living with their mother in New York; their father was living with his mistress in Paris. Eleanor knew only that "something was wrong with my father, and from my point of view nothing could be wrong with him."

ABOVE Eleanor at ten, with the pony that was a gift from her absent father. By the time this photograph was taken, at her grandmother Hall's summer home in 1894, her mother and her little brother Elliott Jr. were dead, and she wished only to be left alone to live in what she called "a dream world in which I was the heroine and my father the hero." Within weeks, her father, too, would die.

RIGHT Eleanor at fourteen, with her surviving brother, Gracie Hall Roosevelt. She wrote to him nearly every day when he was sent off to Groton School because, she said, she wanted him to feel that he belonged to someone.

OPPOSITE, TOP Fifteen-year-old Eleanor (back row, third from right), surrounded by her schoolmates during her first year at Allenswood School. Her headmistress had already singled her out as "Excellent. The most amiable girl I have ever met; she is nice to everybody, very eager to learn and highly interested in all her work."

OPPOSITE, BOTTOM Tiger-claw necklace: Elliott Roosevelt shot the tiger from which these claws were taken in 1881, and had them mounted in India as a gift for his mother. Eleanor inherited it and wore it at formal occasions throughout her life.

vestre. When Eleanor's grandmother Hall thought she might benefit from a year or two away from her increasingly erratic uncles, Bamie suggested she be sent to Allenswood, Souvestre's boarding school, now located just outside London.

The three years Eleanor spent there were the happiest of her life, she remembered. It was at Allenswood, a cousin recalled, "that [she] for the first time was deeply loved, and loved in return." Eleanor was especially proud when she was elected captain of the field hockey team and eventually became the most admired girl in the school.

But it was her relationship with Mademoiselle Souvestre that meant the most to her. The headmistress was intellectually alive, socially conscious, independent minded. "Why was your mind given you," she liked to ask her students, "but to think things out for yourself?" She devoted herself to the tall, diffident American orphan and brought out all the tact, intelligence, discipline, energy, and empathy that would characterize Eleanor later in life. "Whatever I have become," Eleanor would say many years later, "had its seeds in those three years of contact with a liberal mind and strong personality."

Midnight Rambles

At eight thirty in the morning on Monday, May 6, 1895, thirty-seven-year-old Theodore Roosevelt started up the steps of New York police headquarters at 300 Mulberry Street. A knot of eager reporters rushed along behind, trying to keep up. "Where are our offices?" he shouted. "What do we do first?"

It was a rhetorical question. The New York Police Department was famously corrupt, and the new Fusion mayor of New York had appointed Roosevelt one of four police commissioners with orders to clean it up. He was elected president of the board but was powerless to act without the consent of his three fellow members.

At first, Roosevelt was wildly popular. His favorite exclamations became his watchwords—"Bully!" and "Dee-lighted!" Roosevelt forced the police commissioner and his chief lieutenant to resign rather than have him look into their finances. Newspapermen couldn't get enough of him. "Mr. Roosevelt . . . shows a set of teeth calculated to unnerve the bravest of the Finest," wrote Arthur Brisbane of the New York *World*. "They are broad teeth, they form a perfectly straight line. The lower teeth look like a row of dominoes. . . .

They seem to say tell the truth . . . or he'll bite your head off. . . . But Mr. Roosevelt's voice is the policeman's hardest trial. It is an exasperating voice, a sharp voice, a rasping voice. It is a voice that comes from the tips of the teeth and seems to say in its tones, 'What do you amount to anyway?'"

He sometimes affected a distinctive costume—straw hat, pink shirt, black sash with tassels—and he took reporters with him as he prowled New York at night, on the lookout for policemen who dared doze or drink on duty. "These midnight rambles are great fun," he said. "My whole work brings me in contact with every class of people. . . . I get a glimpse of the real life among the swarming millions."

But things began to go wrong when Roosevelt took it upon himself to "rigidly enforce" a Sunday law that was supposed to shutter all of Manhattan's fifteen thousand saloons on the Sabbath. In doing so, he struck at the heart of police graft, but he also alienated German workingmen who looked forward to a stein of beer on their one day off. When thirty thousand of them paraded to protest, Roosevelt insisted on attending, and when an angry marcher called out, *"Wo ist der Roosevelt?"* he leaned forward in the reviewing stand and shouted back, *"Hier bin ich!"* A reporter asked how he could uphold a statute the public opposed. "I do not deal with public sentiment," he said. "I deal with the law."

Roosevelt's action led to a mass exodus of German Americans to the Democrats at the next New York election—and added to the enmity of the man who controlled the state's Republican Party. Ex-Senator Thomas Collier Platt was known as the "Easy Boss" because of his hushed, courteous manner, but behind the scenes he was cold-eyed and immovable. Platt saw Roosevelt as "a perfect bull in a china shop," and tried to have him removed from his post. Roosevelt's fellow commissioners also eventually grew to resent his noisy prominence and began to vote down his proposals.

When Republican Senator William McKinley of Ohio was elected president in 1896, Roosevelt lobbied him hard for a new federal post: assistant secretary of the navy. He'd been interested in the sea—and sea power—since boyhood. McKinley was an amiable, cautious conservative, privately worried that Roosevelt was "too pugnacious . . . always getting into rows with everybody." When McKinley asked Platt for his opinion, the Easy Boss said he'd be delighted to see Roosevelt return to Washington.

The Peacefulness
and Regularity of Things

Franklin Delano Roosevelt was fifteen that spring and finishing up his first year at Groton School. It had not been easy for him. Nothing in his upbringing had prepared him for life among other boys away from home. "In thinking back to my earliest days," he once remembered, "I am impressed by the peacefulness and regularity of things. . . . Hyde Park was the center of the world."

Some children are loved; Franklin Roosevelt was adored. His mother kept him in dresses and long curls until he was nearly six, and then dressed him in kilts and miniature sailor suits. She gave him his daily bath until he was almost nine. Nannies and tutors came and went. His infrequent playmates were mostly the children of other country gentlemen up and down the river.

When he and his father rode around the farm each morning, the Roosevelt

ABOVE The parents of five-year-old Franklin talked him into wearing a kilt before dropping into a Washington, D.C., photographer's studio in 1887. A few days later, they visited Mr. James's friend Grover Cleveland in the White House. As they were leaving, the weary president shook Franklin's hand and said, "My little man, I am making a strange wish for you. It is that you may never be president of the United States."

tenants doffed their hats and called the boy "Master Franklin." His father taught his son to shoot and sled, to sail an iceboat on the frozen Hudson, and to steer the family yacht through the cold Canadian waters around their summer home on Campobello Island off the coast of Maine. And he passed on intact his unfailing good humor. Franklin called him "Popsy."

A reporter would one day ask Sara if she had always wanted her son to become president. "Never, oh never!" she answered. Her ambition for him had been loftier, she said: "The highest ideal I could hold up before our boy—to grow up to be like his father, straight and honorable, just and kind, an upstanding American."

Then, in 1890, when Franklin was eight, Mr. James suffered a heart attack. He recovered, but his doctors warned that his survival depended on being shielded from all unnecessary worry. That warning brought Sara and her son still closer together in a loving conspiracy to keep Mr. James alive.

From birth, Franklin had been what his grandfather Delano called "a very nice child, always bright and happy." Now, his impulse toward unwavering cheer intensified. Unpleasantness was not to be acknowledged. The Roosevelts

ABOVE Master Franklin and Mr. James at Springwood in 1891. Franklin rides his pony Debby; his father sits astride Doolittle, the last of the stable of trotters he had once maintained.

spent four summers at a German health spa, Bad Nauheim, where Mr. James took the waters and Franklin did his best to entertain himself while pretending not to notice his father's fellow patients—"half-crippled sufferers," one remembered, "with pallid ghastly faces, limping to the springs on crutches, and looking as if their next step will be into their graves."

Back at Springwood, his parents encouraged him to fill his time with hobbies—photography, and collecting coins and stamps and books about the navy. Like his increasingly celebrated cousin, he shot and classified birds, but then had them professionally preserved. His mother dusted his exhibits once a week. "I dare not trust it to anyone [else]," she said.

When, in September of 1896, his parents escorted him to Groton and left him there, he remained "dry-eyed and resolute" though "white-faced," Sara noted in her diary, but "James and I feel this parting very much. It is hard to leave my darling boy."

OPPOSITE Franklin was lovingly photographed at every stage of his childhood: at six, at the helm of his father's yacht; wearing a sailor suit to please his mother on his tenth birthday; and with his camera on his way to Groton at fourteen.

ABOVE James Roosevelt Roosevelt—known as "Rosy"—at the reins of his own four-in-hand, 1886. Rosy was Franklin's much-older half brother, the product of Mr. James's first marriage, and spent his summers next door to Springwood. His first wife, Helen Astor Roosevelt, is at his side. Their children—Helen and James Roosevelt Roosevelt Jr., known as "Taddy"—sit behind with their governess. Rosy was amiable and fond of Franklin, but he was also idle, showy, and self-indulgent—everything the elder Roosevelts did not want Franklin to become.

Getting On Very Well with the Fellows

I n these times of exceeding comfort," said the Reverend Endicott Peabody, the founder and headmaster of Groton School in Groton, Massachusetts, "the boys need hardness and, it may be, suffering." The school—which Franklin entered at fourteen, in the third form—was meant to drive that lesson home.

Quarters were spartan and claustrophobic. Each day began with an icy shower. Bells sent the boys scurrying from class to class. Peabody encouraged his students to inflict rough and often brutal justice on boys they simply didn't like.

Theodore Roosevelt was a frequent visitor. Peabody was a cousin of his first wife, and had once offered him a job on the teaching staff. He would eventually send all four of his own sons to Groton. Franklin described an appearance by his celebrated cousin to his parents:

JUNE 4, 1897.
Dear Papa and Mama:

After supper tonight Cousin Theodore gave us a splendid talk on his adventures when he was on the Police Board. He kept the whole room in an uproar for over an hour, by telling us killing stories about policemen and their doings in New York.

Ever with lots of love,
FDR

OPPOSITE Groton upperclassmen share a joke while Franklin does his best to seem inconspicuous in a never-before-published photograph, found in the school archives.

TOP Hundred House, where Franklin lived. The six-by-nine-foot cubicles had curtains, not doors, because the headmaster believed privacy for adolescents only led to trouble.

ABOVE The Groton fife-and-drum corps escorts President Theodore Roosevelt's carriage onto the school grounds in 1902, four years after Franklin's graduation. TR's frequent visits to the school were always big events.

RIGHT In his first year at Groton, Franklin managed to win first prize in the high kick, an individual sport peculiar to the school. He kicked a tin pan two feet above his head, he reported to his parents, even though "at every kick I landed on my neck."

Franklin was accustomed to pleasing grownups, and his teachers all liked him. But most of his classmates did not. They found him too cocky, too well mannered, too eager to please. Other students outperformed him in the classroom. He was too slight and inexperienced at playing on a team to do well at sports; he ended up managing the baseball team, not playing on it. He called it "a thankless task."

He could neither excel nor fully fit in. For a boy who had been the object of almost universal admiration, life at Groton was bewildering, disheartening. "I always felt entirely out of things," he would admit many years later; something had gone "sadly wrong" for him at school. But his letters to his parents carefully kept those feelings hidden: unpleasantness was not to be acknowledged. Over and over again, he would assure them, "I am getting on very well with the fellows."

The Supreme Triumphs

Theodore Roosevelt's old friend Henry Cabot Lodge, now a senator from Massachusetts, wrote him that the only thing that had made the McKinley administration hesitate to bring him to the Navy Department was "a fear that you will want to fight somebody at once."

McKinley's concern was understandable. For nearly a decade, Roosevelt had believed no European power should be permitted a foothold in the New World. He'd once favored a war to seize Canada from Britain, and when the people of Cuba rose against their Spanish rulers in 1895, he'd wanted the United States to intervene immediately on their behalf. He also believed that if the United States was to take its rightful place among the world's great powers it would require a navy that could compete with theirs.

His new job as assistant secretary of the navy permitted him to battle for both objectives—and his easygoing boss, Secretary John D. Long, gave him plenty of opportunity to act. Long was the amiable former governor of Massachusetts, easily bored by detail work and eager always to get away to his native state. Theodore dismissed him fondly as "a perfect dear."

Roosevelt had only been on the job for seven weeks when he made his views on warfare clear to the Naval War College. "All the great masterful races have been fighting races," he said. "Cowardice is the unpardonable sin. No triumph of peace is quite so great as the supreme triumphs of war. It may be that at some time in the dim future of the race the need for war will vanish; but that time is as yet ages distant. . . . It is through strife, or the readiness for strife, that a nation must win greatness."

On February 15, 1898, the U.S. battleship *Maine* blew up in Havana harbor. Two hundred and sixty-six Americans died. The cause was unclear. But Roosevelt blamed Spain and called for vengeance. McKinley moved cau-

tiously: he had seen the dead piled up at Antietam, he said, and wished to see no more. Roosevelt privately accused the president of having "the backbone of a chocolate éclair."

Just ten days later, when his boss took still another weekend off, Roosevelt seized the opportunity to cable squadron commanders around the world to be on high alert and directed Commodore George Dewey to be ready to attack the Spanish fleet in the Philippines. When McKinley finally called on Congress for a declaration of war in April, Dewey steamed into Manila harbor and destroyed virtually the entire Spanish fleet anchored there without losing a single American sailor.

Roosevelt was thirty-nine years old and the father of six children when America went to war, and he held an important post in Washington. But he was determined to get to the front nonetheless. His father had stayed out of the Civil War; he would not give his own children any reason to question his sense of duty. "It was my one chance to do something for my country," he remembered, "and . . . my one chance to cut my little notch on the stick that stands as a measuring rod in every family. I would have turned from my wife's deathbed to answer that call."

His wife was in fact seriously ill that spring, recovering from surgery. Secretary Long noted in his diary that all Roosevelt's friends thought he was "acting like a fool." And yet, he added, "how absurd all this will sound if, by some turn of fortune, he should accomplish some great thing and strike a very high mark."

OPPOSITE, TOP AND BOTTOM A tattered American flag flies above the wreck of the USS *Maine* in Havana harbor, 1898. No evidence of Spanish explosives was ever found, but many Americans, including Theodore Roosevelt, saw Commodore Dewey's destruction of the Spanish fleet in Manila Bay (depicted here in a lithograph based on a painting by J. G. Tyler) as just revenge.

ABOVE In a frame from an early motion picture film, Assistant Secretary of the Navy Roosevelt hurries past the White House on his way to work.

The Wolf Rises in the Heart

Roosevelt left the Navy Department, had Brooks Brothers run up a special uniform "in blue Cravenette," ordered a dozen pairs of spare spectacles, and went to war as a lieutenant colonel in the 1st Volunteer Cavalry. Its commander was a regular army officer and close friend, Colonel Leonard Wood. But the outfit quickly became known as "Teddy's Terrors," "Teddy's Cowboy Contingent," and, finally, "Roosevelt's Rough Riders."

There had never been a regiment like it. One thousand eager horsemen, mostly from the West: bronco-busters and Indians and buffalo hunters; sheriffs and marshals and Texas Rangers who had tamed frontier towns—and the cowboys and prospectors who had shot up the same towns on Saturday nights. And serving right alongside them, Irish cops from New York and Protestant clergymen from New England; fox hunters and yachtsmen and British adventurers; the world's best polo player and the amateur tennis champion of the United States.

"You would be amused," Roosevelt wrote to a friend from the Rough Riders' Texas training camp, "to see three Knickerbocker club men cooking and washing dishes for one of the New Mexico companies."

Roosevelt was determined to get into battle before the fighting ended. When the expedition was finally ordered to sail for Cuba from Tampa, Florida, and he was told his men would have to wait for the second wave of transports, he personally commandeered a ship and ordered his men aboard.

Nothing went as planned. Half the unit's horses had to be left behind. The heat soared above 100 degrees. Drinking water was foul. Tinned beef proved inedible.

The landing at Daiquiri was chaotic, even though the Spanish never fired a shot. Horses were forced to swim ashore; one of Roosevelt's two mounts drowned. General William Shafter, the overall commander, weighed more than three hundred pounds and was so crippled by gout he could not walk. The commander of the cavalry division, General Joseph Wheeler, was a onetime Confederate who sometimes forgot he was fighting Spaniards, not Yankees, and was determined that his men, not the infantry, would get the credit for fighting the Spanish first.

The American target—nineteen miles away, seven of them through heavy jungle—was the port city of Santiago de Cuba, where American warships already blockaded the harbor.

Roosevelt and the Rough Riders were in the lead when they were ambushed on a jungle path near the village of Las Guasimas. In a letter home written the following morning, Roosevelt remembered the clash a little differently: "[We] struck the Spaniards and had a brisk fight for 2½ hours before we drove them out of their position. We lost a dozen men killed or mortally wounded and sixty severely or slightly wounded. . . . One man was killed as he stood

ABOVE The hat TR wore up San Juan Heights and a portrait of him in his Rough Rider uniform, commissioned by Edith Roosevelt from the artist Fedor Encke not long after her husband returned from Cuba. "I cannot say that it looks particularly like me," he once said of this portrait, but he preferred it to other portraits because he wanted his children to remember him as a warrior.

OPPOSITE Eager for battle, Roosevelt's Rough Riders crowd the deck of the transport ship *Yucatan* on their way to Cuba, June 14, 1898. One man hung a sign on her hull reading STANDING ROOM ONLY; another added, AND DAMN LITTLE OF THAT.

WILLIAM H. WEST'S BIG MINSTREL JUBILEE

THE CHARGE OF SAN JUAN HILL

WM.H.WEST IMPERSONATING COL.ROOSEVELT, LEADING THE FAMOUS 'ROUGH RIDERS' TO VICTORY.

TOP The minstrel impresario William H. West was just one of scores of American showmen who would find ways to incorporate Roosevelt's victory into their performances.

ABOVE Wounded Spanish troops on San Juan Heights: "Look at all those damned Spanish dead," Roosevelt exulted to a friend as soon as the shooting stopped.

beside me. Another bullet went through a tree behind which I stood and filled my eyes with bark. The last charge I led on the left using a rifle I took from a wounded man; and I kept three of the empty cartridges for the children."

The Rough Riders, aided by the 1st Cavalry and black troops of the 10th Cavalry, forced the enemy to withdraw. They pushed on toward Santiago, where Spanish troops were dug in along the San Juan Heights and on top of a lower summit the Americans would call Kettle Hill.

On the first of July, the order was given to drive them off. The Rough Riders were assigned to support regular troops as they stormed Kettle Hill. The battle began with an exchange of artillery. Spanish shrapnel bruised Roosevelt's wrist and tore the leg from a man standing next to him. Bullets ripped through the air, Roosevelt remembered, "making a sound like the ripping of a silk dress."

He led his men forward. One captain, a former quarterback at Harvard, carried his sabre on one shoulder and a six-shooter in the other. "Oh Jesus, I'm scared," he said. "But, by God, I'll stay with it."

Spanish fire poured down as the Americans splashed across San Juan Creek. Several Rough Riders were hit. Eventually, hundreds of men were stalled at the foot of the hill awaiting orders to attack.

What Theodore Roosevelt was always to remember as his "crowded hour" was about to begin. "All men who feel any power of joy in battle," Roosevelt later wrote, "know what it is like when the wolf rises in the heart." When the orders did not come, Roosevelt mounted his horse, Texas, and led his Rough Riders forward through the milling men. "Are you afraid to stand up when I am on horseback?" he demanded of one private. The man got to his feet and was killed instantly.

"If you don't wish to go forward," he told an officer, "please let my men pass." He waved his hat, spurred his horse, and started up the hillside. A bullet nicked his elbow. His spectacles fell off, and he somehow managed to replace them as he rode.

The Rough Riders followed him, cheering. The regulars they had been supposed to support struggled to keep up. A wire fence forced Roosevelt to dismount. He got through it and kept going. The Spanish began to flee. He shot one Spaniard with a revolver; "doubled him up," he remembered, "neatly as a jackrabbit."

The summit gave him a clear view of the ongoing battle for San Juan Heights. He decided to join that struggle, too, and rushed toward the fighting. But he forgot to give the order to follow. Only five men did. Three were shot down. He ran back, rallied his men, and joined the assault by black and white troops that finally drove the enemy from its fortifications.

All in all, it had been "fun," Roosevelt said, and "the great day of my life." "No hunting trip so far has ever equaled it in Theodore's eyes," a Rough Rider and old friend wrote Edith after the battle. "[He] was just revelling in victory and gore." He thought himself worthy of a Medal of Honor and would lobby hard for it. "I do not want to be vain," he told a friend, "but I do not think that anyone else could have handled this regiment quite as I have handled it." His men agreed. "We were drawn to him," one remembered. "We'd have gone to hell with him."

Even before he sailed for home, letters began to arrive, urging him to run for governor of New York.

TOP Rough Riders pinned down by Spanish fire from the summit of Kettle Hill. Moments later, Theodore Roosevelt would lead them up the slope—and make himself a national hero.

ABOVE Roosevelt's men bury one of their dead. Their colonel was proud that his regiment suffered eighty-nine casualties, "the heaviest loss suffered by any regiment in the cavalry division."

The Coming American

When a reporter called at Sagamore after Roosevelt got home and asked five-year-old Archie where "the colonel" was, the boy answered, "I don't know where the Colonel is but Father is taking a bath."

Reform-minded Independents pressed him to run on their ticket. But his old antagonist Boss Platt now wanted him, too; a war hero was sure to help the Republican slate. Roosevelt rejected the reformers and ran as a regular Republican: "Idealism," he said, must be combined with "efficiency," and that could only be done as part of a major party.

He barnstormed with six uniformed Rough Riders at his side. One of them remembered an early appearance at Carthage, New York: "He spoke for about ten minutes—the speech was nothing, but the man's presence was everything. It was electrical, magnetic—I looked in the faces of hundreds and saw only pleasure and satisfaction—when the train moved away scores of men and women ran after it [it] waving hats and handkerchiefs and cheering, trying to keep him in sight as long as possible."

Every speech was preceded by a bugle call. "You have heard the bugle that sounded to bring you here," Roosevelt would shout. "I have heard it tear the tropic dawn at Santiago." At one whistle-stop, an overenthusiastic veteran introduced him as the man who "led us up San Juan Hill like sheep to the slaughter—and so will he lead you!"

Roosevelt won. "I have played it with bull luck this summer," he told a friend. "First to get into the war; then to get out of it; then to get elected."

No one was prouder of his victory than the Hyde Park Roosevelts who had deserted the Democrats to support him. "Hyde Park gave the Colonel [an] 81 [vote] majority," Mr. James wrote proudly to Franklin. "Last spring, the Democrats carried the town by 91, so we think we did very well by our cousin." Franklin was so thrilled by what the man his mother called "your noble kinsman" had done that when he was told he needed glasses he ordered two sets of lenses, one mounted in a gold-rimmed pince-nez precisely like the ones Theodore Roosevelt wore up Kettle Hill. He only rarely wore the other pair.

Boss Platt feared the new governor harbored "altruistic ideas," and was "a little loose" on questions affecting "the right of a man to run his own business in his own way." Roosevelt promised to consult Platt as he went along, but he had concluded that it was neither wise nor safe for Republicans to take refuge in what he called "mere negation." New circumstances demanded a new kind of reform—progressive reform. The unprecedented but reckless growth that had transformed the country since the Civil War was meant to continue, but the old "natural laws" of the marketplace were no longer adequate; government needed to step in to tame its excesses and maintain necessary order. Wrongs now had to be righted through legislation as well as persuasion.

As governor, Roosevelt intended to strike a "just balance" between what he called "mob rule" and improper corporate influence.

Platt controlled the legislature. But Roosevelt held two press briefings a day to rally support for his positions—and won more battles than he lost. In less than six months, he secured passage of bills that taxed corporations, limited working hours for women and children, improved sweatshop conditions, and created forest preserves in the Catskills and Adirondacks.

Progressive reformers all across the country took notice. "There is no man in America today whose personality is rooted deeper in the hearts of the people than Theodore Roosevelt," wrote William Allen White, the influential editor of the *Emporia Gazette*. "He is more than a presidential possibility in 1904, he is a presidential probability. . . . He is the coming American of the twentieth century."

OPPOSITE, TOP TR campaigns in Cattaraugus. Upstate crowds were so noisily enthusiastic to see the war hero that he sometimes had to beg for quiet, asking them to "let this be as much of a monologue as possible."

OPPOSITE, BOTTOM As this cartoon from *Judge* suggests, there was little love lost between Boss Platt and Theodore Roosevelt. Platt hoped heavy financial backing from businessmen would persuade TR to run a "business government." Things didn't turn out that way.

ABOVE Wearing his military hat, the eager candidate leans down to grasp as many voters' hands as he can. To his left is Emil Cassi, the Rough Rider bugler, holding the horn with which he heralded every one of the 102 speeches the candidate made in a single week.

The Thing Could Not Be Helped

Roosevelt seemed likely to run for a second term as governor in 1900 and hoped to run for president four years later. But then, everything changed. On November 21, 1899, Vice President Garret A. Hobart died of a heart attack. Friends urged Roosevelt to make himself available for the post when McKinley ran for reelection the following year.

He was against it at first. The vice presidency was a purely ceremonial office. He wanted to become president one day. No vice president had been elected to that office since Martin Van Buren in 1836. Mark Hanna of Ohio, McKinley's closest adviser and party chairman, was against it, too. He thought Roosevelt was a "damned cowboy," shrill and unreliable.

But progressive Republicans admired him, as did westerners, and Boss Platt was determined to get him out of New York—and out of his hair—once and for all. "Roosevelt might as well stand under Niagara Falls," he said, "and try to spit the water back as to stop his nomination by this convention."

It nominated him on the first ballot. The only vote cast against him was his own. "The thing could not be helped," Roosevelt explained to Bamie. "The vital thing . . . is to reelect President McKinley and to this I shall bend all my energies." He proved as good as his word, crisscrossing the country—673 speeches in 567 towns in 24 states.

ABOVE The cartoonist J. Keppler Jr. captured the fear vice presidential candidate Theodore Roosevelt struck in the hearts of Republican conservatives. "Don't any of you realize," Senator Mark Hanna asked convention delegates, "that there's only one life between this madman and the presidency?"

RIGHT Campaign poster, 1900. McKinley followed presidential tradition and stayed above the campaign fray, but his Democratic challenger, William Jennings Bryan, barnstormed across the country. Roosevelt was meant to match him, speech for speech. "'Tis Tiddy alone that's running," said Finley Peter Dunne's fictional Irish bartender, Mr. Dooley, "and he ain't running, he's galloping."

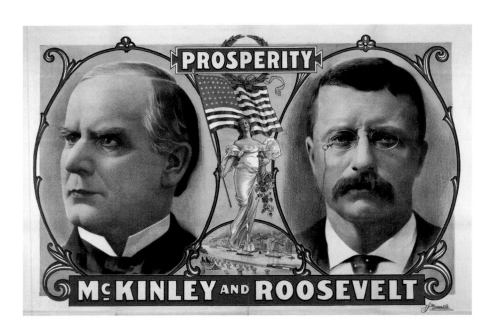

On election night, Roosevelt waited for the returns at Sagamore Hill. When it was clear that McKinley and he had won, a newspaperman congratulated him. "Please don't," Roosevelt said. "This election tonight means my political death." Then, he paused and added, "Of course, gentlemen, this is not for publication."

"The best we can do," Mark Hanna told some of his fellow conservatives, "is pray fervently for the continued health of the president."

ABOVE Theodore Roosevelt stumps for the whole Republican ticket at the Ramapo Iron Works in Hillburn, New York: "I am as strong as a bull moose," he had assured McKinley's campaign manager, "and you can use me to the limit."

LEFT All alone, Vice President Roosevelt waits for a train at the Oyster Bay depot, August 18, 1901. "I hate having him in such a useless & empty position," Edith told a friend. She and Bamie worried what four years of relative inactivity might do to a man so desperate for action. Less than a month after this photograph was taken, everything would change.

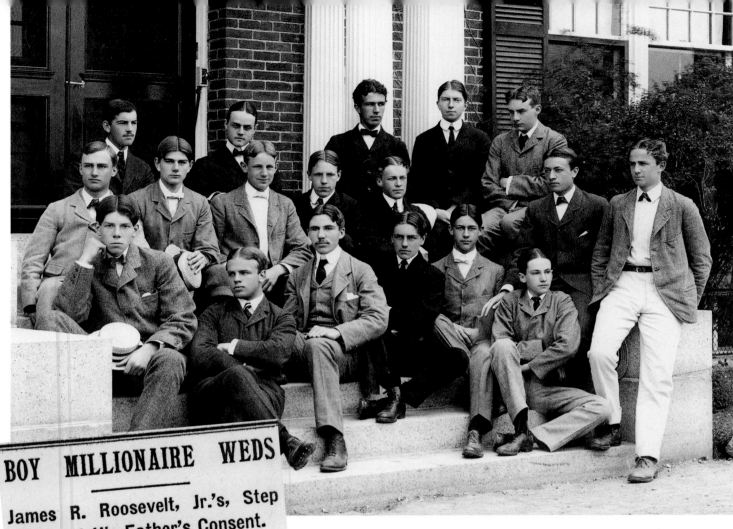

The Disgusting Business About Taddy

Less than three weeks before election day, scandal had hit the Hyde Park Roosevelts. James Roosevelt Roosevelt, the troubled son and namesake of Franklin's half brother, Rosy—known as "Taddy" within the family—had been an embarrassment to Franklin at Groton. At Harvard things got much worse. Taddy stopped attending classes in the spring of his freshman year, disappeared from campus for days at a time, and then vanished altogether. In mid-October, someone tipped off the newspapers that he had secretly married a Manhattan prostitute named Sadie Messinger, "Dutch Sadie" to her customers.

Mr. James, already failing, suffered another heart attack. There had been scandals among the Oyster Bay Roosevelts in the past, but never among his Hyde Park branch of the clan. He could not sleep or stop talking about what his grandson had done. "Tell Franklin to be good and never be like Taddy," he told Sara over and over again. Because of "the

disgusting business about Taddy," Franklin wrote his mother, "one can never again consider him a true Roosevelt." So far as anyone knows, he and Franklin never saw one another again.

Mr. James never recovered from his grandson's indiscretion. Early in the morning on December 8, 1900, with both his sons and Sara at his Manhattan bedside, the long battle she and Franklin had waged to keep him alive finally came to an end. He was buried alongside his first wife in the graveyard behind St. James' Church at Hyde Park.

Franklin did his best to comfort his mother. She was only forty-six. A long lonely widowhood stretched ahead of her. She would find what comfort she could in steady devotion to her son. His successes would be hers, as well.

OPPOSITE, TOP AND LEFT Franklin's half nephew, Taddy, sits with his arms folded, third from the right in this photograph of his Groton class. The notice of his unexpected marriage that so horrified his grandfather appeared in the *New York Times* on October 19, 1900.

ABOVE Franklin and his frail father at Campobello during the last summer of James Roosevelt's life, 1900

Here Is the Task

On the afternoon of September 13, 1901, Theodore Roosevelt was where he liked most to be: in the woods, miles from the nearest town, with his wife and children as companions. That morning, accompanied by two guides, he had climbed New York's highest peak, Mount Marcy in the Adirondacks, and then clambered down again to have a picnic lunch on the shore of a lake named Tear of the Clouds.

Seven days earlier, at the Pan-American Exposition in Buffalo, New York, a young anarchist named Leon Czolgosz had shot President McKinley twice at point-blank range. At the news, Alice Roosevelt recalled, she and her siblings "put on long faces and then my brother [Ted] and I went outside and did a little jig." The idea that her father might now become president, she remembered, was "sheer rapture."

One of McKinley's wounds was only superficial. But the other had pierced both walls of his stomach and was irretrievable in that era before reliable X rays. His condition had quickly stabilized, nonetheless, and he seemed so certain to recover—one of his physicians told the press he was "first rate"— that Vice President Roosevelt had been encouraged to go ahead with his vacation.

But at about 1:25, a park ranger struggled up the slope with a telegram:

THE PRESIDENT IS CRITICALLY ILL.

More messages followed.

HIS CONDITION IS GRAVE.

OXYGEN IS BEING GIVEN.

ABSOLUTELY NO HOPE.

THE PRESIDENT APPEARS TO BE DYING AND MEMBERS OF THE
CABINET IN BUFFALO THINK YOU SHOULD LOSE NO TIME COMING.

Roosevelt started for Buffalo, four hundred miles away. He became president at the moment of the president's death, at two fifteen on the morning of the 14th, but he did not reach Buffalo until one thirty that afternoon and did not take the oath of office in the library of a friend's house until half past three—and then only after he had made sure that space was found for twenty-four reporters. He was the youngest president in American history, at just forty-two years old. "It is a dreadful thing to come into the Presidency this way, but it would be a far worse thing to be morbid about it," he told Henry Cabot Lodge. "Here is the task, and I have got to do it to the best of my ability, and that is all there is about it."

ABOVE The shooting of President William McKinley, as reported by *Leslie's Weekly*. Leon Czolgosz waited in a receiving line, a handkerchief wrapped around his right hand. Inside the handkerchief was a pistol. As McKinley reached out to shake his left hand, thinking his right was injured, Czolgosz pulled the trigger.

Franklin Roosevelt was at sea, returning from a voyage to Europe meant to cheer his grieving mother, when he got the news from a passing ship by megaphone. It was a "terrible shock to all," he noted, but it was also exciting. Cousin Theodore's ascension to the nation's highest office had provided him with vivid evidence of how far an ambitious Roosevelt might rise.

ABOVE Before beginning his vacation, Vice President Roosevelt met with reporters outside the house where the wounded president was then thought to be recovering.

RIGHT Mourning crepe drapes the home of Roosevelt's friend Ansley Wilcox at 641 Delaware Avenue in Buffalo; TR took the formal oath of office as president here on September 14, 1901.

CHAPTER 2

In the Arena

1901–1910

The Gift of Leadership

For the first few nights of his presidency, Theodore Roosevelt slept at the home of his sister Bamie and her husband, Commander William S. Cowles, at 1733 N Street, while the widow of his murdered predecessor packed up to leave Washington.

His first night in the White House was to be September 23, 1901, and since his wife and children had not yet arrived, he asked Bamie and his younger sister, Corinne, and their husbands to join him for dinner. The day before had been the birthday of the man whose memory meant the most to him, his late father, Theodore Roosevelt Sr. "What would I not give if only he could have lived to see me here in the White House," the president said.

Then he noticed that the flowers on the dinner table were saffronia roses, the same variety his father had always worn in his buttonhole. "I feel as if my father's hand were on my shoulder," Roosevelt said, "as if there were a special blessing over the life I am to lead here."

Theodore Roosevelt would prove to be a new kind of president

for a new century. In the decades since the death of Abraham Lincoln, most American presidents had largely been content to be caretakers. Real power lay with the Congress, with the party machines that controlled what did and did not happen on Capitol Hill, and with the financial giants whose power grew steadily after the Civil War and whose orders many senators followed without a second thought.

From the first, Roosevelt was different. "I did not care a rap for the form and show of power," he remembered. "I cared immensely for the use that could be made of the substance."

At first, no one knew precisely in which direction Roosevelt would lead the country. He had pledged to "continue, absolutely unbroken, the policy of President McKinley." But he also had a reputation for independence and unpredictability, and had been taught by his father to view the world in terms of right and wrong—and to see himself always as the defender of the right. "I'm no orator, and in writing I'm afraid I'm not gifted at all," he wrote. "If I have anything at all resembling genius it is the gift of leadership."

PRECEDING PAGES Eager to be elected president in his own right, Theodore Roosevelt strides to the polls in Oyster Bay on election day, 1904.

OPPOSITE, TOP Bamie Roosevelt's N Street home in Washington, D.C., where her brother stayed before moving to the White House.

OPPOSITE, BOTTOM TR on his way to work at the White House for the first time, September 20, 1901. His tall companion is thought to be his brother-in-law, Commander Cowles.

ABOVE TR at his desk in the president's office, a vase of his father's favorite roses at his side

SOUTHERNERS ARE HEATED

President Criticized for Dining With Prof. Washington

MORE THAN SHOCKING

Possible Political Effect of This Crossing of the Color Line.

REVISING CHARLESTON PROGRAM

How Do You Like It?

Within hours of moving into the White House, Roosevelt wired Booker T. Washington, president of the Tuskegee Institute and the best-known, most-admired black man in America, asking him to come and have dinner with him.

Each man wanted something from the other. Jim Crow laws were systematically disenfranchising Negro citizens throughout the South. Washington wanted the new president's assurance that he would continue to appoint African Americans to federal jobs and resist those Republicans who wanted to crack the solid Democratic South by turning the party of Lincoln "Lily White."

©UNDERWOOD & UNDERWOOD

Roosevelt wanted Washington's help in making sure that he—and he alone—controlled black delegates to the Republican national convention in 1904.

A reporter for one of the wire services spotted Washington's name in the visitors' register and immediately filed a story. No black person had ever dined at the White House before. Not only had the president dined with Washington, but he had done so in the company of his wife and his teenage daughter, Alice.

The southern press exploded. "White men of the South," asked the New Orleans *Times-Democrat,* "how do you like it? White women of the South, how do you like it? . . . The Negro is not the equal of the white man. Mr. Roosevelt might as well try to rub the stars out of the firmament as to try to erase that conviction from the hearts of the American people."

The president was astonished at the furor. "I would not lose my self-respect by fearing to have a man like Booker T. Washington to dinner," he wrote, "if it cost me every political friend I have got." Washington remained Roosevelt's most powerful African American ally, but Roosevelt never asked him, or any other black person, to dine at the White House again.

In Duty Bound

By 1901, a handful of men dominated American finance and industry. Through the manipulation of some 250 big interlocking, interstate corporations, or "trusts," they dictated the rates farmers paid to ship their products and the wages and hours and conditions industrial workers had to accept. They decided the cost to consumers of everything from coal to whiskey, canned meat to lamp oil. And they destroyed small businessmen who dared try to compete with them.

J. Pierpont Morgan, the New York financial titan, who had been a friend of the president's father, spoke for most of the men who ran the trusts. "I owe the public nothing," he said.

That attitude was anathema to Theodore Roosevelt. He had a patrician's scorn for mere wealth and an inbred sense of responsibility toward society. But for all the fire of his rhetoric, he remained a man of the middle, seeking always to stake a position somewhere between what he saw as reaction on one side and revolution on the other. "I have been in a great quandary over Trusts," he wrote a friend. "I do not know what attitude to take. I do not intend to play a demagogue. On the other hand, I do intend . . . to see that the rich man is held to the same accountability as the poor man, and when the rich man is rich enough to buy unscrupulous advice from very able lawyers this is not always easy."

For five months, Roosevelt continued to honor his pledge to maintain the consistently pro-business policies of his predecessor, following the advice given by McKinley's old Ohio ally, Senator Mark Hanna: "Go slow."

JACK AND THE WALL STREET GIANTS.

Then, without warning, on February 18, 1902, Roosevelt ordered his Justice Department to move against J. P. Morgan's latest creation, the Northern Securities Company, whose goal was the monopolistic control of all the railroads between the Great Lakes and the Pacific Ocean.

Wall Street was stunned. So was Morgan. He hurried to the White House.

"If we have done anything wrong," he told the president, "send your man to my man and they can fix it up."

"That can't be done," the president said.

"We don't want to fix it up," his attorney general, Philander Knox, added. "We want to stop it."

Morgan asked if the administration planned to attack any of his other interests.

Not unless they'd done something wrong, Roosevelt said.

The Supreme Court would eventually uphold Roosevelt's action, finding that Northern Securities had been in illegal restraint of trade. The president would never directly challenge Morgan again, but he would invoke the Sherman Antitrust Act against forty other trusts during his presidency, more than all three of his predecessors combined. "The great corporations," he wrote, "are the creatures of the State, and the State not only has the right to control them, but it is in duty bound to control them wherever need of such control is shown."

He did not believe that economic concentration in itself was bad, but he was confident the federal government had the power—and the moral duty—to curb its worst excesses.

OPPOSITE Theodore Roosevelt takes his antitrust message to River Point, Rhode Island; and (LEFT) Rutland and (ABOVE) Randolph, Vermont. In August of 1902, with congressional elections fast approaching, the president undertook a two-week tour through New England, explaining that he felt he had no choice but to bring the great corporations under the "real, not the nominal, control" of the national government because, as he told crowd after crowd, "the government is us . . . you and me!" "Not since the Great Emancipator," said the *New York Times,* "has a Chief Magistrate of the United States delivered to the American people a message of greater present concern."

ABOVE Trolley passengers look on helplessly a second or two before their car slams into the president's carriage in downtown Pittsfield, Massachusetts. "Did you lose control of the car?" Roosevelt asked the engineer afterward. "If you didn't, it's a God-damned outrage!" The engineer claimed he'd had the right of way but was sentenced to six months in jail for his recklessness.

RIGHT Onlookers crowd around the mangled carriage after the president and his party had moved on. A local jeweler and sometime cameraman named Wheeler did a brisk business selling souvenir photographs of the accident's aftermath.

A Wonderful Escape

Wednesday, September 3, 1902, was to be the final day of the president's New England tour and he was scheduled to speak at Pittsfield, Massachusetts. The motorman of a suburban trolley filled with people hoping to hear him suddenly stepped up his speed to get there first. The trolley slammed into the president's landau, hurling it forty feet across the road and throwing its passengers into the air. The governor of Massachusetts was unhurt, but the president's bodyguard, William Craig of the Secret Service, was killed, crushed beneath the trolley's wheels. Roosevelt was thrown out, landed on his face, and injured his left shin. He was back on his feet within seconds, cursing and shaking his fist in the motorman's face. The next morning's newspapers hailed his "Wonderful Escape from Death," but his face was badly swollen and his leg injury turned into a dangerous abscess. Twice, Roosevelt would have to endure surgery to have it drained and the bone beneath it scraped, and he was forced to spend several weeks in a wheelchair, confronted with a crisis that threatened the nation's economy—and his own political survival.

ABOVE The carriage itself. Despite the death of his Secret Service man and his own injuries, Roosevelt finished out his day of speech making and hand-shaking. "It takes more than a trolley accident to knock me out," he said later, "and more than a crowd to tire me."

Made for the People

America ran on anthracite coal, most of it mined from Pennsylvania hillsides. It was a nightmarish business. Sixteen-hour days. The constant threat of cave-ins. Boys as young as ten breaking big chunks into small ones. Low wages that had not been raised for more than twenty years—and company-owned stores intended to swallow up what little money the miners could scrape together. And dominating all of it, mineowners adamantly opposed to change. Coal mining is a "business not a religious, sentimental, or academic proposition," said George F. Baer, president of the Philadelphia and Reading Coal and Iron Company. "The rights and interests of the laboring man will be protected and cared for—not by the labor agitators, but by the Christian men to whom God in his infinite wisdom has given . . . control of the property interests of the country."

OPPOSITE Coal smoke blankets the Homestead Steel Works, operated by U.S. Steel on the Monongahela River.

ABOVE Strikers at Olyphant, Pennsylvania, some of the 147,000 members of the United Mine Workers who downed their tools in the spring of 1902. Many were immigrants, and some ten thousand of them would return to their homelands rather than continue to endure conditions in American coalfields.

Back in the spring, the United Mine Workers, led by young John Mitchell, called for a strike. More than 140,000 men laid down their tools. Management refused even to hear their grievances. The price of coal rose from five to thirty dollars a ton. Winter was coming. Homes would remain unheated—and the administration was sure to take the blame. Roosevelt's close friend Republican Senator Henry Cabot Lodge of Massachusetts didn't think there was anything the president could do—but urged him at least to "appear" to do something.

Appearances alone didn't interest Theodore Roosevelt. He summoned both sides to Washington to discuss what he called "a matter of vital concern to the whole nation." The White House was being renovated, so the talks were held in the temporary White House on Lafayette Square. The face-to-face meeting failed to budge the owners. Roosevelt privately denounced their "wooden-headed obstinacy and stupidity," and sent word that unless they accepted binding arbitration he would contact the Republican governor of Pennsylvania and ask him formally to request ten thousand federal troops to seize the mines and get them working again.

A conservative congressman confronted the president. "What about the Constitution of the United States?" he asked. How could private property be put to public purposes without due process of law? Roosevelt grasped his visitor's lapels. "The Constitution was made for the people and not the people for the Constitution," he said.

The mineowners retreated—but only slightly. They agreed to follow the recommendations of a presidential commission—provided no member of the United Mine Workers sat on it. Roosevelt was determined that labor have a voice and appointed the head of the Order of Railroad Conductors instead. The owners objected until the president told them, with a straight face, that he was naming him as a "sociologist," not a union man. Roosevelt remembered "the mixture of relief and amusement I felt when I thoroughly grasped the fact that while they would heroically submit to anarchy rather than have Tweedledum, yet if I would call it Tweedledee they would accept it with rapture; it gave me an illuminating glimpse into one corner of the mighty brains of these 'captains of industry.'"

The mineowners still refused to recognize the union, but they did agree to a 10 percent pay raise and a nine-hour workday. The strike ended. American homes would be heated that autumn—and the Republicans would maintain majorities in both houses of Congress.

Roosevelt was jubilant. He was the first president to mediate a labor dispute, the first to treat labor as a full partner, the first to threaten to employ troops to seize a strike-bound industry. And it had all worked.

"I feel like throwing up my hands and going to the circus," he said.

OPPOSITE During the coal strike, city workers dole out shovels of scarce fuel to shivering residents of Manhattan's Lower East Side. A police officer keeps New Yorkers from trying to take more than their share.

ABOVE Members of the president's Anthracite Coal Commission clamber into a coal car while investigating conditions in the mines at Meadville, Pennsylvania.

LEFT The president, surrounded by miners after the strike ended: "I am President of the United States," he said, "and my business is to see fair play among all men, capitalists or wage workers."

The Greatest Disappointment

"It has been very chilly [here] for the past week," Franklin wrote to his mother from Harvard that October, "and the buildings have been cold through lack of fuel, but now that the strike is settled the coal has begun to come in small quantities. In spite of [the president's] success in settling the trouble, I think that [he] makes a serious mistake in interfering—politically, at least. His tendency to make the executive power stronger than the Houses of Congress is bound to be a bad thing, especially when a man of weaker personality succeeds him in office."

Franklin was a Harvard sophomore now, and echoing the conservative opinions of classmates whose well-to-do parents were appalled at the president's willingness to deal directly with labor. His mother disagreed. "One cannot help loving and admiring him the more for it," she told her son, "when one realizes that he tried to right the wrong."

After Franklin's father died in 1900, Sara moved to Boston to be closer to her son. She interested herself in every aspect of his life, exulted in his successes, and overlooked his failures, just as she always had.

Successes did not come easily. He was not an outstanding student or especially well liked by his classmates. Many of them thought him an overeager lightweight, just as his schoolmates at Groton had. He became editor in chief of the *Crimson,* and scored a scoop when he learned his famous cousin was coming to Cambridge, but when he ran for class

This certifies that Mr. *F. D. Roosevelt*

is a member of the

HARVARD REPUBLICAN CLUB

of Harvard University, and is entitled to a shingle.

....President.

ABOVE, LEFT Franklin's celebrated surname and his father's honorary membership were not enough to get him past the door of the exclusive Porcellian Club, the narrow building with the fanlight at 1320–24 Massachusetts Avenue in Cambridge—a fact that deeply wounded him.

ABOVE, RIGHT FDR's membership card in the Harvard Republican Club. He joined in 1900 to show his support for the McKinley-Roosevelt ticket and would remain a Republican for at least two years. The "shingle" to which the card entitled him was a placard to hang on his wall as a sign of his enthusiasm for his famous cousin.

OPPOSITE, LEFT AND TOP Franklin as a Harvard freshman, and as a senior seated (center) with the staff of the *Harvard Crimson* during his term as its president. His successor in that position remembered that Roosevelt seemed to "like people . . . and made them instinctively like him. Moreover, in his geniality there was a kind of frictionless command."

marshal he lost. Still too slight for sports, he led cheers at a football game—though he admitted it made him feel "like a damned fool waving my arms and legs before several thousand amused spectators."

He was elected to several clubs, and fully expected an invitation to join Harvard's most exclusive organization, the Porcellian. He was a "legacy," after all: his own father had been an honorary member; his cousin Theodore belonged.

But Franklin was blackballed. As always, he was reluctant to let anyone know how hurt he was, but fifteen years later, he would confide to a young relative that his rejection by Porcellian had been the "greatest disappointment" of his life.

He was disappointed in love, as well. Alice Sohier was the beautiful seventeen-year-old daughter of a wealthy North Shore yachtsman—the "love-

liest" debutante of her year, Franklin remembered—and after courting her for several months he asked her to marry him. One day he hoped to be president like his fifth cousin, he told her—and he hoped to have no fewer than six children, the same number that now tumbled across the White House lawn.

Alice turned him down. Later, she would tell her granddaughter that she had rejected his proposal in part because "I did not wish to be a cow."

Franklin never told his mother about Alice, and to ensure that she did not know too much about his private life had begun using a secret code in his terse diary. Within weeks of his parting with Alice Sohier in the late summer of 1902, cryptic new messages began to appear in the diary's pages, involving someone identified only as "E."

OPPOSITE Franklin (at center, arms folded) and fellow members of the Harvard class of 1904 at their sixth class reunion at Nahant, Massachusetts

ABOVE, LEFT Eighteen-year-old Alice Sohier dressed for presentation at the Court of St. James's in London in the spring of 1903, a year after she rebuffed Franklin's proposal. "She had flocks of beaux," a family member recalled. "She was having too good a time to be very serious about marriage."

ABOVE, RIGHT Westmorely Court, the most opulent building on Harvard's Gold Coast, where, for four years, Franklin shared a suite with a fellow Grotonian, Lathrop Brown

Teddy's Bear

As soon as the 1902 congressional elections were over, President Roosevelt set off for the Mississippi Delta in hopes of shooting a black bear.

His guide was Holt Collier, a former slave and scout for the Confederacy who claimed to have accounted for some three thousand bears over a long lifetime. Collier's hounds found a bear and chased it into a muddy watering hole. Collier blew a bugle, the signal for Roosevelt to come and shoot it. Before he could get there, the cornered bear killed one dog and wounded two more. To save the rest of his pack, Collier smashed his gun over its head, then tied the dazed, wounded animal to a tree until the president could get there.

When he finally did, he refused to fire. It wasn't sporting to shoot a bear that could not get away, he said, and he asked that someone else put it out of its misery. Collier killed it with a knife.

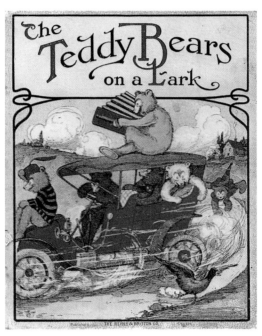

The president was not pleased with the experience. "I have just had a most unsatisfactory experience in a bear hunt in Mississippi," he wrote. "There were plenty of bears, and if I had gone alone . . . I would have gotten one or two. But my hosts, with the best of intentions, insisted upon turning the affair into a cross between a hunt and a picnic, which always results in a failure for the hunt and usually in a failure for the picnic."

A rumor spread that the lassoed bear had been a cub, and that that was the reason the president had held his fire. A cartoonist captured that version. A Brooklyn stationer's wife made two stuffed toys modeled after the cartoon cub and called them "Teddy's Bear." Soon, manufacturers both in the United States and overseas were turning out toy bears of their own.

The Teddy bear would become Roosevelt's most enduring symbol—and helped permanently saddle him with "Teddy," a name he said he detested. "No man who knows me calls me by [that] nickname," he complained to a friend that winter, "and if it is used by anyone it is a sure sign he does not know me."

OPPOSITE, LEFT, TOP AND BOTTOM TR and companions setting out in search of a black bear, and a guide bringing in the dead bear Roosevelt had refused to kill

OPPOSITE, RIGHT Clifford Berryman's cartoon in the *Washington Post* transformed the grown bear into a cuddly cub and caught the public's fancy.

ABOVE, LEFT AND RIGHT The proud owner of an early Teddy bear and the cover of one of countless books indirectly inspired by the president's misadventure in Mississippi

Breathing the Free Western Air

In the spring of 1903, Theodore Roosevelt undertook a marathon eight-week tour of the West—14,000 miles, 25 states, 150 cities and towns, 260 speeches. He was exhausted but exhilarated as he set out, suffering again from asthmatic wheezing and eager to breathe what he called "the free western air." With an eye toward ensuring his nomination for president in 1904, he preached about everything from the need for a big navy to the sacred duty he believed every woman had to bear children.

But as he moved from one spectacular landscape to the next, his central message was the importance of preserving them for the future. "We are not building this country of ours for a day," he said. "It is to last through the ages." The United States was fast becoming an urban and industrial country. Americans needed their unspoiled forests and hills, canyons and deserts to refresh and restore themselves. National Parks represented "essential democracy" at work, allowing every American to share in a legacy that belonged to everyone.

Before Theodore Roosevelt left office—and over the objections of conservatives like House Speaker Joseph G. Cannon of Illinois, who liked to say, "Not one cent for scenery"—he would create five National Parks, fifty-one bird sanctuaries, four national game refuges, and eighteen National Monuments. All in all, he set aside more than 280,000 square miles of federal land under one kind of protection or another—an area larger than the state of Texas and nearly half the size of the Louisiana Purchase—and created the United States Forest Service to help ensure that the development of natural resources proceeded in a responsible, sustainable way.

TOP TR begins his western trip by climbing into the locomotive of his train at Altoona, Pennsylvania. He rode next to the engineer for forty-nine miles, and then thanked him for the "bully" start to his cross-country journey.

ABOVE At Yellowstone, Roosevelt (left) and the writer John Burroughs enjoy Old Faithful—which the New York *World* called the president's "only rival in intermittent but continuous spouting."

OPPOSITE Roosevelt keeps an eye on the photographer as he and his party roll through the Wawona Tunnel Tree in the Mariposa Grove of Giant Sequoias, now part of Yosemite National Park.

"Surely our people do not understand even yet the rich heritage that is theirs," he wrote. "There can be nothing more beautiful than the Yosemite, the groves of giant sequoias and redwoods, the Canyon of the Colorado, the Canyon in the Yellowstone, the Three Tetons; and our children must see to it that they are preserved for their children and their children's children forever with their majestic beauty unmarred."

ABOVE Surrounded by symbols of the nation and the wildness he loved, Roosevelt calls for conservation at Newcastle, Wyoming. "He gave himself very freely and heartily to the people wherever he went" on his western tour, John Burroughs remembered. "He could easily match their western cordiality and good-fellowship."

LEFT Troopers of the all-black 9th Cavalry—called "buffalo soldiers" by the Plains Indians—struggle to control the surging crowds eager to greet the president's carriage (lower left) as it crosses the Presidio Golf Course in San Francisco. He moved on to Yosemite the next day, but the solitude the West had once provided for him was no longer easy to find.

I Took the Canal Zone

The American expansionism Roosevelt had advocated since long before his days at the Navy Department had succeeded beyond his dreams. The United States was now a world power. It had annexed Hawaii, driven Spain from the New World, dominated Cuba, and nearly finished subjugating the Philippines.

But one great expansionist vision remained unfulfilled. For more than half a century, American and European investors had dreamed of a Central American canal linking the Atlantic to the Pacific. Roosevelt believed such an inter-ocean pathway was now indispensable for the full exercise of American naval power.

There were two rival routes: one through the mountains of Nicaragua (the late James Roosevelt had invested heavily in it), and a shorter path across the Isthmus of Panama in Colombia, where a French company had stalled and thousands of workers had already died of yellow fever.

When the French company offered to sell its rights to the Panama route for a reasonable price, Roosevelt agreed to buy them, then instructed his secretary of state, John Hay, to negotiate a treaty with Colombia. It called for a payment of $10 million, plus an annual rental fee for a six-mile "Canal Zone" across the isthmus.

But the Colombian senate unanimously refused to ratify the treaty—and then demanded double the price. Roosevelt was enraged. "I do not think that the Bogota lot of jack rabbits should be allowed permanently to bar one of the future highways of civilization," he said.

Roosevelt divided the world into what he called "civilized" powers—industrialized and mostly white—and "uncivilized" nations that produced raw materials, bought products instead of manufacturing them, and were incapable of self-government.

The great enemy of civilization was what he called "chaos." To combat it, he believed, it was the duty of "civilized and orderly powers" to police the rest. Britain should be responsible for India and Egypt, he believed. Japan—which Roosevelt numbered among the "civilized" nations because it had become an industrial and military power—should control Korea and the Yellow Sea.

And the United States—and only the United States—must police the Caribbean. When the dictator of Venezuela defaulted on his country's loans and German warships steamed in to shell her ports and blockade the coast, Roosevelt threatened war to make Germany back off, then took over Venezuelan customs collecting until the debts were paid.

OPPOSITE Rusting French equipment and a section of the unfinished canal across the Isthmus of Panama, abandoned after twenty-two years of effort by the Panama Canal Company. Where the French despaired, Roosevelt saw opportunity.

ABOVE Theodore Roosevelt in 1903. Despite his bellicose reputation, Roosevelt was proud that during his seven and a half years in the White House "not a shot had been fired against a foreign foe." (The bloody Philippine insurrection inherited from McKinley didn't count in his mind because the islands were then American territory, not a foreign country.)

In Roosevelt's view, the refusal of the Colombian senate to honor the government's commitment was just the latest embodiment of the kind of "chaos" he deplored. He was determined to end it—and get an American canal under way. He would not attack Colombia directly; Congress wouldn't stand for it. But again and again over the previous fifty years the people of the narrow, jungle-covered Province of Panama had asserted their wish to be independent of Bogotá.

Philippe Bunau-Varilla was a tiny, fastidious Frenchman, a lobbyist for the French canal builders and in touch with rebels eager to rise against Colombian rule. He visited Roosevelt in the White House. It was a delicate conversation: What did the Frenchman think was going to happen in Panama Province?

"Mr. President," his visitor said, "a Revolution."

Roosevelt was careful to say nothing about how the United States might respond. He didn't need to. The Frenchman had "no assurances in any way," TR remembered. "[But] he is a very able fellow, and it was his business to find out what he thought our Government would do. I have no doubt that he was able to make a very accurate guess, and to advise his people accordingly. In fact, he would have been a very dull man had he been unable to make such a guess."

HARPER'S WEEKLY
JOURNAL OF CIVILIZATION

New York, Saturday, November 21, 1903

VOL. XLVII.   No. 2448

Copyright, 1903, by HARPER & BROTHERS. All rights reserved

HELD UP THE WRONG MAN

ABOVE *Harper's Weekly* defends Roosevelt's decision to strong-arm Colombia and tacitly support the secession of Panama.

RIGHT General Esteban Huertas (center), the diminutive commander of the Colombian garrison at Panama City, was paid $65,000—more than a million and a half dollars in today's terms—to persuade the soldiers shown here not to resist the revolution.

THE NATIONAL MOTTO GALLERY.

The rebels proclaimed their independence. An American cruiser landed troops to neutralize the handful of Colombian troops the revolutionaries hadn't already bought off. It was all over within seventy-two hours.

Roosevelt was presiding at a cabinet meeting at 11:35 on the morning of November 6, 1903, when a messenger brought him the happy news. By the time lunch was served, the United States had recognized the brand-new Republic of Panama.

American work on the great canal would soon begin. Years later, Roosevelt would boast that "I took the Canal Zone and let Congress debate and while the debate goes on, the Canal does, too. And now instead of discussing the Canal before it was built, which would have been harmful, they merely discuss me—a discussion which I regard with benign interest."

ABOVE Clifford Berryman of the *Washington Post* saw TR's action in Panama as the latest in a long line of heroic American deeds, while, for *Puck*, Grant Hamilton depicted Roosevelt as an enthusiastic and distinctly un-American imperialist.

E Is an Angel

For Thanksgiving that year, Franklin and his mother traveled to the Delano family homestead at Fairhaven, Massachusetts, rather than face the prospect of being at Springwood without Mr. James. After dinner, Franklin took Sara for a walk in the garden. He had something to tell her. He had fallen in love with Eleanor Roosevelt, the orphaned daughter of the president's late younger brother, Elliott Roosevelt.

He had asked her to marry him.

She had said yes.

Sara was stunned. They were too young, she thought: Franklin was just twenty-one; Eleanor only nineteen. And if they married she feared she would be left alone.

Franklin and Eleanor did their best to reassure her. "You know, dear

mummy, that nothing can ever change what we have always been & always will be to each other," he wrote. "Only now you have two children to love & to love you." Eleanor echoed that sentiment: "It is impossible for me to tell you how I feel toward Franklin. I can only say that my one great wish is always to prove worthy of him. . . . I know just how you feel and how hard it must be, but I do want you to learn to love me a little."

Loving her a little was the best Eleanor Roosevelt dared wish for.

"[Franklin] had always been so secure in every way," she remembered, "and then he discovered that I was perfectly insecure." Everything in her upbringing had seemed calculated to make her feel that way. When she was seventeen, her grandmother had insisted she come home from Allenswood to prepare for her debut in New York society. She spent a summer at Tivoli, where one of her drunken uncles had become so uncontrollable that he could not be discouraged from spraying buckshot from his bedroom window at anyone who dared venture onto the lawn. Three locks had to be installed on her bedroom door. "It was not a very good preparation for being a gay and joyous debutante," she remembered.

One of the young men who sought her out to dance that season remembered that "the spirit of competition [among his fellow suitors] was distinctly present." Her own memories were different. "I imagine that I was well-dressed, but there was absolutely nothing about me to attract anybody's attention. . . . I was tall, but I did not dance very well. . . . By no stretch of the imagination could I fool myself into thinking that I was a popular debutante."

On November 17, 1902, just five weeks after Franklin had said goodbye to the beautiful Alice Sohier, he attended the New York Horse Show at Madison Square Garden. Several Roosevelt cousins had been invited to sit in his stepbrother Rosy's special box, including Eleanor. She and Franklin had seen one another casually at family events over the years, but now he asked to see her again—and again and again—noting each meeting in his diary with an "E," precisely as Theodore Roosevelt had once kept the courtship of his second wife secret in his journal.

A little over a year later, he invited her to Cambridge for the Harvard-Yale game. Franklin led the cheers. That evening, he wrote another entry in his special code: "After lunch I have a never to be forgotten walk to the river with my darling."

He had proposed. With her help, he said, he could make something of himself.

She had asked him, "Why me? I am plain. I have little to bring you." But she had also said yes.

When Franklin told his mother his big news a few days later, she asked him to keep the engagement a secret for a year to see if his feelings for Eleanor and hers for him were truly lasting, just as her father had insisted that she and Mr. James let time pass before announcing their engagement.

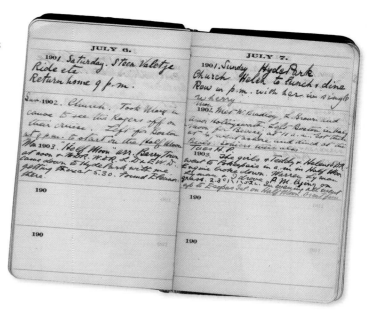

OPPOSITE In June of 1903, Eleanor, seated second from the right, came to Springwood for a four-day house party. Franklin, wearing a straw hat, stands nearby. All the guests, invited by his mother, were relatives by blood or marriage.

ABOVE Two weeks later, after another encounter with the cousin with whom he'd fallen in love, Franklin used an amateurish private code to write "E is an Angel" in his diary. The cipher was intended to keep his mother from knowing what was on his mind.

Bedlam Let Loose

Within days of becoming president, Theodore Roosevelt had issued an executive order changing the official name of his new residence from the Executive Mansion to what most people had always called it—the "White House." The place was in dreadful shape: shabby, cramped, still lit by gaslight with an elevator that rarely worked and floors so shaky that whenever a large gathering was expected, the floors of the public rooms had to be shored up with timbers.

The fashionable New York architect Charles F. McKim was called in to renovate and rebuild: much of the interior had to be gutted, and the executive offices of the president were to be moved from the second floor into a new building.

In May 1902, Roosevelt ordered that it all be done in six months. He moved to a bedroom across Jackson Street until he could join his family at Sagamore Hill for the summer. "The house is torn to pieces," McKim wrote that summer, "bedlam let loose cannot compare with it."

When work was finished in the fall of 1902, the Roosevelt White House had an almost royal air: the coachmen's buttons bore the initials "T.R."; Edith met weekly with the cabinet wives to decide who was and who was not to be invited to dinner; those asked to accompany the president on his frequent rides through Rock Creek Park were instructed to stay behind him and not get closer than ten yards. Critics spoke of an "Imperial Court," and some White House dinner guests complained that the president monopolized the conversation: "Hardly an observation was made by anyone else at the table," one wrote, "and, in fact, it would only have been possible by the exercise of a sort of brutal force."

"I do not think that any two people have ever got more enjoyment out of the White House than Mother and I," TR told Ted. "We love the house itself without and within, for its associations, for its stateliness and its simplicity. . . . We almost always take our breakfast on the south portico now, Mother looking very pretty and dainty in her summer dresses."

ABOVE AND RIGHT John Singer Sargent's portrait of Theodore Roosevelt, painted in the White House. TR loved it and had it hung in the expanded entrance hall. Henry Adams thought it was "good Sargent and not very bad Roosevelt. It is not Theodore, but a young intellectual idealist with a taste for athletics, which I take to be Theodore's idea of himself."

OPPOSITE, TOP Workers roofing the new Executive Office Building, where the president's offices would eventually be located. The building was meant to be a temporary structure but has remained in place ever since—the West Wing.

OPPOSITE The people of France presented Edith Roosevelt with this portrait by Théobald Chartran. The first lady is seated in the White House garden with the south portico of the White House in the background.

FAR RIGHT The expanded State Dining Room, lit by a brand-new electric chandelier, its walls a menagerie of the president's hunting trophies

The Steam-Engine in Trousers

Theodore Roosevelt was the first president to have been born in a city, and the first to be known by his initials—"T.R." He was so many things at once that one admirer called him "polygonal": moral crusader and canny politician; birdwatcher and big-game hunter; historian and expansionist and naturalist; omnivorous reader and hands-down the most prolific writer in presidential history. (In addition to his thirty-five books he would write some 150,000 letters before he was through.)

He moved fast, talked fast, seemed to harbor an opinion on every topic—and to be more than happy to express any or all of them. "I always believe in going hard at everything," he told one of his sons. "My experience is that it pays never to let up or grow slack and fall behind."

"His personality," said one visitor, "so crowds the room that the walls are worn thin and threaten to burst outward. You go to the White House. You

ABOVE TR takes a fence. When a photographer failed to capture his first jump, the president was happy to repeat the process for the camera. Photographs of him playing tennis on the new courts just outside his office were forbidden, however, because he feared voters would find the game effete.

ABOVE, RIGHT Roosevelt mounts a chair to make sure a Denver crowd can see as well as hear him. "He has only one limiting and devouring ambition," a French observer wrote, "which is to move and convince. . . . He is a workman who puts the best of his energy into driving rivets. He hammers out understandings."

shake hands with Roosevelt and hear him talk—and then go home to wring the personality out of your clothes."

An admirer hailed him as "a stream of fresh, pure bracing air from the mountains, [sent] to clear the fetid atmosphere of the national capital." Another called him "a steam-engine in trousers." But the novelist Henry James, who had known him for years, dismissed him as "the monstrous embodiment of unprecedented and resounding Noise." Mark Twain thought him a showoff, a "little imitation cowboy." And the biographer Gamaliel Bradford felt that he was always "playing a game. . . . Forcing optimism, forcing enjoyment with the desperate instinctive appreciation that if he let the pretense drop for a moment, the whole scheme of things would vanish away."

Whatever they thought of him, no one was ever able to ignore him. "Roosevelt has the knack of doing things and doing them noisily, clamorously," a reporter wrote, "while he is in the neighborhood the public can no more look the other way than the small boy can turn his head away from a circus parade followed by a steam calliope."

ABOVE Roosevelt takes time out to chat with the traveling press. He understood the importance of newspapermen as no president had before him. He made certain they had their own press room in the renovated White House, allowed them to interview him during his daily shave, parceled out important news on Sunday evenings so that it got big play on Monday mornings—and banished reporters who he felt had betrayed him to the "Ananias Club," named for the New Testament figure struck dead for lying.

"TERRIBLE TEDDY" WAITS FOR "THE UNKNOWN."

A Festival of Rejoicing

The Democrats played into Roosevelt's hands in 1904, nominating Alton B. Parker of New York for president, an able jurist but also, as the president said privately, "a neutral-tinted individual."

Roosevelt promised voters what he called a "Square Deal," favoring neither capital nor labor, rich nor poor. "If the cards do not come to any man," he said, "or if they do come, and he has not got the power to play them, that is his affair. All I mean is that there shall be no crookedness in the dealing."

By late October, a big Roosevelt victory seemed so likely that some of the big-time financiers who feared him scurried to write handsome checks for his campaign. Still, he worried he might not be elected president in his own right. "If things go wrong," he wrote his son Kermit, "never forget that we are very, very fortunate to have had three years in the White House, and that I have had a chance to accomplish work such as comes to very, very few men in any generation; and that I have no business to feel downcast or querulous merely because when so much has been given me, I have not had even more."

THE GOOD OLD DAYS.

PUCK

"TAKE YOUR CHOICE, GENTLEMEN."

OPPOSITE "'Terrible Teddy' Waits for 'The Unknown.'" Even the cartoonist, J. Keppler Jr., no admirer of Roosevelt, understood that his popularity in 1904 was so great that it didn't much matter which candidate the Democrats sent into the ring against him.

ABOVE In Keppler's "The Good Old Days," a frustrated TR—muzzled by his own pledge in the interest of what he called "civic decency" to stick to the custom that kept incumbent presidents from active campaigning—thinks back to 1900, when, as a vice presidential nominee, he'd been free to speak before an estimated three million Americans.

LEFT "Take Your Choice, Gentlemen." Puck sought to make the presidential contest a choice between TR and militarism and Alton B. Parker and the Constitution.

THE SACRED ELEPHANT.

ABOVE Republicans march to an easy victory in Keppler's "The Sacred Elephant." Henry Cabot Lodge acts as Emperor Roosevelt's mace bearer, carrying his Big Stick, while his vanquished enemies, including J. P. Morgan, seek to placate him with tribute.

OPPOSITE "Always Incisive, Decisive and Precise." Roosevelt's election-night pledge not to run for a third term, even though he'd served less than two, was seen as a selfless act by his admirers. Roosevelt himself soon realized it had been a terrible mistake.

Edith Roosevelt invited a few friends for dinner on election night—"a little feast," she called it, "which can be turned into a festival of rejoicing or into a wake as circumstances warrant." By seven thirty, it was clear that her husband would win by a landslide; it turned into the largest in history up to that time. "Have swept the country," he wired a friend. "I had no idea there would be such a sweep."

At this moment of personal triumph—and without consulting anyone—he made the worst blunder of his political career. The Constitution said nothing about how many terms a president might serve. But because George Washington had refused to stand for a third term, none of his successors had dared try to break that precedent. Roosevelt could have argued that he would not really have had two full terms since he had shared his first with the assassinated William McKinley. But he viewed that as a mere technicality. "The wise custom which limits the President to two terms regards the substance, and not the form," he told the press. "Under no circumstances will I be a candidate for or accept another nomination."

As he spoke, Edith and Alice visibly flinched. At the pinnacle of his power, Theodore Roosevelt had made himself a lame duck. He himself quickly came to regret what he'd said. "I would cut my hand off," he told a friend, "if I could recall that written statement."

ALWAYS INCISIVE, DECISIVE AND PRECISE.

We Are Greatly Rejoiced

On December 1, 1904, less than three weeks after Franklin Roosevelt had proudly cast his first presidential vote for his cousin Theodore, he and Eleanor finally announced their engagement. The newspapers paid most attention to the president's niece. She had "more claim to good looks than any of the Roosevelt cousins," one reported. Franklin was identified only as a member of the New York Yacht Club who had failed to be elected class marshal at Harvard.

The year of secrecy about their relationship had been hard on both Franklin and Eleanor. They had had to meet without arousing the curiosity of friends or relatives—or talkative servants. And they could never be alone together. "Oh, boy dear, I want you so much," Eleanor wrote after plans for one meeting had to be canceled.

Franklin's mother made things still more difficult. She promised her son she would "love Eleanor and adopt her fully when the right time comes," but meanwhile she had looked for ways to keep them apart, even taking her son on a Caribbean cruise in the hope that he might get over his infatuation.

OPPOSITE Although the official announcement of her son's engagement was still three months away, Sara allowed Eleanor to visit him at Campobello in August 1904. The month went "Oh! So quickly," Eleanor remembered, and when she left the island, a neighbor told her, Franklin "looked so tired and I felt everybody bored him."

ABOVE Eleanor and her future mother-in-law. When the engagement was finally revealed, Alice Roosevelt Longworth thought it "simply too nice to be true," but another cousin worried for Eleanor: "To have lived through such unhappiness and then to [plan to marry] a man with a mother like Cousin Sally . . . A more determined and possessive woman than I have ever known."

ABOVE Rivington Street on Manhattan's Lower East Side, where Eleanor taught calisthenics and "fancy dancing" to the children of Jewish and Italian immigrants at the College Settlement House. When Franklin visited her there, her students gathered around to ask if he were her "feller"—an expression, she later said, "which meant nothing to me at the time."

Meanwhile, Eleanor had discovered the rewards of useful work. Like many debutantes of her era, she joined the Junior League and volunteered to teach immigrant children in a Settlement House—on Rivington Street on New York's Lower East Side. Unlike most of her contemporaries, she took her work seriously. She rode public transportation, worked overtime, and sometimes turned down invitations rather than miss a class.

One afternoon, when Franklin dropped by to visit, a little girl fell ill. Eleanor asked him to carry her home. He did and never forgot the sights and foul smells of the tenement in which she lived. "My God," he told Eleanor. "I didn't know anyone lived like that."

Eleanor loved her work, found fulfillment in helping others that she never found elsewhere. But she was willing to give it up for marriage, hoping to find in her husband a confidant and to find in his mother something like the loving mother she had never had. It was a bargain she would sometimes come to regret.

As the months went by, Eleanor's Oyster Bay cousins began to suspect the truth. "Eleanor and Franklin are comic," one wrote after a chaperoned visit. "They [avoid] each other like the black plague and [deceive] us sweetly in every direction. . . . I would bet they are engaged." His cousins liked Franklin— the president's daughter Alice especially enjoyed his high spirits—but they also sometimes called him "Feather Duster" behind his back and would never be sure he was quite up to Eleanor.

When the engagement was finally announced, TR wrote Franklin and expressed nothing but delight.

Dear Franklin,

We are greatly rejoiced. I am as fond of Eleanor as if she were my daughter; and I like you, and trust you, and believe in you. . . . You and Eleanor are true and brave and I believe you love each other unselfishly; and golden years open before you. May all good fortune attend you both. . . .

Give my love to your dear mother.

Your affectionate cousin,
Theodore Roosevelt

ABOVE At Tiffany's, "after much inspection and deliberation," Franklin secretly purchased this engagement ring to give to Eleanor on her twentieth birthday, October 11, 1904, some five weeks before their engagement was to be announced. "You could not have found a ring I would have liked better," she assured him. "I love it so I know I shall find it hard to keep from wearing it!" The large white diamond weighs approximately 3.40 carats.

ABOVE, LEFT Eleanor's official engagement portrait. The gossip sheet *Town Topics* reported that she was "attractive . . . unusually tall and fair," with a "charming grace of manner that has made her a favorite since her debut."

The First Inauguration in the Family

The president invited the newly engaged couple to join the rest of the Roosevelts at his inauguration on March 4, 1905. "Franklin and I went to our seats on the capitol steps just back of Uncle Ted and his family," Eleanor recalled. "I was interested and excited but politics still meant little to me, though I can remember the forceful manner in which Uncle Ted delivered his speech. . . . I told myself I had seen an historic event—and I never expected to see another inauguration in the family."

Franklin never took his eyes off the president.

Afterward, Rough Riders escorted TR to the reviewing stand for the inaugural parade. Cowboys and grateful coal miners marched past. So did Geronimo and a contingent from Harvard in caps and gowns. The president refused to take shelter from the icy wind and stamped his feet in time to the music. At the reception that followed he shook 8,150 well-wishers' hands, still thought to be a presidential record.

LEFT AND ABOVE In this never-before-seen detail from a panoramic glass-plate image of TR's inauguration, his worshipful young cousin Franklin can be seen peering over the crowd to see his hero take the oath of office.

A Royal Alliance

Thirteen days after his inauguration, on March 17, President Roosevelt was to lead the St. Patrick's Day Parade up Fifth Avenue in Manhattan. Franklin and Eleanor Roosevelt chose that day to marry in a cousin's parlor on East Seventy-sixth Street so that TR could be present to give his brother's daughter away.

"The wedding of Miss Eleanor Roosevelt and Franklin Delano Roosevelt, her cousin, took on the semblance of a National 'Event,'" wrote a *New York Times* reporter who watched the guests arrive. "The presence of President Roosevelt, the bride's uncle, Miss Alice Roosevelt and Mrs. Roosevelt, and, as some rather enthusiastic if not discreet woman observed, the entire family in every degree of cousinship, made it very much like a 'royal alliance.'"

Alice Roosevelt remembered that "Father always wanted to be the bride at every wedding, the corpse at every funeral, and the baby at every christening." When the Reverend Endicott Peabody asked, "Who giveth this woman in marriage?," the president shouted back, "I do!" Once Franklin and Eleanor had exchanged their vows, he slapped the groom on the back. "Well, Franklin," he said, "there's nothing like keeping the name in the family." Then he hurried into the room where refreshments were served and held forth for an hour and a half.

The newlyweds were largely overlooked. But as they left, one of the guests exclaimed at how handsome the bridegroom was. Another answered, "Surprising for a Roosevelt."

OPPOSITE, LEFT A newspaper notice of the Roosevelts' wedding and their wedding certificate. Franklin's headmaster at Groton, Rev. Endicott Peabody, performed the ceremony. The witnesses were Eleanor's aunt and uncle, the president and first lady of the United States.

OPPOSITE, TOP Eleanor in her wedding dress. No photographs of the wedding itself have survived.

ABOVE Franklin designed the gold stickpins worn by his groomsmen; the three ostrich feathers of the Roosevelt family crest are inlaid with diamonds.

LEFT The newlyweds at Springwood, where they went immediately after the wedding. "My precious Franklin & Eleanor," Sara wrote that evening. "It is a delight to write to you together & to think of you happy at dear Hyde Park, just where my great happiness began."

A Scrumptious Time

Franklin and Eleanor's honeymoon lasted more than three months. Wherever they went, they took turns writing home to Franklin's mother, whom they both now called "Dearest Mama."

> R.M.S. *OCEANIC*
> *Dearest Mama:*
>
> *Eleanor has been a* wonderful *sailor and hasn't* missed *a single meal or* lost *any either.*

> R.M.S. *OCEANIC*
> *The stewardess informed me . . . that my husband must be English, he was so handsome and had the real English profile! Of course it is a great compliment but you can imagine how Franklin looked when I told him.*

At Brown's Hotel in London they were escorted to the royal suite because they were the president's kin. Eleanor was embarrassed. Franklin was delighted—and eagerly photographed its splendor. "We . . . went to the Alcazar on the Champs Elysées," Eleanor reported. "It was very funny and very vulgar, but as we couldn't hear very much the vulgarity didn't matter, and the crowd was most amusing."

ABOVE Eleanor poses for Franklin while holding his hat and consulting a tourist map in a Venetian gondola. "We saw churches until my husband would look no more," she remembered.

TOP, CENTER A postcard from Eleanor to her mother-in-law pronounces the cathedral at Ulm, Germany, "very fine."

TOP, RIGHT Franklin snapped this photograph of the royal suite at Brown's Hotel in London, to which the honeymooners had been assigned because of their illustrious surname. Eleanor was "horrified" at the expense and embarrassed to find that "in some way we had been identified with Uncle Ted." FDR was delighted.

From Venice, Franklin explained that "I had telegraphed ahead for an excellent gondolier [and we] went the whole length of the Grand canal. . . . I had expected to be disappointed . . . but the reality is far more wonderful than the pictures I had made."

PALACE HOTEL, ST. MORITZ
We had a lovely day and Franklin climbed to the highest peak and took some photographs. . . . Even very near the top there were beautiful wild flowers and Franklin . . . picked a number of them and the wild jasmine smells sweeter than anything I ever had.

Franklin assured his mother that he and Eleanor were having a "scrumptious time." But there were private hints of strain as well. Eleanor grew jealous when she chose not to accompany him up an Italian mountainside and he went anyway, in a party that included an attractive New York milliner who happened to be staying at their hotel. For his part, Franklin sleepwalked, suffered nightmares, and developed persistent hives.

ABOVE, LEFT Eleanor's maternal aunt "Tissie," Elizabeth Hall Mortimer (left), and her two daughters surprised the honeymooners at their hotel in St. Moritz, Switzerland. The Roosevelts would meet relatives and friends of their family all over Europe.

ABOVE Franklin, haggard and suffering from hives, photographed by Eleanor, in the Papadopoli Gardens in Venice

露国艦隊の敗戦　其貳　旅順港外大海戦真図

戰敗の隊艦國露　其貳　圖眞戰海大外港順旅

露國艦隊

レトヴヰザン
ツェザレウィチ
グロンボイ
ロ　シ　ア
オスウラビヤ
バ　ヤ　ン
ドミットリ
ドンスコイ
セヴストポール
ペレスウィチ
クーリック
ポベータ
ボルタワ
ドロゴブスク
外二軍艦二十四隻
外三水雷艇十三隻

日本艦隊

日露戰闘畫報第貳

三　初
笠　朝　高
日　吉　笠
砂　富　八
置　常　淺
野　磐　千
士　手　出
島　雲　吾
閑　妻　八
滄　雲　朝
曙　汐　村
雷　雨　逆
鳥　村　白
敷　島
笠
日　進
軍艦十六隻
水雷艇四隻
青雲堂石版部致版

The loss of Russian fleet of war vessels.　*The Illustrated war of Japan & Russia. 1904*

A Mighty Good Thing

From one of the last stops on FDR's honeymoon, Osberton Hall, a British country house owned by old friends of his parents, he wrote excitedly to his mother, "Everyone has been talking about Cousin Theodore, saying that he is the most prominent figure of present day history, and adopting toward our country in general a most respectful and almost loving tone."

Everyone was talking about the American president because he had just succeeded at something no other statesman had dared attempt: helping to end a conflict that threatened to disrupt the balance of power in the Pacific. For two years, Russia and Japan had been at war over which would dominate Korea and Manchuria. Russia had found itself on the losing end. Japan occupied Korea, took Port Arthur and Mukden in Manchuria, and sank most of

ABOVE A 1904 Japanese woodcut shows Japanese warships battering the Russian fleet during the siege of Port Arthur. It was the first modern clash of steel battleships on the high seas and a great victory for Japan.

the czar's fleet in the battle of Tsushima. But its victories had been won at a fearful cost.

Theodore Roosevelt persuaded both sides to send representatives to a conference near Portsmouth, New Hampshire, in August of 1905. Before talks began, he invited them aboard the presidential yacht, provided a stand-up lunch so that no one could claim he'd been slighted by the seating arrangements, and proposed a toast to which he insisted there be no responses, asking "in the interests of all mankind that a just and lasting peace may speedily be concluded."

Then he worked behind the scenes to hammer out the agreement that came to be called the Treaty of Portsmouth. Each side could claim some kind of victory: Russia abandoned all claims to Korea; Japan dropped its demand for payment for the costs of the war; the disputed island of Sakhalin was split in two. Roosevelt's friend and frequent critic Henry Adams declared him "the best herder of Emperors since Napoleon."

"This is splendid, this is magnificent," Roosevelt told a friend after it was signed. "It's a mighty good thing for Russia, and a mighty good thing for Japan, and mighty good for me, too!"

For all that he had done he would win the Nobel Prize for Peace.

ABOVE While a twenty-one-gun salute echoes off Oyster Bay, President Roosevelt hurries aboard the presidential yacht *Mayflower* on August 5, 1905, determined to get peace talks between Japan and Russia under way.

LEFT Aboard ship, Roosevelt poses for an official photograph, flanked by Russian and Japanese diplomats. "I think we are off to a good start," he said that evening. "I know perfectly well that the whole world is watching me, and the condemnation that will come down on me, if the conference fails, will be world-wide, too. But that's all right."

The White House Gang

ABOVE Archie and Quentin await orders from the White House police force. "Not one of my children ever wants to be told or directed about anything whatever," Edith once complained, and her husband was no help. "He thinks children should be given entire freedom for their own inclinations."

OPPOSITE, TOP The president and his family in the summer of 1903 (left to right): Quentin, TR, Ted Jr., Archie, Alice, Kermit, Edith, and Ethel

OPPOSITE, BOTTOM Harvard freshman Ted Jr. being helped off the field at Harvard with a broken nose. When sportswriters suggested that Yale players had deliberately tried to injure the president's son, Ted indignantly denied it in a letter to his father: "They played a clean straight game. . . . They beat us by simply and plainly outplaying us."

The country was as obsessed with Roosevelt's family as it was with him, and newspapermen competed to find fresh copy about its members. "The other day," the president wrote in August of 1905, "a reporter asked Quentin something about me, to which that affable and canny young gentleman responded, 'Yes, I see him sometimes; but I know nothing of his family life.'"

Everything the Roosevelt children did seemed to make headlines.

Theodore Jr.—"Ted"—was an eighteen-year-old Harvard freshman. His father had pushed him so hard when he was small that Edith and a physician had had to intervene. He remained a "regular bull terrier," his proud father wrote, stoical enough to have finished a Groton football game despite a broken collarbone, but combative enough to relish what the president called "sanguinary battles with outsiders." Photographers now dogged his steps, and his father urged him not to let his temper get the better of him.

Sixteen-year-old Kermit was at Groton. But the White House was still home to fourteen-year-old Ethel and eleven-year-old Archie. Both were quiet and sweet-tempered.

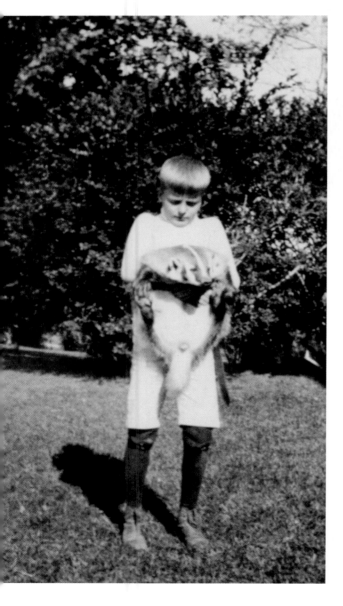

Seven-year-old Quentin was sweet-tempered too. "A roly-poly, happy-go-lucky personage," his father wrote, "the brightest of all the children." But he was also mischievous and irrepressible, a "fine little bad boy," according to his mother, fond of big words that he bit off just as his father did, and accustomed to giving orders to the band of small boys who called themselves "the White House gang."

The children's pets were allowed to roam everywhere—rabbits, raccoons, exotic birds, a kangaroo rat, dogs, a cat that attacked the Speaker of the House, and snakes that Quentin enjoyed bringing into cabinet meetings. The children rolled giant snowballs down the White House roof and onto the heads of policemen, spattered Gilbert Stuart's portrait of George Washington with spitballs, and used mirrors to reflect sunlight into the eyes of clerks trying to work in the neighboring State, War, and Navy Building—until the president himself ordered semaphore men stationed on its roof to signal them to stop "and report to me right away."

The president often saw himself as one of the gang. "I came up-stairs," he once reported to "Darling Kermit," "[and found] Archie . . . driving Quentin by his suspenders which were fixed to the end of a pair of woolen reins. Then

they would ambush me and we would have a vigorous pillow-fight, and after ten minutes of this we would go into Mother's room, and I would read them the book Mother had been reading them. Archie and Quentin are really great playmates."

OPPOSITE, LEFT Archie and a pet badger his father brought home from his western tour. It looked like "a mattress with legs," the president wrote. Archie assured nervous visitors that it bit only legs, "not faces."

OPPOSITE, TOP Quentin, the youngest and liveliest of the Roosevelt children. "His tow head was always mussed," a member of the White House Gang of small boys he led recalled. "His head seemed too large for his body. He was as irrepressible mentally as he was physically, and, either way, there was no holding him back."

ABOVE Quentin rides Algonquin, the calico pony he and a footman once smuggled into the White House elevator and up to the second-floor family quarters to cheer up his brother Archie, who was mourning the loss of a favorite dog.

RIGHT An illustrated letter from Theodore to his son Kermit at Groton depicts a White House pillow fight in which the president of the United States took a prominent and enthusiastic part.

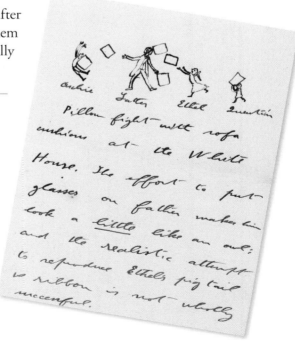

Never Anything but Trouble

Alice was twenty-one in 1905, the daughter of Theodore Roosevelt's first wife. Her early life had been divided among her mother's parents, her aunt Bamie, and her father's other children at Sagamore Hill. Like her cousin Eleanor, she felt she had never had a real home of her own.

"Father doesn't care for me one-eighth as much as he does for the other children," she once confided to her diary. "It is perfectly true that he doesn't, and Lord, why should he? We are not in the least congenial, and if I don't care overmuch for him and don't take a bit of interest in the things he likes, why should he pay any attention to me or the things I live for, except to look on them with disapproval."

Edith and Theodore had urged her to remain ladylike, tractable, reserved—to behave the way Eleanor did. Instead, Alice set out to be "conspicuous." The "First Daughter"—the first teenage girl to grow up in the White House in a quarter of a century—was attractive, outspoken, and desperate to be noticed. She did everything—or almost everything—a young woman of her age and standing should not have done. She smoked. She bet on the horses, took long unchaperoned automobile rides in a bright red roadster, jumped into a swimming pool fully clothed, flirted with battalions of wealthy young men in New York and Newport, and wore a green snake as a wriggling fashion accessory to divert attention during one of her father's meetings with the press.

Her face was everywhere—candy boxes, song sheets, the front pages of newspapers around the world. The German navy named a ship for her. Overseas crowds hailed her as "Princess Alice." She couldn't get enough of it. "The family was always telling me, 'Beware of publicity!'" she remembered. "And there was publicity hitting me in the face every day. . . . And once stories got out, or were invented, I was accused of courting publicity. I destroyed a savage letter on the subject from my father. . . . There was he, one of the greatest experts in publicity there ever was, accusing me of trying to steal his limelight."

One evening, a troubled young man had driven his carriage up to Sagamore Hill and insisted on seeing the president. When the Secret Service told him to go away, there was a struggle. A pistol was found. Roosevelt stepped out onto the porch to see what all the fuss was about. An agent said the intruder was a harmless lunatic, convinced he was destined to become the president's son-in-law.

"Of course, he was crazy," Roosevelt later told the family. "He wants to marry Alice."

Republican Congressman Nicholas Longworth of Ohio did want to marry Alice, and she accepted his proposal. He was sixteen years older than she, drank too much, and had a reputation as a ladies' man, but he was also a member of Porcellian and, Alice's father assured the king of England, "much the best violinist ever to come out of Harvard University."

Their wedding at the White House on February 17, 1906, was the social event of the year. Eleanor was pregnant and unable to attend. But Franklin

ABOVE Portrait of the first daughter by Edward Curtis, 1905. "Ever since she debuted into society," the *New York Times* wrote, "there has been constant danger that she would stampede the cabinet with her poodle and pet garter snake or demoralize the senate with one of her skirt dances and acrobatic stunts."

OPPOSITE Alice at play. "I can be President of the United States," her exasperated father once told a friend, "or I can attend to Alice. I cannot possibly do both!"

and Sara rode together up the White House driveway and stood side by side inside to watch the exchange of vows.

Afterward, the president, his new son-in-law, and thirty-eight other members of Porcellian slipped into a private dining room for the ceremonial toast to the groom that club tradition called for. Franklin had to stand outside with the other guests. Later, when the official photograph was being made, he helped adjust Alice's veil, then stepped back before the camera clicked.

As the newlyweds left the White House, Alice embraced her exhausted stepmother. "Mother, this has been quite the nicest wedding I'll ever have," she said. "I've never had so much fun."

Edith answered, only half in jest, "I want you to know that I'm glad to see you leave. You have never been anything but trouble."

SCENE AT THE MOMENT WHEN BISHOP SATTERLEE SAID: "I PRONOUNCE THEE MAN AND WIFE."

TOP Bystanders watch as, one by one, carriages drop off some of the seven hundred wedding guests, Franklin and his mother among them. "The number of people at the wedding will be so great," the president had complained as the lists were drawn up, "that we shall be fortunate if we escape a riot."

RIGHT Breathless wedding coverage from the front page of the *Washington Times*, February 17, 1906

OPPOSITE Congressman Nicholas Longworth, Alice Roosevelt, and her father pose for the official wedding photograph. "Alice looked remarkably pretty," Sara Delano Roosevelt reported to Eleanor, "and her manner was very charming." The lace that trimmed the bride's satin gown came from the wedding dress worn by her late mother, Alice Lee, when she married Theodore Roosevelt twenty-six years earlier.

A SHORT INTERVIEW IN THE WHITE HOUSE

Now, Mr. Railroadman, stock watering must stop—

Rates are too high—

They must come down

Safety must be guaranteed—

I hope I impress my meaning on you—

Good day!

I Attack Inequities

In June of 1906, Theodore Roosevelt seemed almost invincible. In his most recent message to Congress he had called for a series of what he called "national solutions to National problems." Then, employing both the power of what he was the first to call the "bully pulpit" to rally public support, and his hard-won ability to outthink and outmaneuver the opposition behind the scenes, he'd pushed through a series of bills that made good on some of the most important of those promises. "I attack," he once wrote. "I attack inequities. I try to choose the time for an attack when I can get the bulk of the people to accept the principles for which I stand."

Over the furious objections of the railroads—and the powerful Republican senators they controlled—Roosevelt won passage of the Hepburn Act. It empowered the Interstate Commerce Commission to limit the rates the railroads could charge to move goods from place to place—and for the first time in American history gave the rulings of a federal agency the force of law.

With indirect help from crusading journalists, he pushed through the Pure Food and Drug Act, which demanded that the producers of everything from patent medicines to canned tomatoes accurately label their products. And when the meat-packing trust tried to block a meat inspection bill, Roosevelt released part of the appalling findings of a federal investigation into industry practices and then threatened to make public the rest if they didn't back down. They did.

Roosevelt enraged those whom he denounced as "malefactors of great wealth"—especially those who had contributed to his 1904 campaign in hopes of having some control over his policies. "We bought the son of a bitch," one said, "but he wouldn't stay bought."

The Antiquities Act Roosevelt had also signed in June of 1906 empowered the president to provide protection for prehistoric ruins as well as "objects of scientific interest" on federal lands—without having to ask permission of Congress. He immediately reinterpreted the act so that he could also save as National Monuments some of the country's most extraordinary natural wonders—including Devil's Tower and the Muir Woods, Mount Olympus, and more than 800,000 acres of the grandest canyon on earth.

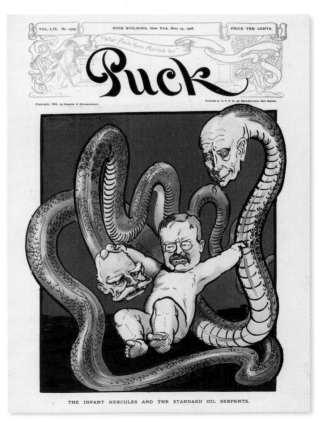

ABOVE Theodore Roosevelt at the peak of his power in 1906

OPPOSITE "A Short Interview in the White House." *Puck* often opposed Theodore Roosevelt, but its stable of cartoonists found him irresistible, nonetheless.

RIGHT "The Infant Hercules and the Standard Oil Serpents." In 1906, TR attacked Standard Oil for profiting from secret rail rates and found himself locked in combat with two formidable opponents, John D. Rockefeller (with the forked tongue), and Nelson W. Aldrich, who was both the father-in-law of Rockefeller's son and the Senate whip of the president's own party.

A Colossal Blunder

On August 16, 1906, Theodore Roosevelt received a telegram from the mayor of Brownsville, Texas. Black troops of the 25th United States Infantry (Colored) stationed at nearby Fort Brown had shot and killed a white bartender, he charged, had wounded a white police officer, and then had vowed to "repeat this outrage." He demanded that the guilty be punished and the regiment immediately be stationed elsewhere.

The soldiers denied any wrongdoing. The regiment's white commanding officer backed them up; his men had all been safely in their barracks on the night in question. An all-white Texas grand jury had failed to indict any of the soldiers.

Roosevelt ordered the inspector general—a white South Carolinian—to investigate.

The president had made a few symbolic gestures toward civil rights. He had denounced the lawlessness of lynching, and when whites in Indianola, Mississippi, forced his black appointee as postmistress to resign, he closed the post office and made Indianola residents travel twenty miles to get their mail. But he also made much of his Confederate ancestry whenever he was in the South and privately thought it would take black people "many thousands of years" to match the intellectual powers of white people.

The inspector general's report on the Brownsville incident recommended that the president declare at least some of the accused guilty. "The colored soldier," he charged, is inherently "secretive," and too "aggressive in his attitude toward social equality." Since none would confess, all should be dismissed.

Booker T. Washington hurried to the White House and begged the president not to do anything before he could undertake an investigation of his own. To act without actual evidence of guilt and without giving the troops any chance to defend themselves, he said, would be a "colossal blunder."

Roosevelt contemptuously dismissed Washington's appeal. He waited until November 7—the day after hundreds of thousands of black voters cast their votes for his party's congressional candidates all across the North—and then dismissed all 167 men from the service. None would get a penny in pension. One of the sergeants had fought alongside Roosevelt in Cuba; he remembered splitting his rations with the colonel himself after the battle of Las Guasimas.

Roosevelt angrily denounced critics of his Brownsville decision as naive "sentimentalists," but when the time came to write his autobiography, he chose to make no mention of the case.

ABOVE After Brownsville, W. E. B. Du Bois urged black voters to abandon TR and his party. "What, after all, do we have to thank Roosevelt for?" he asked the readers of the *Horizon: A Journal of the Color Line,* and then answered his own question: "For asking a man to dine with him," for appointing perfectly well-qualified black men to a handful of federal jobs, "and for saying, publicly, that the door of opportunity ought to be held open to colored men." But, Du Bois continued, "the door once declared open, Mr. Roosevelt, by his word and deed since has slammed most emphatically in the black man's face."

OPPOSITE *Harper's Weekly* comments on the injustice done to the men of the 25th U.S. Infantry. More than six decades later, Augustus F. Hawkins, a black congressman from Los Angeles, introduced a bill that persuaded the Department of Defense to grant honorable discharges to all 167 of the men who had been dismissed. By then, just two members of the battalion were still living.

HARPER'S WEEKLY

A JOURNAL OF CIVILIZATION

Vol. LI.   New York, Saturday, January 12, 1907   No. 2612

DISHONORABLY DISCHARGED

While Our Civilization Lasts

The Brownsville controversy was soon buried by the news that TR and Edith had made a three-day surprise visit to the Panama Canal, the first time a sitting president had ever set foot on foreign soil. "ROOSEVELT IS THERE," declared the *Washington Post.*

TR described it all in a letter to Kermit: "We worked from morning till night. The second day I was up at a quarter-to-six and got to bed at a quarter of twelve, and I do not believe that in the intervening time, save when I was dressing, there were ten consecutive minutes when I was not busily at work in some shape or form. For two days there were uninterrupted tropic rains without a glimpse of the sun . . . so that we saw the climate at its worst. It was just what I desired to do."

Wearing a Panama hat and a seaman's sou'wester over his white tropical suit, TR seemed oblivious to the steady deluge that at its height deposited three inches of rain in less than two hours. He inspected hospitals, barracks, and kitchens; ate with workers rather than the dignitaries waiting for him at Panama City's grandest hotel; ordered the train that was supposed to keep him dry and safe to stop again and again so that he could jump down to ask the men how they were being treated or wade through the mud to see for himself what they were doing. "I went over everything that I could possibly go over in the time at my disposal . . . ," he remembered, "and spent a day in the Culebra Cut where the greatest work is being done." Thousands of men were at work there, blasting, digging, and scooping out an artificial valley a third of a mile wide across the Continental Divide. "With intense energy men and machines do their task," Roosevelt told his son, "the white men supervising matters and handling the machines, while the tens of thousands of black men do the rough manual labor where it is not worthwhile to have machines do it. . . . American canal-builders and the thousands of men laboring under them are changing the face of the continent, are doing the greatest engineering feat of the ages, and the effect of their work will be felt while our civilization lasts."

ABOVE, LEFT Ignoring the relentless rain, Theodore Roosevelt strides ashore at La Boca, Panama, November 15, 1906.

OPPOSITE Roosevelt at the controls of a ninety-ton Bucyrus steam shovel that could lift eight tons of rock and earth in a single scoop

LEFT Roosevelt and Manuel Amador, the Panamanian president who had led the uprising against Colombia, meet on the steps of the Metropolitan Cathedral in Panama City. "To reorganize the great work [of digging the Canal], to grasp . . . its immense magnitude, a superior man was necessary," Amador told TR through his interpreter, "and you were this man." The rain-soaked riders in the foreground are Panamanians wearing Rough Rider uniforms because it was thought that would please the American president.

A Christmas present to Franklin &
Eleanor from Mama
Number & Street not yet
quite decided —
19 or 20 feet wide — [1905]

A Heart Well-Nigh Broken

In the winter of 1908, Franklin and Eleanor Roosevelt moved into the six-story New York townhouse his mother had built for them at 49 East Sixty-fifth Street. With them came their first two children, two-year-old Anna and eleven-month-old James, Eleanor's younger brother, Hall—and six servants.

Sara and three more servants occupied the house's twin at number 47. The Roosevelt family crest was carved above the common entrance and open doors on three floors connected the households.

Sara had hired the staff. She and her son had also overseen the construction and furnishing. Eleanor had played almost no part. Not long after they moved in, Franklin found her weeping. He asked what was wrong. "I said I did not like to live in a house which was not in any way mine," she remembered, "one that I had done nothing about and which did not represent the way I wanted to live. Being an eminently reasonable person, he thought I was quite mad and told me so gently, and said I would feel different in a little while and left me alone until I should become calmer."

Eleanor did calm down, she recalled, but her outburst was the first sign that in the interest of her marriage she had simply been "absorbing the personalities of those around me and letting their tastes and interests dominate me"—and that she resented it.

Franklin delighted in his children. Eleanor seemed mostly puzzled by them. "I had never had any interest in dolls or in little children," she remembered, "and I knew absolutely nothing about handling or feeding a baby." Nannies hired and fired by her mother-in-law saw to such details. "Brother fell out of his chair this morning," Eleanor noted one day. "Anna did not come to breakfast because she said, 'No, I won't.'" Misbehavior alarmed her; so did the nurses who told her how to handle it.

OPPOSITE, LEFT, BOTTOM AND TOP Sara Delano Roosevelt's 1905 Christmas note promising to build Franklin and Eleanor a brownstone, and the twin houses into which she and they moved three years later

OPPOSITE, TOP RIGHT Eleanor and her mother-in-law at Springwood the following year

ABOVE Family portrait, 1908: Eleanor and James, Franklin and Anna

LEFT Franklin takes Anna for a walk at Campobello, while Eleanor and Anna's nurse look on.

Franklin was home only in the evenings. He had finished Columbia Law School, passed the New York bar, and, with the help of family connections, had gone to work as a clerk for the Wall Street firm of Carter, Ledyard and Milburn. The law itself didn't interest him much. A member of the firm recalled that he "tended to dance on the top of the hills" and leave to others the hard work on the slopes below.

But "thanks to Uncle Ted," his wife remembered, he was already interested in politics, and so he did enjoy getting to know all kinds of people he'd never encountered at Groton or Harvard—ambulance chasers and penniless plaintiffs and witnesses, both credible and incredible.

A few months after the Roosevelts moved to Sixty-fifth Street, Eleanor gave birth to a third child, at eleven pounds "the biggest and most beautiful of all the babies," she remembered. They named him Franklin Jr. and immediately registered his name at Groton.

That summer, Eleanor and several servants took the three children to Campobello. Sara had bought the younger Roosevelts their own "cottage" on the island, entirely separate from hers. There was no electricity, no telephone; all the cooking had to be done on a small coal stove. Eleanor loved it. It was hers, the first real home she had ever known.

But as the weeks went by, it became clear that something was wrong with the baby's heart. Doctors were consulted, first on the island, then in Hyde Park, finally in Manhattan. No one seemed able to do anything.

Sara recorded the baby's final hours in her journal.

November 1st. At a little before 7 A.M., Franklin [called my room] "Better come, Mama, Baby is sinking." I went in. The little angel ceased breathing at 7:25 . . . Franklin and Eleanor are most wonderful, but poor Eleanor's mother's heart is well-nigh broken. She so hoped and cannot believe her baby is gone from her.

November 2. I sat often beside my little grandson. It is hard to give him up and my heart aches for Eleanor.

Franklin Roosevelt Jr. was buried in the family plot at St. James' Church in Hyde Park. It seemed "cruel," Eleanor wrote, "to leave him out there in the cold. . . . I reproached myself very bitterly for having done so little about the care of this baby. I felt he had been left too much to the nurse and I knew too little about him, and that in some way I was to blame."

Within a month of her baby's burial, Eleanor would find herself pregnant again.

ABOVE During the early years of her motherhood, Eleanor wore this locket marked by her and her husband's initials and the year of their engagement. The dents were caused by one teething baby after another.

OPPOSITE Eleanor and the first Franklin Jr., photographed at Campobello in the summer of 1908

Oughtn't We All Be Proud?

America's place in the wider world continued to matter most to Theodore Roosevelt. U.S. relations with Japan had deteriorated since he'd helped end the Russo-Japanese War.

Americans living along the Pacific coast had not helped. The San Francisco school board voted to segregate Japanese from white children. The California legislature called for cutting off Japanese immigration altogether. Newspapers issued dire warnings about a "Yellow Peril." Asian immigrants and their descendants were burned out, beaten, killed.

The president got the school board to change its policy and under a so-called "Gentleman's Agreement" persuaded Japan quietly to limit the outflow of emigrant workers on its own. But Japanese sea power was growing and Japanese sensibilities had been hurt.

When Roosevelt thought he detected what he called "a very, very slight undertone of veiled truculence in [Japanese] communications," he felt it was time to show "that I am not afraid of them."

He resolved to send sixteen American warships around the world to remind everyone that "the Pacific is as much our home waters as the Atlantic"—and to impress the voters with the U.S. Navy's new importance, as well. Thanks in large part to Roosevelt's resolve, America's naval power was now second only to Great Britain's.

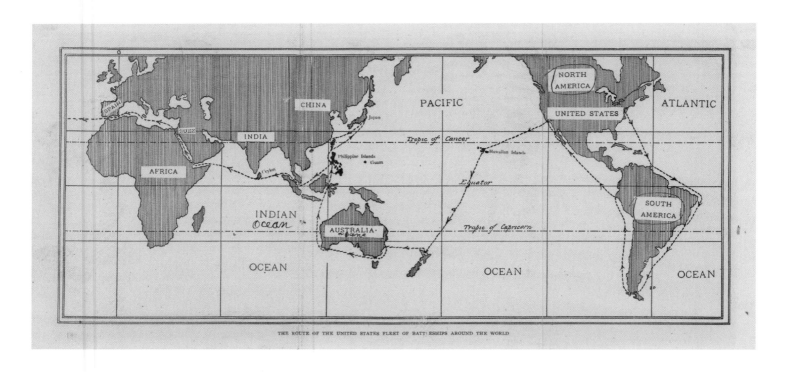

THE ROUTE OF THE UNITED STATES FLEET OF BATTLESHIPS AROUND THE WORLD

OPPOSITE, TOP The Great White Fleet of sixteen battleships and their escorts leaves Hampton Roads, Virginia, on December 16, 1907.

OPPOSITE, BOTTOM Americans followed the progress of the thirty-seven-month round-the-world voyage on newspaper maps.

ABOVE The fleet visited twenty ports of call, including (TOP LEFT AND RIGHT) Havana and Rio de Janeiro; (ABOVE, LEFT AND RIGHT) Wellington and Sydney.

"The Nations Pride"

Enjoying himself in Candy Ceylon

When Congress balked at approving the money for such a long voyage, he ordered the Great White Fleet to set sail across the Pacific anyway, confident that in the end legislators would not want to be responsible for keeping fourteen thousand American sailors from coming home again. "I determined on [sending the fleet] precisely as I took Panama, without consulting the Cabinet. A council of war never fights, and in a crisis the duty of a leader is to lead."

Looking back, Roosevelt believed the fourteen-month voyage of the Great White Fleet—steaming into twenty ports on six continents—had been "the most important service that I rendered to peace."

The ceremony celebrating the fleet's return on February 22, 1909, would be one of the high points of Roosevelt's life. "Did you ever see such a fleet?" he asked everyone around him. "Isn't it magnificent? Oughtn't we all be proud?"

But the president remained a realist about the prospects for a permanent peace in the Pacific. "Sooner or later, the Japanese will try to bolster up their power by another war. Unfortunately for us, we have what they want most, the Philippines. . . . When it comes, we will win over Japan, but it will be one of the most disastrous conflicts the world has ever seen."

CLOCKWISE, FROM ABOVE The Great White Fleet's voyage continues: TR was most keen that Japan be impressed by American naval power; sailors went ashore wherever their ships anchored, including Ceylon and Egypt; the sight of the fleet steaming past the Rock of Gibraltar inspired an insurance company to adopt it as its symbol; thousands of New Yorkers poured into Riverside Park to see the anchored fleet lit up at night.

OPPOSITE, BOTTOM On February 22, 1909, the fleet returned to Hampton Roads, where President Roosevelt climbed onto the gun turret of the fleet's flagship, the USS *Connecticut,* and welcomed her crewmen home. "Another chapter is complete," he said that day, "and I could not ask a finer concluding scene for my administration."

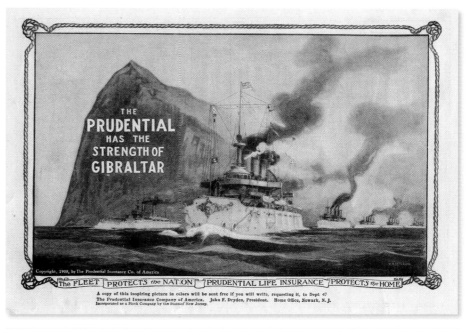

VOL. LX. No. 1535. PUCK BUILDING, New York, August 1, 1906. PRICE TEN CENTS.

"What Fools these Mortals be!"

Puck

THE CROWN PRINCE.

My Future Is in the Past

Theodore Roosevelt had accomplished a great deal during his seven years as president: the breakup of National Securities, the coal strike settlement, the Panama Canal, an end to the Russo-Japanese War, millions of wild acres preserved for future generations to enjoy. "I do not believe that any president has ever had as thoroughly a good time as I have had," he wrote. "Or ever has enjoyed himself as much."

But privately he was not satisfied. He could not class himself as a great president, because he had faced no great crisis while in office. "A man has to take advantage of his opportunities, but the opportunities have to come. If there is not war, you don't get the great general; if there is not the great occasion, you don't get the great statesman; if Lincoln had lived in times of peace, no one would know his name."

Now, hampered by his own pledge not to run again in 1908, Roosevelt hand-picked a successor, his good friend and secretary of war, William Howard Taft of Ohio, who promised to remain true to the progressive principles the president had laid down. The country seemed to want that, too. Taft won easily.

As he left the White House, Roosevelt did his best to seem cheerful, but when a friend assured him that he had not finished with politics he said, "My dear fellow, for Heaven's sake don't talk about my having a future. My future is in the past."

He was just fifty years old. "I want him to be the simplest American alive after he leaves the White House," Edith wrote. "And the funniest thing to me is that he wants to be also and says he is going to be, but the trouble is he has really forgotten how to be."

OPPOSITE Keppler heralds the nomination of Theodore Roosevelt's chosen successor, Secretary of War William Howard Taft. "Taft will carry on the work substantially as I have carried it on," Roosevelt assured a British friend. "His policies, principles, purposes and ideals are the same as mine. . . . In leaving, I have the profound satisfaction of knowing that he will do all in his power to further every one of the great causes for which I have fought and that he will persevere in every one of the great governmental policies in which I most firmly believe."

ABOVE, LEFT Roosevelt and President-elect Taft (in top hats) climb the snow-covered Capitol steps on inauguration day. "I knew there would be a blizzard when I went out," Roosevelt told a newspaperman.

ABOVE William Howard Taft. "Mr. Taft was so nice and big and beaming over his victory," Edith Roosevelt wrote after election day, "that it did one good to look at him."

Bwana Mkubwa Sana

All his life, Roosevelt had dreamed of hunting big game in Africa. Now, with his son Kermit at his side, he could make that dream a reality—and not be tempted to answer reporters' questions about how his successor was doing. On that subject he promised to be "silent as an oyster."

When the former president sailed for Africa, J. P. Morgan was supposed to have said, "Every American hopes that every lion will do its duty."

The Roosevelt safari reminded onlookers of a military campaign. A vast American flag flew over the ex-president's tent. Skilled white hunters served as guides. Three naturalists from the Smithsonian Institution saw to the steadily growing collection of specimens. Two hundred and six porters carried supplies, including cans of California peaches and Boston baked beans, ninety pounds of jam, four tons of salt to cure animal skins, and sixty miniature volumes, ranging from *Alice in Wonderland* to *The Federalist*—specially bound in pigskin, Roosevelt explained, so that dust and dents and bloodstains would "merely [make them] look as a well-used saddle looks." His tent was cared for by two men; two more saw to his horses; another pair were responsible for his

guns and ammunition. To his face, they all called him "Bwana Makwuba Sana," or "Very Great Master." Among themselves he was "Bwana Tumbo," "The Master With a Big Stomach." When Roosevelt overheard the second title and asked about it, he was told it meant "The Man with Unerring Aim."

For good luck, the ex-president carried a gold-mounted rabbit's foot, given to him by his friend the former heavyweight champion John L. Sullivan.

He didn't need it. Together, his and Kermit's rifles accounted for 512 animals and large birds, including twenty rhinoceroses, seventeen lions, eleven elephants, and nine giraffes—and not including countless smaller birds felled by their shotguns. They kept only a dozen trophies for themselves, Roosevelt said, and "shot nothing that was not used either as a museum specimen or for meat." The expedition would eventually send home crates and barrels containing 11,397 preserved creatures, "not . . . a tenth," Roosevelt wrote, "nor a hundredth, part of what we might have killed, had we been willing."

He reveled in all of it, but he was away from his wife for eleven months and he missed her. "Oh sweetest of sweet girls," he wrote toward the end of the safari on the twenty-fourth anniversary of their engagement, "last night I dreamed that I was with you, that our separation was but a dream; and when I [woke] up it was almost too hard to bear. Well, one must pay for everything; you have made the real happiness of my life; and so it is natural and right that I should constantly [be] more and more lonely without you. . . . Do you remember when you were such a pretty engaged girl, and said to your love, 'No, Theodore, that I cannot allow'? Darling, I love you so. . . . How very happy we have been for these last twenty-three years." He signed his letter, "Your own lover."

ABOVE Edith Roosevelt, for whom TR began to yearn while in Africa

OPPOSITE Shielded from the harsh noonday sun, Roosevelt devours one of the sixty miniature volumes in his personally selected "Pigskin Library." His British-made tent was so comfortable and so spacious, Roosevelt told a white hunter, that it made him feel "a little effeminate."

RIGHT Reporters waylay TR at the end of his safari on March 11, 1910, hoping to elicit his views. "We have nothing to say and will have nothing to say on American or foreign policy questions," he told them. "I will give no interviews and anything purporting to be an interview with me can be accepted as false as soon as it appears."

The Force of His Personality

In March of 1910, Theodore Roosevelt finally steamed up the Nile and out of the African interior. Reunited with Edith at Khartoum, he began a one-man, three-month parade across North Africa and Europe—making headlines wherever he went.

He upset Egyptians by telling them that they were not ready for independence from Great Britain. From the pulpit of an Amsterdam church he recited a Dutch nursery rhyme he remembered learning in his grandfather's house. Near Berlin, he watched maneuvers with Kaiser Wilhelm and took the opportunity to warn him that a war between Germany and England would be "an unspeakable calamity."

At the Louvre in Paris, he passed up Rubens's full-bodied nudes because he did not feel they should be viewed in mixed company.

At the Sorbonne, Roosevelt set forth his concept of leadership:

It is not the critic who counts; not the man who points out how the strong man stumbles, or where the doer of deeds could have done them better. The credit belongs to the man who is actually in the arena, whose face is marred by dust and sweat and blood; who strives valiantly; who errs, and comes short again and again, because there is no effort without error and shortcoming; but who does actually strive to do the deeds; who knows the great enthusiasms, the great devotions; who spends himself in a worthy cause; who, at the best knows in the end the triumph of high achievements, and who at the worst, if he fails, at least fails while daring greatly, so that his place shall never be with those cold and timid souls who know neither victory nor defeat.

Everywhere, crowds cheered him as if he still held office. The trip was both exhilarating and exhausting. "Father is so tired that whenever we go in a motor he falls asleep," Edith wrote home. "The people are quite mad about

OPPOSITE, TOP TR, Edith, and their party explore the battlefield of Omdurman near Khartoum, where in 1898 British lancers undertook the last great cavalry charge of the nineteenth century.

OPPOSITE, BOTTOM On his way to pick up an honorary degree from Cambridge University, Roosevelt spots a miniature Teddy bear placed in his path by cheering students, its tiny paw extended in welcome.

ABOVE Roosevelt maintains an uncharacteristic silence while a top-hatted guide points out the finer points of the oversized history paintings that line museum walls at Versailles.

him and stand around the hotel to see him go in and out. . . . [Though it was midnight,] I had to send him out on our balcony before they would disperse."

King Edward VII of England died while Roosevelt was still abroad, and President Taft asked TR to represent the United States at the London funeral. "With Roosevelt and the Kaiser at King Edward's funeral," a former White House aide wrote, "it will be a wonder if the poor corpse gets a passing thought."

One day, TR and Edith managed to slip away from onlookers and make an unannounced visit together to St. George's Church on Hanover Square, where they had quietly been married twenty-eight years before.

Taft watched Roosevelt's progress warily. "I don't suppose there was ever such a reception as that being given Theodore in Europe now," he wrote. "It illustrates how his personality has swept over the world, for after all no great event transpired during either of his administrations, and no startling legislation was enacted into law. It is the force of his personality that has passed beyond his own country and the capitals of the world and seeped into the small crevices of the universe."

ABOVE Kaiser Wilhelm II and TR look on as twelve thousand Prussian soldiers stage a five-hour mock battle. "Well, my dear Roosevelt," the Kaiser told his guest, "you are the first private citizen that has ever reviewed the Prussian troops!"

ABOVE Roosevelt, in top hat and morning coat, brings up the rear of the parade of befeathered royals attending the funeral of King Edward VII in London. After a week of their company, he said, he feared that "if I met another king I should bite him."

LEFT *Collier's,* the muckraking weekly that had helped awaken the public to the need for the kind of reforms Roosevelt had championed, welcomes him home.

All Franklin's Plans

No one followed Theodore Roosevelt's travels with more interest than Franklin Roosevelt did. He was bored with the law just as the ex-president had once been, and eager to follow the political path his cousin had blazed.

Other young members of the Roosevelt clan harbored the same ambition. Theodore Robinson, who had married Rosy's daughter, Helen, was already running for the New York Assembly; Joseph Alsop Jr., married to the ex-president's niece, was considering a run in Connecticut; Theodore Roosevelt Jr. was just twenty years old, still too young to run for office but already being called the "Crown Prince" in the newspapers; his three younger brothers might choose to run someday as well. All of them were sure to run as Republicans.

If Franklin were to have a chance, it would be best to run as a Democrat— the party in which his late father had always felt most at home. And so when Judge John E. Mack, the Democratic Dutchess County district attorney, dropped by the Wall Street law firm where Franklin was working and asked if he'd be interested in running for the state legislature, he jumped at the chance. No Democrat could win in Dutchess County unless he could peel votes away from the Republicans: Who was more likely to do that than a personable young man named Roosevelt?

Franklin saw no need to ask for his wife's advice. Her husband always lived "his own life exactly as he wanted it," she remembered. "I listened to all Franklin's plans with a great deal of interest. It never occurred to me that I had any part to play. I felt I must acquiesce in whatever he might decide to do and be willing to go to Albany. . . . I was having a baby, and for a time at least that was my only mission in life." Only one thing held Franklin back. He wanted to be sure his cousin Theodore would not object to a member of the family running for office on the Democratic ticket.

TR sailed into New York Harbor on the morning of June 18, 1910, aboard the German passenger ship *Kaiserin Auguste Victoria*. More than a million New Yorkers waited to welcome him home, including scores of reporters eager to ask him what he thought of President Taft and whether he would ever consider running for the White House again himself.

The revenue cutter *Manhattan* drew up alongside, prepared to take the Roosevelts ashore. Among the newspapermen, old friends, and family members, on her top deck were Franklin and Eleanor. At some point during the day's festivities, Franklin asked the ex-president for his blessing. He gave Franklin the go-ahead. It was too bad he was choosing to run as a Democrat, TR said, but he knew Franklin could be counted on to battle the bosses in whatever party he chose.

"I'm so fond of that boy," Theodore had once told Sara Delano Roosevelt, "I'd be shot for him."

OPPOSITE Theodore Roosevelt tips his hat to the crowd as he returns from his triumphal tour of Europe. There to greet him are friends, politicians, and family members, including Franklin and Eleanor, standing together at the far right.

CHAPTER 3

The Fire of Life

1910—1919

I'm Not Teddy

I n the early autumn of 1910, voters living along the back roads of upstate Dutchess County, New York, were startled by something altogether new—a bright red two-cylinder Maxwell touring car, draped with bunting. The car's owner, a Poughkeepsie piano tuner, was behind the wheel. Next to him was an eager young candidate for the state senate, Franklin Delano Roosevelt of Hyde Park.

He was a twenty-eight-year-old lawyer who had never run for anything before, and a Democrat running in a traditionally Republican district. But he was also the fifth cousin of the most popular man in America, former president Theodore Roosevelt. Young Roosevelt promised "a strenuous campaign." It proved so strenuous that he spent one afternoon across the state line in Connecticut, pumping the hands of baffled farmers who couldn't vote for him even if they'd wanted to.

He professed to be "dee-lighted" by everything, just as his cousin always was. "I'm not Teddy," he liked to tell the crowds. "A little shaver said to me the other day that he knew I wasn't Teddy—I asked him why, and he replied, 'Because you don't show your teeth.'" But he did. A Democratic committeeman remembered that from the first he'd been "a topnotch salesman because he wouldn't immediately enter into a topic of politics when he met a party . . . he would approach them as a friend and would lead up to that with that smile of his."

The midterm elections proved a disaster for the Republicans nationally. Democrats captured the House for the first time in sixteen years. And, as Franklin's proud mother kept a tally of her boy's triumph, the Democratic tide helped sweep him into the New York State Senate. FDR was on his way.

PRECEDING PAGES Colonel Roosevelt acknowledges cheers from New York supporters during his Progressive crusade in 1912.

ABOVE William Yawkey, members of his family, and the Maxwell in which Franklin Roosevelt's political career began. For five wearying weeks, Yawkey drove the eager state senate candidate up and down Dutchess County so that he could speak, a friend remembered, wherever "a group of farmers could be brought together."

RIGHT One of the five hundred placards Roosevelt paid to have printed up and distributed throughout the county. Women could not yet vote, William Yawkey remembered, but large numbers of them turned out at FDR's evening rallies to see him anyway: "He might have stepped out of a magazine cover picturing a typical college man of the day," Yawkey said, "descended from the best honest-to-goodness American stock."

Franklin D. Roosevelt

Franklin D. Roosevelt

For State Senator
Counties of Columbia, Dutchess and Putnam

LEFT AND BELOW FDR meets the voters, 1910. Eleanor is just behind him in the lower picture, wearing a large hat. His enthusiasm sometimes got the better of him. When he ended one roadside speech by saying, "When I see you again I will be your state senator," a bearded farmer shouted, "Like hell you will!" FDR enjoyed telling that story all his life.

Quiescence . . . Is an Impossibility

Two weeks after his party's spectacular defeat at the polls in 1910, Theodore Roosevelt traveled to Washington to make a speech and stopped by the White House. President Taft and his wife were out of town. Roosevelt remembered every servant and gardener by name, asked about their families, and exclaimed over a piece of the corn bread he'd especially loved while living at the White House, brought to him hot from the kitchen.

When he was shown into the handsome new Oval Office that had been built within the West Wing, he strode across the room and sat down in the president's chair. It seemed very "natural" to be sitting there, he said. He had once pledged not to try to occupy that chair again, but now he had begun to change his mind.

Edith hoped to keep "Father safely caged" at Sagamore Hill. "Put it out of your mind, Theodore," she told him. "You will never be president of the United States again." But, as his friend James Bryce wrote, "Quiescence for [Roosevelt] is an impossibility. He is a sort of comet . . . but much denser in

OPPOSITE, TOP AND BOTTOM TR takes to the air. When the colonel visited an aviation meet near St. Louis in 1910, the pioneer aviator Arch Hoxsey asked if he'd like to join him in his flying machine. Roosevelt eagerly agreed to be buckled in. As they flew over the grandstand, Hoxsey felt the plane cant alarmingly; Roosevelt was leaning out to wave at the crowd in the grandstand below. They stayed up for three minutes and twenty seconds. "It was great! First class!" TR said when he was back on the ground. "I wish I could stay up for an hour." He was the first prominent American politician ever to fly. Hoxsey died in a crash at another air show less than two months later.

ABOVE Seated in his automobile aboard a Hudson River ferry, gawked at by fellow passengers and at least one photographer, the colonel's attention remains fixed on his book, one of the two or three he often read every day. Not a moment was to be wasted.

LEFT TR indulges in a favorite exercise. His fondness for felling trees was so great that once, as he left Bamie's breakfast table at Farmington, Connecticut, with his ax over his shoulder and fueled by a dozen cups of black coffee, his sister had to remind him that the oak trees that shaded the town green were off-limits.

PUCK BUILDING, New York, April 10th, 1912.   PRICE TEN CENTS.

VOL. LXXI. No. 1832.   Copyright, 1912, by Keppler & Schwarzmann. Entered at N.Y.P.O. as Second-class Mail Matter

Puck

THE NEW TATTOOED MAN
He Makes an Exhibition of Himself.

substance, and not so much attracted by as attracting the members of the system which he approaches."

Roosevelt's lifelong need for action—for being heard and being admired, as well—had a lot to do with his change of heart. But so did substance. Like other progressives within the Republican Party he had grown more and more disappointed by the conservative path Taft had chosen to follow. Amiable, well meaning, and enormous—he weighed over 330 pounds—Taft had backed away from meaningful tariff reform, retreated in the face of timber and mining interests eager to get at national forests, and refused to intervene in legislative matters on the grounds that it would violate the constitutional doctrine of separation of powers.

Roosevelt felt both personally and politically betrayed by the man he'd chosen to succeed him and whom he had now come to consider "utterly helpless as a leader." Social justice in America, TR said, in advocating what he called a "New Nationalism," could only be achieved through a strong federal government headed by someone who saw it as his duty to act as "the steward of the public interest"—someone like himself.

But Taft's Republican Party did not see things that way. It was actually a collection of strong state parties. Those state parties controlled their state legislatures, which were, in turn, largely controlled by the interests—banks in New York, timber in Michigan, copper in Montana, and railroads everywhere. And when Roosevelt said that special interests should be driven out of public life, party stalwarts were understandably alarmed. Old friends and once-friendly editorialists denounced him. "I fear things are going to become very bitter before long," President Taft told an aide.

His combative spirit was aroused. By the end of 1911, Roosevelt was no longer willing to say that he would not challenge Taft. He did not wish to run, he said; but if there were "a genuine popular demand" he would not "shirk a plain duty if it came unmistakably as a plain duty."

ABOVE Keppler's "The New Tattooed Man" perfectly captures Roosevelt's dilemma as the 1912 presidential election approached: How could a man so prone to moral preachments go against his own solemn vow never to run for president again? It also artfully echoes Bernhard Gillam's celebrated series of cartoons showing Republican presidential nominee James G. Blaine tattooed with his own transgressions twenty-eight years earlier (page 31).

OPPOSITE Standing on a flag-draped table, the colonel delivers the most important speech of his political career, August 31, 1910. Before some ten thousand eager listeners gathered in a grove at Osawatomie, Kansas, he called for a "New Nationalism." "The man who wrongly holds that every human right is second to his profit," Roosevelt said, "must now give way to the advocate of human welfare, who rightly maintains that every man holds his property subject to the general right of the community to regulate its use to whatever degree the public welfare may require it." He made headlines all across the country—and made anxious the occupants of the Taft White House.

Roosevelts Run True to Form

Franklin Roosevelt's debut in Albany was nearly as noisy as his cousin's had been the year he was born. "Senator Roosevelt is less than thirty," said the *New York Times*. "He is tall and lithe. With his handsome face and his form of supple strength he could make a fortune on the stage and set the matinee girl's heart throbbing with subtle and happy emotion. But no one would suspect behind that highly polished exterior the quiet force and determination that now are sending shivers down the spine of Tammany's striped mascot."

Theodore Roosevelt had made his reputation by embarrassing the bosses of his own Republican Party. Franklin lost no time in taking on Tammany Hall, a decision not calculated to make him popular among his fellow Democratic senators.

When the political boss of the Bowery saw Franklin's name on the list of Democratic newcomers, he said, "Well, if we've caught a Roosevelt, we'd better take him down and drop him off the docks. The Roosevelts run true to form."

A seat in the United States Senate for New York opened up. In those days, U.S. senators were still chosen by their state legislatures. The Democrats were in control in New York and their boss, Charles Murphy, had already made his choice—a Buffalo millionaire named Billy Sheehan, personally charming, privately corrupt—and the outnumbered Republicans had agreed not to put up a fight.

But a band of twenty-one reform-minded Democrats resolved to block Sheehan with a nominee of their own. Franklin joined their ranks and—because he alone was wealthy enough to rent a house rather than a room in Albany—the rebels met in his library each morning, producing so much blue cigar smoke that Eleanor had to move the children to the top floor.

The press found the idea of a new Roosevelt repeating his celebrated cousin's Albany battles irresistible. "It's the most humanly interesting political fight for many years," wrote the Albany stringer for the *New York Herald*, Louis Howe. Franklin thought so, too. He denounced Tammany Hall as a "noxious weed," its members as "hopelessly stupid" and "beasts of prey." Tammany spokesmen responded that Franklin was a snob, a secret Republican, anti-Catholic. "There's nothing the matter with Sheehan," Manhattan Assemblyman Alfred E. Smith said, "except he's an Irishman."

The stalemate dragged on for more than two months—and might have gone on even longer if a fire hadn't gutted the state capitol building, requiring the weary and impatient Democrats to caucus in cramped quarters across the street.

Finally, after sixty-four days, the Tammany boss named a new candidate, an Irish American judge every bit as pliant as Sheehan. Roosevelt and the remaining insurgents gave in—and then worked hard to make a defeat seem like a victory. "I have just returned from a big fight," Franklin told the press,

"a fight that went 64 rounds, and there was fighting every second of those 64 rounds. . . . This fight was a free-for-all . . . and many on the other side got good and battered. . . . The battle ended in harmony, and we have chosen a man for the people who will be dictated to by no one."

Theodore Roosevelt was impressed. "We are all really proud of the way you have handled yourself," he wrote from Sagamore Hill. "Good luck to you."

Eleanor was fascinated by the Sheehan battle and pleased at her own ability to function apart from her mother-in-law in a wholly new world. She organized a big reception for constituents, supplied food and drink every evening for Franklin and his fellow insurgents, and got to know all kinds of people—including a number of politicians who were unable to resist her but couldn't stand her husband. "Here in Albany," she recalled, "began . . . a dual existence for me which was to last all the rest of my life. Public service, whether my husband was in or out of office, was to be part of our daily life from now on."

In the state senate, Roosevelt "was a very uncertain factor," one reformer remembered. "No one could ever tell how he was going to vote." He battled hard for a direct primary that would have allowed voters, not bosses, to choose their senators—a cause for which Theodore Roosevelt had actively campaigned—but then backed away at the last minute from a reform charter for New York City. After a fire at the Triangle Shirtwaist Company killed 146 women, a special commission produced a flood of thirty-two reform bills. Roosevelt voted for all of them, but when the most hotly contested vote came—on a bill setting a fifty-hour-per-week work limit for women and children—he didn't bother to show up for the debate and later pretended he had helped to lead it.

And throughout, he maintained an earnest, pious air, compounded by what one observer remembered as "the unfortunate habit—so natural that he was unaware of it—of throwing his head up [which], combined with his great height, gave him the appearance of looking down his nose at most people."

"Awful arrogant fellow, that Roosevelt," Big Tim Sullivan, a ward boss, said. Looking back many years later, Franklin himself agreed. "You know," he told an old friend, "I was an awfully mean cuss when I first went into politics."

ABOVE In the grisly aftermath of the Triangle fire, grieving friends and family members try to identify their dead, laid out on the floor of the Twenty-sixth Street morgue. Although the doors of the sweatshop had been locked when the fire broke out, no one was found legally at fault in the trial that followed, and the owners of the building were allowed to collect $65,000 in insurance on their damaged property.

OPPOSITE As late as 1913, when this photograph was taken in Washington, FDR still struck some observers as smug and superior. Many years after FDR had died, a ninety-year-old Tammany veteran would remember him as "a patronizing son of a bitch."

We Stand at Armageddon

On February 24, 1912, Theodore Roosevelt announced that he was once again a candidate for president of the United States. "My hat is in the ring," he said, "the fight is on and I am stripped to the buff."

His son-in-law, Ohio Congressman Nick Longworth, said that at the prospect of a return to action, TR suddenly seemed ten years younger, "in such wonderful spirits, that he behaved like a boy." But Edith saw what was coming: she was sure the Old Guard would deny him the Republican nomination and could see no "possible result which could give me aught but keen regret."

But Roosevelt was determined to run, and seven out of nineteen Republican governors promised their support.

State party machines still picked most delegates to the Republican convention, but a dozen states were slated to hold direct primaries that year. If Roosevelt could demonstrate in those that voters overwhelmingly wanted him, he reasoned, the bosses would be unable to resist.

The fight went on for almost four months—bitter, damaging, personal. Roosevelt called Taft a "puzzlewit," "a fathead," "disloyal to every canon of decency and fair play." "Once Roosevelt gets into a fight," one friend explained, "he is completely dominated by the desire to destroy his adversary."

"I don't want to fight," Taft said. "But when I do fight, I want to hit hard. Even a rat in a corner will fight." He denounced Roosevelt as a "freak," a "demagogue," "the most dangerous man we have had in this country since its origin." But his heart wasn't in it. One evening, a reporter came upon an exhausted Taft aboard his train. "Roosevelt was my closest friend," the president said, and began to weep.

When the primary season ended, Roosevelt had captured nine states—including Taft's own home state of Ohio. It was clear that most Republican voters wanted change.

But just as Edith had predicted, when the party met in the Chicago Coliseum in June, the Old Guard regulars who ran things were immovable. They awarded all but 19 of the 254 contested delegates to Taft. Roosevelt declared that he was being robbed and told his followers not to bother sitting through the roll call. They walked out. "The parting of the ways has come," Roosevelt said. The Republican Party must stand "for the rights of humanity or else it must stand for special privilege." The next day, he appeared before his supporters and prepared them for battle: "the victory shall be ours, and it shall be won as we have already won so many victories, by clean and honest

LEFT, TOP AND BOTTOM The gaudy spectacle of Theodore Roosevelt's return to presidential politics, splitting the Republican Party and threatening to unseat the incumbent president he himself had helped elect, was catnip to cartoonists. J. Keppler Jr. drew Roosevelt as Edgar Allan Poe's raven, squawking "Nevermore" to President Taft's prospects for reelection. In his "It's Comin' After Us—A Graveyard Is No Place to Be on Halloween," the angry ghost of the once-united Republican Party pursues the men who have torn it apart.

THE AMERICAN NEWSPAPER OFFICE.

WHEN ROOSEVELT IS OUT OF POLITICS.

WHEN ROOSEVELT IS BACK IN POLITICS.

ABOVE In "The American Newspaper Office," cartoonist Samuel D. Ehrhart spoke for nearly everyone in the press; whatever reporters and publishers thought of TR, he always produced excitement—and reams of copy. He was, as a writer for the *New York Times* said, "a fountain of perennial energy, a dynamic marvel."

RIGHT Keppler's "Will the History of Napoleon's Return Repeat Itself?" Here, TR, as the ex-emperor of France, returns from exile on the island of Elba and is confronted by an army commanded by Taft but made up of men who had once been loyal to him. In Napoleon's case he dared them to shoot him, many soldiers came over to his side, and the Bourbon king was forced to flee.

ABOVE On August 6, 1912, TR returns in triumph to Chicago, the city where the Republican Party had denied him its nomination two months earlier. In "A Confession of Faith," the two-hour formal acceptance speech he made to the Progressive Party convention, he dismissed the two traditional parties as "husks, . . . boss-ridden and privilege-controlled," and promised bold action to protect what he called "the crushable elements" at the bottom of the American ladder. California Governor Hiram Johnson was picked as his running mate. The proceedings ended with chorus after chorus of "Praise God from Whom All Blessings Flow."

RIGHT The quasi-religious fervor of the Progressive Party is evident in these handouts: Progressives were called upon to sing "hymns," not campaign songs, and to follow a "creed" rather than a platform.

PROGRESSIVE BATTLE HYMNS

"We Stand at Armageddon and We Battle for the Lord"

"For there is neither East nor West,
Border nor Breed nor Birth,
When two Strong men stand face to face,
Though they come from the ends of the earth."
—Kipling

TEN CENTS

THE PROGRESSIVE CREED
I AM A PROGRESSIVE

Because I believe that the civilization which we enjoy, has been achieved by going forward rather than by "standing pat," by foresight rather than hindsight.

Because I believe that human rights are more sacred than property rights, and that both should be protected by honest laws enforced by honest men.

Because I believe that social and political justice for all is not impossible, and is worthy the consecrated effort of every one who demands a "square deal" for himself and is willing to give it to others.

Because I believe that prosperity is based on honesty, and that the command: "Thou shalt not steal!" applies to political delegates and public money as well as to private property.

Because I believe in the Common Good of our common country rather than in party loyalty or sectional pride, in moral principles rather than in political bosses, in the people who make the laws rather than the laws themselves.

Because I believe in Theodore Roosevelt and Hiram Johnson, the men, the politicians and the statesmen, and know by their past records and public service that they are worthy of my confidence and my vote.

fighting for the loftiest of causes. We fight in honorable fashion for the good of mankind; fearless of the future; unheeding of our individual fates; with unflinching hearts and undimmed eyes. We stand at Armageddon, and we battle for the Lord!"

They cheered him for forty-five minutes. If they wished to form a new Progressive Party and have him make the fight, he told them, "I will make it, even if only one state should support me."

Roosevelt's blood was up. He championed positions far more radical than any he had espoused before, positions that had been put forward for decades by Americans who felt left out. The Progressive platform recognized a woman's right to vote and labor's right to organize, and promised to curtail campaign spending, defend natural resources, limit the workday to eight hours and the workweek to six days, and provide federal insurance for the elderly, the jobless, and the sick. (Only the aspirations of African Americans were ignored: Roosevelt rejected a plank drafted by W. E. B. Du Bois calling for an end to lynching and segregation because he believed it would kill any hope of winning white votes in the South; Du Bois was so angered that he urged black voters to vote for the Democratic nominee; Roosevelt's old ally Booker T. Washington sadly said he'd stick with Taft.)

If judges dared interfere with the new laws, Roosevelt said, they should be recalled by the voters. "When a judge decides a constitutional question, when he decides what the people as a whole can and cannot do, the people should have the right to recall that decision if they think that it is wrong."

Roosevelt was confident he could beat Taft, but his hope of defeating the Democrats rested on their picking what he called "a reactionary." Two of the three leading candidates were just the kind of opponents he'd hoped for, but after forty-six ballots the Democrats settled on Woodrow Wilson, the former president of Princeton University and governor of New Jersey. He'd only been in politics for two years, but he appealed to reformers because he'd beaten his own party machine to pass progressive legislation in his state. TR dismissed him as "merely a less virile me," but both men understood that Wilson was the worst possible opponent from Roosevelt's point of view. "Nothing new is happening in politics except Mr. Roosevelt," Wilson said, "who is always new, being bound by nothing in the heavens above or in the earth below. He is now rampant and very diligently employed in splitting [his] party wide open—so that we may get in."

ABOVE Woodrow Wilson on the stump. "Of course I do not for a moment believe that we shall win," TR told Kermit once the Democrats had picked their nominee. "The chances are overwhelmingly in favor of Wilson, with Taft and myself nearly even, and I hope with me a little ahead."

LEFT Roosevelt campaign paraphernalia, 1912. TR's followers officially called themselves Progressives, but because their nominee was fond of saying he was "strong as a bull moose," they would be remembered as the Bull Moose Party.

Your Slave and Servant

ABOVE Louis Howe (left) at work as an Albany
stringer for the *New York Herald* a year or two
before he was asked to take over State Senator
Franklin Roosevelt's campaign for reelection in
1912. Howe "had an enormous interest in . . .
having power," Eleanor once explained to a friend,
"and if he could not have it . . . himself, he wanted
it through someone he was influencing, he loved
power."

The 1912 election would divide the Hyde Park Roosevelts from their Oyster Bay cousins for the first time. Franklin's mother told her son how much she wanted him to be reelected to the state senate "because I know how honest and fearless you are and that nothing will change when you are honest and right." But she also hoped the Bull Moose Party would endorse him. "Of course it ought to, to be true to its principles."

Franklin Roosevelt could not help but admire the battle Theodore Roosevelt was waging. "It is indeed a marvelous thing," he told an old friend. But he was already enlisted in the opposing army. Long before the Bull Moose Party was created, he had been a vocal supporter of Woodrow Wilson.

In the end, Sara visited Progressive headquarters and sent money to TR's campaign. Eleanor remained of two minds. "Franklin is . . . well satisfied with Mr. Wilson's nomination," she wrote a close friend. "But I wish [he] could be fighting now for Uncle Ted, for I feel he is in the Party of the Future."

Franklin would be unable to fight for himself or anyone else that fall. He was up for reelection, but he and Eleanor had both come down with typhoid fever and were confined to their house on East Sixty-fifth Street.

Luck brought him an able stand-in. That fall, the same red Maxwell that had introduced Franklin Roosevelt to his constituents two years earlier prowled Dutchess County again in search of votes—but this time it was carrying a very different kind of passenger.

Louis McHenry Howe was a veteran Albany newspaperman, gruff and diminutive, chain-smoking and so famously homely he sometimes answered the phone by saying, "Medieval Gnome here." Howe loved politics and political maneuvering, was drawn to power but knew he could never win it for himself, and came to believe that the closest he could ever get was to make himself indispensable to young Franklin Roosevelt. He had already begun to address his employer, only partly joking, as "Beloved and Revered Future President."

Howe crisscrossed Roosevelt's district. He shook hundreds of hands, promised jobs on behalf of the candidate wherever he could, and introduced a shrewd innovation: mimeographed "personalized" letters to farmers, fishermen, and apple growers promising each group special legislation. And he placed newspaper ads denouncing Republican bosses and promising support for woman suffrage.

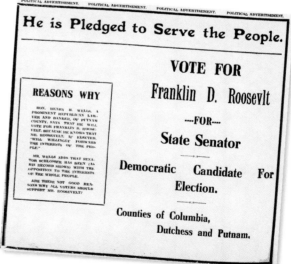

Dear Mr. Roosevelt . . .

Here is your first ad. . . . As I have pledged you in it I thought you might like to know casually what kind of a mess I was getting you into. Please wire O.K., if it's all right.

Your slave and servant,
Louis Howe

ABOVE, LEFT AND RIGHT Ill with typhoid in the fall of 1912, FDR needed to find a way to be reelected without displaying the kind of ebullient charm he demonstrates here, greeting his former pastor on a street in Oswego. Advertisements like the one above, written by Louis Howe and paid for by the candidate, helped turn the trick—and won their author a lifelong job.

The Great Fight for Righteousness

From the first, Theodore Roosevelt's third-party campaign was crippled. Many of those who had urged him to challenge Taft—including five of the seven Republican governors—backed off when he became a Bull Moose. Those who did rally to him were devoted but disorganized and often amateurish.

Taft mostly stayed off the campaign trail, convinced his cause was hopeless, but he issued statements denouncing what he saw as Roosevelt's dangerous radicalism. "One who so lightly regards constitutional principles, and especially the independence of the judiciary," was unfit for the presidency, he said, adding, "I say this sorrowfully, but I say it with the conviction of the truth."

Conservative newspaper publishers, Republican and Democratic alike, shared Taft's alarm. TR, said the *Houston Post,* had been "the first president whose chief personal characteristic was mendacity, the first to glory in duplicity, the first braggart, the first bully."

Roosevelt and Wilson each traveled the country by train, and TR sometimes delivered thirty whistle-stop speeches a day, shadowboxing through the caboose to maintain his energy before stepping out onto the platform. He professed to love what he called "the deluge of travel and dust."

Again and again, he denounced his Democratic opponent as a secret advocate of state's rights, a false progressive masquerading as a friend of an active federal government. But when an aide suggested that something be made of rumors concerning the married Democratic candidate's relationship with a divorcée, TR laughed it off: "You can't cast a man as Romeo who looks and acts so much like an apothecary clerk."

Both he and Wilson shared Wilson's view that "the President is at liberty in both law and conscience to be as big as he can," and both men lashed out at the giant trusts and monopolies at every stop. But Roosevelt's "New Nationalism" called only for their regulation, while Wilson's "New Freedom" seemed to suggest that his policies would actually break them up.

OPPOSITE Roosevelt campaigns. "As this movement has developed," he said, "instead of my growing less radical, I have grown more radical. . . . This country will not be a good place for any of us to live in if it is not a reasonably good place for all of us to live in."

On the evening of October 14, Theodore Roosevelt was in Milwaukee standing in his open automobile in front of the Gilpatrick Hotel, waving his hat to the crowd. A delusional German immigrant named John Schrank, standing just seven feet away, aimed a pistol at his chest. He had been stalking his target for a month, convinced the ghost of William McKinley was directing his hand, that it was his sacred duty to prevent Roosevelt from winning a third term.

Schrank's bullet hit him in the chest. "He pinked me," Roosevelt said. He dabbed at his mouth, found no blood, concluded his lungs were undamaged, and insisted on delivering his scheduled speech despite his wound. "Friends," he said from the podium, "I shall ask you to be as quiet as possible. I don't know whether you fully understand that I have just been shot. . . . The bullet is in me now, so I cannot make a very long speech." Pale and sometimes swaying at the podium, he went on for more than an hour before his aides could get him to stop and agree to go to a local hospital. From there, he was rushed by train to Chicago, where better care was available.

The news spread fast. Edith Roosevelt heard it while attending the theater in New York. He sent her a telegram urging her to stay home. He'd been far more seriously injured falling off horses, he said. But she hurried west anyway; assurances like that had been made about William McKinley, too.

Franklin and Eleanor Roosevelt, still recovering from typhoid, anxiously telephoned the *New York Times* that evening to get the latest bulletins on TR's condition. Woodrow Wilson suspended his campaign. Even Roosevelt's enemies were impressed by his courage.

He was out of action and under his wife's strict care for almost two weeks. "This thing about ours being a campaign against boss rule is a fake," Roosevelt joked to a reporter. "I was never so boss-ruled in my life."

On election day, Roosevelt easily beat Taft. But Woodrow Wilson won the presidency, and his party gained control of both the Senate and the House of Representatives for the first time in almost two decades. Roosevelt was gracious to the winner, but privately he was wounded. "There is no use disguising the fact that the defeat at the polls is overwhelming," he told Kermit. "I had expected defeat, but I had expected that we would make a better showing. . . . I try not to think of the damage to myself personally."

"I cannot bear to have Father beaten," Edith confided to her diary at Sagamore Hill. "It makes me so choky . . . when I think of [him] almost being assassinated . . . and the people being such cold fishes."

TOP, LEFT An ambulance brings TR from Chicago's North Western Depot railroad station to Mercy Hospital. Once he was settled in room 314 he called in the reporters who had been traveling with him. How did he feel? one asked. Roosevelt laughed. "I feel as well as a man feels who has a bullet in him!"

TOP, RIGHT Roosevelt's family rushed to his side, including his sons Kermit and Quentin. Their father assured them that his time in the hospital was "a positive spree."

CENTER Eight days after he was wounded, Roosevelt gingerly climbs down from the train that carried him home to Oyster Bay.

RIGHT Theodore Roosevelt casts his ballot, November 5, 1912. By dinnertime it was clear that while he had beaten Taft, his own strong showing had ensured a victory for Wilson. TR assured the press that "like every good citizen" he accepted the result "with good humor and contentment," but Edith wrote Kermit that his father's "disappointment went deeper than he admits to himself."

I'd Like It Bully Well

On the same day that Theodore Roosevelt was defeated, Franklin Roosevelt was easily reelected to the New York State Senate.

Recovered from their illness, Franklin and Eleanor went to Washington for Woodrow Wilson's inauguration, where Josephus Daniels, the new secretary of the navy, sought Franklin out. Roosevelt had been an early supporter of the new Democratic president. He had a reputation as a reformer. He had a lifelong interest in sailing and the sea. And, most important, he bore the country's most famous name.

"How would you like to come to Washington as assistant secretary?" Daniels asked. He was offering him Theodore Roosevelt's old job.

"I'd like it bully well!" Franklin said.

Theodore Roosevelt sent his congratulations right away.

Dear Franklin:

I was very much pleased that you were appointed as Assistant Secretary of the Navy. It is interesting to see that you are at another place which I myself once held. I am sure you will enjoy yourself to the full as Assistant Secretary and that you will do capital work. . . .

New York Democratic bosses were as glad to see Franklin leave the state senate for Washington as Republican bosses had been to see Theodore Roosevelt run for vice president fourteen years before.

He was just thirty-one, the youngest assistant secretary of the navy in history, seven years younger than Theodore Roosevelt had been when he first sat at the same desk, so young and so young looking that a dinner companion who didn't catch his name thought him a "naughty little boy, just out of college."

He and his new boss seemed hopelessly mismatched. The new assistant secretary had attended Groton and Harvard, learned to sail aboard his father's yacht, and, like his cousin Theodore, believed in a strong defense and a big navy.

Josephus Daniels was a newspaper editor from North Carolina who called battleships "boats," seemed most concerned with banning wine from officers' messes throughout the fleet, and was a close ally of Wilson's secretary of state, William Jennings Bryan, who believed strong defenses were a provocation and promised that the United States would never go to war on his watch.

Not long after Franklin took up his new duties, his boss went off on an inspection tour, leaving him in charge.

"There's a Roosevelt on the job today," Franklin told a reporter. "You remember what happened the last time a Roosevelt occupied a similar position?"

What had happened then, of course, was the Spanish-American War.

Eleanor, sensitive always to any feeling among her Oyster Bay relatives

that she and Franklin might unfairly be exploiting their link with Theodore Roosevelt, was appalled. It was a "horrid little remark," she told her husband.

Franklin did not apologize.

Secretary Daniels had already noted in his diary that Franklin's "distinguished cousin TR went from the Navy Department to the Presidency. May history repeat itself," Daniels said.

Franklin could not have agreed more. He and Eleanor rented Theodore Roosevelt's sister Bamie's home at 1733 N Street. TR had spent the first few nights of his presidency there, and afterward had walked there so often to talk things over with his shrewd sister that the press called it the "little White House." It would be Franklin Roosevelt's headquarters for the next several crowded, frenetic years.

Eleanor brought to it all the organizational skills she'd learned in Albany, seeing to the needs of her growing household, entertaining her uncle's old friends, getting to know new people from all over the country who might be helpful to her husband's ambitions. "My calls began [in the autumn of] 1914," she recalled, "under poor auspices, for I was feeling miserable again, as another baby was coming along. . . . Somehow or other I made my rounds every afternoon, . . . [and] from ten to thirty calls were checked off on my list day after day. Mondays, the wives of the Justices of the Supreme Court; Tuesdays, the members of Congress."

Franklin's official duties at the department included procurement, budgets, and overseeing the 65,000 civilians who worked in the navy yards. But he was not content with that. "I get my fingers into about everything," he said, "and there's no law against it."

Franklin reveled in the trappings of his new job. Seventeen guns greeted him whenever he stepped aboard a ship. He affected a navy cape and designed an official assistant secretary's flag for himself. And whenever he could get away to his summer home on Campobello Island, he liked to come and go by destroyer, guiding the big warship through the narrows with his own sure hand at the wheel.

ABOVE Franklin and Eleanor lead a delegation from the Navy Department into the Brooklyn Navy Yard not long after FDR became assistant secretary in 1913. The tall civilian bringing up the rear is Livingston Davis, a raffish but admiring Harvard classmate whom Roosevelt had appointed as his personal assistant.

OPPOSITE Roosevelt, wearing a derby, returns to Brooklyn eleven months later for the laying of the keel of Battleship #39—which, the *New York Times* explained, was meant to be "the world's biggest and most powerful . . . superdreadnought ever constructed." She would be christened the USS *Arizona* in 1915. Twenty-six years later, at Pearl Harbor, she would virtually be destroyed by Japanese aircraft, with the loss of more than eleven hundred members of her crew.

My Last Chance to Be a Boy

After Theodore Roosevelt's defeat as the Progressive Party's candidate for president in 1912, he undertook another great adventure: an expedition into the Amazon rain forest to chart the course of a newly discovered jungle waterway. The expedition's leader was Cândido Rondon, the Brazilian explorer who had discovered its headwaters and given it its name—"Rio de Duvida"—the "River of Doubt." No one knew where it led.

Roosevelt's twenty-four-year-old son Kermit, now a trained engineer, went with him. The depression Kermit had first experienced as a child had deepened, and, like his late uncle Elliott, he had begun drinking to obliterate it. His mother wanted him to take care of his father; his father hoped this dangerous mission would provide his son with the kind of action that had always eased his own bouts of melancholy.

The expedition was the fifty-five-year-old Theodore Roosevelt's "last chance to be a boy," he said. Instead it would nearly kill him—and turn him into an old man.

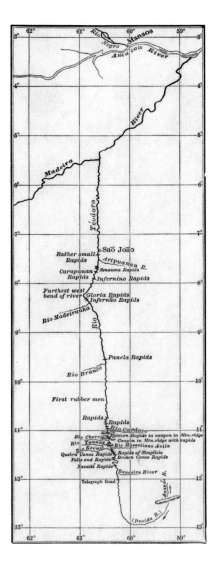

The Roosevelt party—twenty-two men and seven dugout canoes—would not see another human being for forty-eight days. Flesh-eating piranhas prowled the river; so did fifteen-foot caimans. Insects swarmed so thickly Roosevelt had to wear protective gear to write articles for *Scribner's*. Termites ate part of his pith helmet. Rain fell in sheets. Roosevelt noted that everything that didn't rot, rusted.

The expedition soon ran out of food—and found it hard to replenish its supply. The animals off which they had expected to live were furtive, invisible.

Unseen Indians of the Cinta Larga tribe, who sometimes killed and ate strangers who dared intrude into their forest, stalked the party—and shot one of the expedition's dogs full of arrows. Five out of seven dugout canoes were lost in the fast-moving water. New ones had to be carved from hollowed trees and hauled by land around rapids and waterfalls. One man was swept away by a torrent.

Roosevelt and Kermit both contracted malaria, and things got steadily worse. Two of the new canoes got trapped by the rushing water. Roosevelt,

LEFT, TOP Roosevelt's canoe starts down the River of Doubt, February 27, 1914. A companion left behind remembered watching "the dark forest . . . shut out our erstwhile leader and his Brazilian companions" and wondering "whether or not we would ever see them again."

LEFT, BOTTOM Roosevelt, wreathed in mosquito netting and wearing specially made gauntlets, struggles to write an account of his day's travels.

ABOVE A map of the river the expedition explored, based on TR's own notes

already ill, waded in to help free them and gashed his leg—the same leg that had been injured in the trolley accident nine years earlier. The wound became infected. Soon he could no longer stand.

The expedition struggled on and soon came to a series of six rapids. The men somehow had to find a way to leave the river and move through the rain forest. Roosevelt told his son that the party should go on without him. The ex-president of the United States intended to swallow a lethal dose of the morphine he always carried with him into the wilderness; he did not want to be a burden. But Kermit would not hear of it. He was a Roosevelt too. He would sooner have died himself than leave his father behind, alive or dead.

Roosevelt changed his mind: "I saw that if I did end [my life], that would only make it more sure that Kermit would not get out. For I knew he would not abandon me, but would insist on bringing my body out, too. That, of course, would have been impossible. . . . So there was only one thing for me to do, and that was to come out myself."

Kermit's weeks of working alongside the expedition's porters and paddlers paid off. He used his engineering skills to lower the dugouts down the steep canyon walls, and kept his men moving forward.

But there was still more trouble. A porter shot and killed a companion and fled into the forest. A deep gorge and an apparently impassable series of new rapids stretched on ahead.

Theodore was helpless now, forced to be paddled along beneath a makeshift tent. His fever rose to 104. He grew delirious, reciting the same few lines of poetry over and over again: "In Xanadu did Kubla Khan a stately pleasure-dome decree . . ." The expedition's doctor cut open his leg to save his life. Roosevelt endured the surgery without anesthetic.

Finally, on April 26, after a month and a half in the wilderness, they came upon a six-man relief party that had been sent to help them out of the rain forest.

The River of Doubt, which turned out to be almost half as long as the Rhine, was renamed "Rio Roosevelt."

New Yorkers gave Roosevelt another big welcome when he returned home, but friends were shocked by his appearance. He had lost fifty-five pounds—roughly a quarter of his weight—could barely make himself heard when speaking, and leaned on a cane he bravely called "my Big Stick." "As he limped down the companionway," a reporter for the *New York Sun* wrote, "the impression was strong that the Colonel had endured the greatest hardships of his life." It now seemed likely that his public life really had finally come to an end.

ABOVE Kermit Roosevelt, a victim of malaria himself, would find himself struggling to keep his father alive.

ABOVE In this battered photograph, a makeshift canvas tent shields Roosevelt from the sun as he is paddled downriver. Suffering from malaria and a badly infected leg, he was unable even to sit up and considered committing suicide rather than slow the expedition's return to civilization.

LEFT Roosevelt returns to New York, fifty-five pounds lighter than he had been when he set out for South America. He was "thinner and older-looking," a newspaperman wrote, "and there was something lacking in the power of his voice." An old friend would be more blunt: "The Brazilian wilderness stole away ten years of his life."

The Complete Smash-up

I n early August of 1914, five weeks after the assassination of Archduke Franz Ferdinand in Sarajevo, Germany declared war on Russia and France and sent troops across the Belgian border. Britain declared war on Germany. Russia then went to war against the Austro-Hungarian Empire.

"A complete smash-up is inevitable," FDR told Eleanor. A "great black tornado trembles on the edge of Europe and the whole question of peace and war trembles in the balance," Theodore Roosevelt told a friend. "It is not a good thing for a country to have a professional yodeler, a human trombone like Mr. Bryan as Secretary of State, nor a college president [like Mr. Wilson] as head of the nation, with . . . a hypocritical ability to deceive plain people . . . and no real knowledge or wisdom concerning internal and international affairs."

By the end of the year almost all of Europe and parts of Asia would be engulfed in what would be called the Great War.

President Wilson called for "strict and impartial neutrality," and insisted that strengthening American armed forces would only serve to provoke the belligerents. The British fleet blockaded Germany to choke off armaments. In retaliation, the Germans loosed submarines and warned that they would sink enemy vessels on sight.

All of the Roosevelts sided with England and her allies from the moment the first gun was fired. "Even I long to go over into the thick of it and right the wrong," Franklin told an old British friend. "England's course has been magnificent—Oh, if that German fleet would only come out and fight!" But as an official in the Wilson administration, Franklin had to keep such thoughts to himself.

Theodore Roosevelt did not. "More and more," he wrote, "I come to the view that in a really tremendous world struggle, with a great moral issue involved, neutrality does not serve righteousness; for to be neutral between right and wrong is to serve wrong."

ABOVE German troops march into Brussels, August 20, 1914. "The infantry marched singing, with their iron-shod boots beating out the time," an American witness wrote. "At times two thousand men were singing together in absolute rhythm and beat. It was like the blows from giant pile-drivers."

OPPOSITE Theodore Roosevelt broods on a beach within the Breton National Wildlife Refuge off the coast of Louisiana, set aside by him while president. Now, convinced that the United States must enter the war just beginning in Europe, he remained a private citizen, powerless to act.

Fifth Cousin by Blood, and Nephew by Law!

In the spring of 1915, as the war intensified, Theodore Roosevelt found himself in a Syracuse courtroom—on trial for libel. In a recent speech, he'd said that when it came down to a struggle between "popular rights and corrupt and machine-ruled government," the interests of the Republican and Democratic bosses of New York were "fundamentally identical."

The Republican boss, William Barnes, immediately sued Roosevelt for libel. TR cast about among old friends and allies for those willing to testify to the truth of his charge. Most backed away, unwilling to risk the wrath of one boss or the other.

Franklin was different. During the 1911 state senate battle over Billy Sheehan, he'd seen collusion between the bosses of both parties firsthand and was more than willing to say so in court on behalf of the man who continued to be his hero. When a lawyer asked Franklin what relation he was to the former president, he grinned. "Fifth cousin by blood," he said proudly, "and nephew by law!" "I shall never forget the capital way in which you gave your testimony," the ex-president told Franklin afterward.

The trial continued, and Theodore Roosevelt was asleep in his Syracuse hotel room on the night of May 7th when the telephone rang. A newspaperman was calling. A German submarine had sunk the British passenger ship *Lusitania* off the coast of Ireland. More than 1,100 men, women, and children had drowned, including 128 American citizens. Did Roosevelt have a comment? Two German Americans sat on the jury that would decide Roosevelt's fate. But he could not keep from speaking out. "This represents not merely piracy," he told the reporter, "but piracy on a vaster scale of murder than the old-time pirates ever practiced. . . . It seems inconceivable that we can refrain from taking action in this matter, for we owe it not only to humanity but to our own national self-respect."

It took the jurors two days, but in the end all twelve exonerated Roosevelt—who went right back on the attack.

OPPOSITE, TOP LEFT AND RIGHT Two views of the defendant in the courtroom: Roosevelt was such a voluble, intimidating witness in his own defense that the plaintiff's lawyer begged the judge to make the ex-president "confine himself to words and not answer with his whole body"—to stop treating him like a "mass meeting."

OPPOSITE, BOTTOM Leaving the courthouse, Roosevelt tips his hat to the well-wishers who gathered outside every day to get a glimpse of him.

RIGHT "Enlist," a poster published by the interventionist Boston Committee of Public Safety, shortly after the Germans sank the *Lusitania* with hundreds of civilians aboard

ABOVE, RIGHT Theodore and Franklin Roosevelt make their way to the Syracuse courthouse, the only known photograph of FDR in close proximity to the man he most admired on earth. The man between them is one of TR's attorneys, William H. Van Benschoten.

The Visitor

Franklin and Eleanor Roosevelt had houses in New York City and Washington, D.C., and on Campobello Island. But for their four children—Anna, James, Elliott, and the second Franklin Jr.—it was Springwood, their grandmother's house at Hyde Park, that provided sanctuary from their parents' increasingly turbulent world. "Hyde Park was very definitely my most favorite place in life," Anna recalled. "Hyde Park was home and the only place I ever thought was completely home."

In 1915, Sara Delano Roosevelt greatly expanded Springwood to accommodate her growing family and the nurses and maids that traveled with them. The house now included so many bedrooms she sometimes called it "our hotel." The renovated first floor, modeled after the country houses of the Roosevelts' aristocratic friends in England, was meant to be a showcase for her son and his collections: his stuffed birds; his naval prints and books; his albums filled with stamps.

When he was there, Franklin acted just as his own father had: he rode with his children, swam and sledded, and took them iceboating on the Hudson.

But his visits with the family were always brief. "I do so wish the holiday had been longer and less interrupted while it lasted," he once wrote Eleanor.

ABOVE Eleanor Roosevelt at Springwood, photographed by her daughter, Anna. "It was my husband's home and my children had a sense that it was their home," Eleanor remembered. "But for me . . . it was not home."

ABOVE Springwood rebuilt, photographed by Margaret Bourke-White. The expansion of the Roosevelt home to better suit a rising statesman was planned by Franklin and his mother: "Do not speak of it to Eleanor," Sara told her son while plans were being drawn up. "It is too uncertain and I want to surprise her if I do it."

LEFT Sara ran her household from the claustrophobic parlor she called her "snuggery." She could see who was coming and going from here, gave instructions to her servants, and received morning visits from her grandchildren.

ABOVE On the Springwood terrace. Sara puts a protective arm around her grandson Franklin Jr., 1917. "We quickly learned," James recalled, "that the best way to circumvent 'Pa and Mummy' was to appeal to Granny." When their parents objected, Eleanor recalled, "she looked at us quite blandly and said she hadn't realized we disapproved. She never heard anything she did not want to hear."

OPPOSITE, TOP LEFT Anna and James attend a suitably decorous tea party on their grandmother's lawn.

OPPOSITE, RIGHT John and Franklin Jr. with their harvest. "Granny's idea of teaching . . . self-sufficiency," James remembered, "was to provide the land, the seeds . . . and lots of advice, then purchase my crop at prices 50 percent above market value." When FDR gently objected that 150 percent of parity seemed unrealistically high, his mother looked hurt and said that surely "dear James should be encouraged in his display of initiative."

OPPOSITE, BOTTOM Roosevelt children in their grandmother's rose garden

"I felt Tuesday as if I was really getting back to earth again—and I know it is hard for us both to lead this kind of life—but it is a little like a drug habit—almost impossible to stop."

Eleanor liked the new Springwood at first. It was "very home-like and for the chicks," she told a friend, ". . . ideal." But it remained her mother-in-law's home, she remembered many years later, and "I was only a visitor."

Sara ran everything. She called her grandchildren "our children." She weighed them, dressed them, saw to their manners, showered them with gifts, and offered what Anna remembered as "consistent, warm, spontaneous love"—the kind of love Eleanor had never known when she was a girl and now found hard to provide to her own children. "Up to a point," she once wrote, "it is good for us to know that there are people in the world who will give us love and unquestioned loyalty. . . . I doubt, however, if it is good for us to feel assured of this devotion without the accompanying obligation of having to justify this devotion by our behavior."

Sara had firm views about her daughter-in-law, as well. "If you'd just run your comb through your hair, dear," she once told Eleanor in front of dinner guests, "you'd look so much nicer."

On March 11, 1916, Eleanor gave birth to John Aspinwall Roosevelt. She had now borne six children, five of whom had lived. There would be no more. She was thirty-one years old. The decade during which, she said, "I was always just getting over a baby or about to have another" was over. She was ready to resume a life of her own, to find a new kind of fulfillment, on her own terms.

The Cry of a Broken Heart

Theodore Roosevelt hoped somehow to obtain both the Progressive and the Republican presidential nominations in 1916. But the Old Guard of his old party had not forgiven him for 1912. And, while most Americans sympathized with Britain and France, they still remained reluctant to get involved in a far-off war.

The Republicans chose instead the austere, mildly progressive Supreme Court Justice Charles Evans Hughes. Roosevelt privately called him "the bearded lady." But the next day, when Roosevelt's name was placed in nomination at the Progressive Party convention, he sent a telegram from Sagamore Hill declining the honor and urging his followers to abandon their new party and vote Republican.

The delegates were stunned. When the telegram was read, William Allen White recalled, "for a moment there was silence. Then there was a roar of rage. It was the cry of a broken heart such as no convention ever had uttered in this land before. . . . I had tears in my eyes. . . . I saw hundreds of men tear the Roosevelt picture or the Roosevelt badge from their coats, and throw it on the floor."

In November, Wilson would win a narrow victory on the slogan "He Kept Us Out of War." "We are passing through a streak of yellow in our national life," Roosevelt told his sister. The Progressive Party disintegrated without its

hero. Some members returned to the Republicans; some became Democrats. A number of the social and economic reforms Roosevelt and the Progressives had championed had already become law thanks to Woodrow Wilson's shrewd political skills: a new antitrust statute, workmen's compensation, a ban on most child labor, the Federal Reserve Board, and the Federal Trade Commission.

But making a reality of other planks in the old Progressive platform would have to wait for another time—and another Roosevelt.

ABOVE McKee Barclay, cartoonist for the *Baltimore Sun,* captures the bitterness Progressives felt when Roosevelt declined their presidential nomination and openly supported the Republicans who had scorned him four years earlier. "Around me," Oswald Garrison Villard wrote from the Progressive convention, "men of the frontier type could not keep back their tears at this self-revelation of their idol's selfishness, the smashing of their illusions about their peerless leader."

A Very Exclusive War

Even the sinking of the *Lusitania* had not persuaded Wilson that entry into the war was inevitable. "There is such a thing as being too proud to fight," he had declared, and then had engaged Germany in a long exchange of diplomatic messages that had further infuriated Theodore Roosevelt.

But the president had also agreed to double the defense budget in the interest of what he now called "preparedness." Theodore Roosevelt called it "half-preparedness."

Meanwhile, Franklin organized a fifty-thousand-man Naval Reserve, relentlessly drove shipyards to greater efforts, laid the keels of new battleships, complained again and again about Secretary Daniels being "too damned slow for words"—and surreptitiously slipped damaging information about his boss and the administration's defense efforts to the ranking Republican on the House Military Affairs Committee. If the public ever turned on the administration for having been too slow in preparing for war, Franklin was determined that he would not be blamed. And he shared his cousin Theodore's conviction that the United States not only would, but should, get into the war.

By early 1917, the battle lines had been frozen for nearly three years, along a line that stretched 450 miles from Belgium to Switzerland. In an attempt to strangle British supply lines and break the deadlock, Germany began waging unrestricted submarine warfare on all vessels, including American merchant ships.

Wilson severed relations with Germany. Then, an intercepted German telegram to the Mexican president promised that in exchange for help in the

ABOVE A French soldier hit at Verdun, one of nearly 100,000 casualties suffered during the ten-month battle

OPPOSITE At Plattsburgh on the shore of Lake Champlain, the Colonel preaches his brand of militant preparedness to hundreds of well-to-do young men—college students, businessmen, his own son, Ted Jr., and his son-in-law Richard Derby—who, at their own expense, underwent officer training in readiness for American intervention in the Great War.

event of war with the United States, Texas, Arizona, and New Mexico would be returned to Mexico. Wilson still seemed reluctant to take further action. "My God, why doesn't he do something?" Theodore Roosevelt said. "If he does not go to war with Germany [now] I shall skin him alive."

On March 18, the Germans torpedoed three American merchant ships. Wilson polled his cabinet as to what he should do. All ten members voted for war. Josephus Daniels cast his vote with tears in his eyes.

On the evening of April 2, 1917, Woodrow Wilson finally asked Congress for a declaration of war. "It is a fearful thing to lead this most peaceful people, into the most terrible and disastrous of all wars. . . . But the right is more precious than peace, and we shall fight for the things we have always carried nearest our hearts."

Franklin sat next to Secretary Daniels on the House floor. Eleanor was in the gallery, listening "breathlessly," she remembered, and then "returned home still half-dazed by the sense of impending change."

Franklin, eager to do his part and mindful always of TR's example, volunteered to serve overseas. President Wilson told him to stay where he was. "Neither you nor I nor Franklin Roosevelt," Wilson told Josephus Daniels, "has the right to select the place of service to which our country has assigned us."

A few days later, Theodore Roosevelt called at the White House to see Wilson and to try—like Franklin—to get into the war. The Allies were desperate, he said. It would take time to build and train an American army. He was sure he could raise a division of volunteers virtually overnight, just as he had during the Spanish-American War, then lead it into battle and inspire the Allies to hold on. All his previous criticism was now "dust in a windy street," he assured Wilson. All he wanted to do was help. Wilson was kind but noncommittal. "He is a great big boy," Wilson told an aide after Roosevelt had left. "There is a sweetness about him. . . . You can't resist the man." But he had the secretary of war formally turn him down. Theodore Roosevelt was half blind, in bad health, out of touch with military developments—and an amateur. "The business now at hand," Wilson said later, "is undramatic, practical and of scientific definitiveness and precision."

Roosevelt was deeply wounded. "This is a very exclusive war," he told a friend, "and I have been blackballed by the committee on admissions."

You Must Do What You Think You Cannot Do

The war was my emancipation and education," Eleanor Roosevelt recalled. "Instead of making [social] calls, I found myself spending three days a week in a canteen down at the railroad yards, one afternoon a week, distributing free work for the Navy League, two days a week, visiting the naval hospital, and contributing whatever time I had left to the Navy Red Cross and the Navy Relief Society. I loved it. I simply ate it up."

The war liberated all of what Eleanor called her "executive ability." In order to undertake the war work that consumed her, she had to organize her busy household to function without her. She often rose at five in the morning and spent twelve hours without a break at the Union Station Red Cross canteen making coffee and jam sandwiches for the doughboys passing through. "Sometimes I wondered if I could live that way another day," she wrote. "Strength came, however, with the thought of Europe and a little sleep, . . . you could always begin a new day."

One day, the Red Cross asked Eleanor to inspect St. Elizabeths Hospital, a mental facility filled with sailors and Marines suffering in the aftermath of battle. The prospect terrified her. Her experiences with her alcoholic father and uncles made her frightened of anyone without what she called "the power of self-control." She never forgot the sound of the door locking behind her or the sight of the dark ward filled with shattered men, some chained to their beds, muttering, staring.

They continued to frighten her, but she came back to see them, week after week, and lobbied the government and raised private funds to improve the conditions under which they lived.

"You must do what you think you cannot do," she wrote. She would keep doing that all her life.

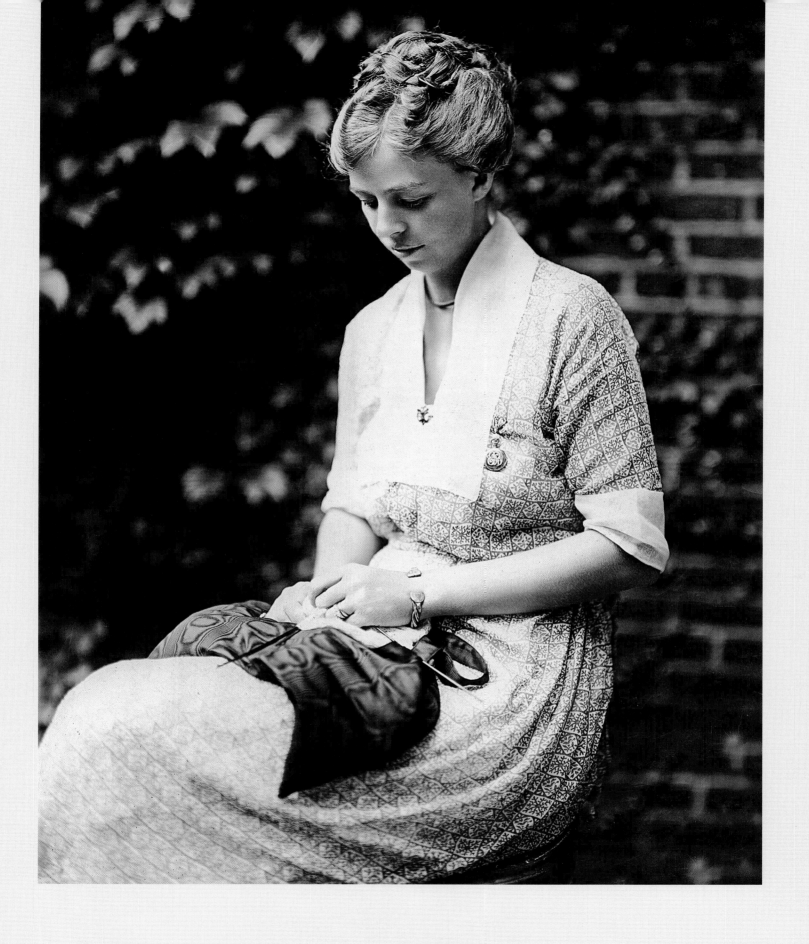

Uncuriously Enough,
His Name Is Roosevelt

On July 4, 1917, Franklin addressed the annual Tammany Hall celebration in New York. He assured his mother afterward that it had been a "purely patriotic" event, part of the larger war effort. In fact, it was a signal to Boss Murphy and the big-city Democrats that once the fighting ended, he would no longer be their enemy. To succeed in postwar politics, he would need the bosses he had once fought so hard.

Meanwhile, he did all he could to strengthen and speed up the navy. Daniels overruled his plan to build hundreds of small craft to patrol American harbors that were not under any real threat—"I fear buying a lot of junk," he wrote—but when the secretary also opposed a far grander scheme to eliminate the submarine menace by laying half a million nets and mines between Scotland and Norway, Franklin went over his head

ONLY THE NAVY CAN STOP THIS

The U. S. Navy Publicity Bureau gratefully acknowledges its indebtedness to the New York Herald for the reproduction of Mr. Rogers' cartoon.

Printed by the U. S. Navy Publicity Bureau, N. Y.

to the president himself to win approval. Seventy-one thousand mines would be put in place before the war ended. "Mr. Daniels has one, only one, virile-minded, hard-fisted, civilian assistant," wrote the *Chicago Post*. "Uncuriously enough, his name is Roosevelt."

Privately, Franklin continued to be scornful of his slow-moving boss and never abandoned hope of supplanting him as secretary, but he also learned lessons from Daniels that would prove essential to him later—how to work his will with Congress, and how to keep control out of the hands of ambitious military men who assumed they knew better than civilians.

OPPOSITE, TOP This photograph of FDR consorting with his old enemy, Boss Murphy of Tammany Hall, appalled his mother's resolutely Republican older brother, Warren Delano III. "Uncle Warren says one of the papers has pictures of you and Murphy side by side," Sara told him. "All this rather upsets me, I confess." FDR reassured her, but he was uncomfortable, too; Murphy proudly wears his Tammany sash; Roosevelt has taken his off and holds it, rolled up as small as possible, in his fist.

OPPOSITE, BOTTOM, AND ABOVE A few days after the United States entered the war, Franklin marches the Washington Senators onto the field and raises the flag at Griffith Stadium. He was grateful that his post kept him in the public eye but worried that failure to serve in uniform might hurt his peacetime political prospects.

ABOVE, LEFT W. A. Rogers's poster was meant to rally American support for the war and yield volunteers for the navy.

ABOVE Archie Roosevelt recovering from his wounds in an American hospital in Paris. At the news that he'd been wounded, his mother drank a toast to him at Sagamore Hill and then, tears in her eyes, smashed her glass, saying, "That glass shall never be drunk from again!"

ABOVE, RIGHT Major Theodore Roosevelt Jr. and his wife, Eleanor, who was in France, organizing YMCA canteens for the doughboys. He'd been gassed near Cantigny, then shot in the back of the left kneecap; he was forced to walk with a cane for the rest of his life.

OPPOSITE, TOP LEFT Kermit in a British uniform in Mesopotamia. Married now, and with an infant son, he confessed that he didn't "like the war at all, but as long as it's going on I want to be the first in it." He'd joined the British army because he thought it would take too long for U.S. forces to get into action.

OPPOSITE, TOP RIGHT Quentin, the last of the Roosevelt boys to face combat, in the cockpit of his plane

OPPOSITE, BOTTOM Alice Roosevelt Longworth buys war bonds from Girl Scouts in Washington, D.C.

The Lion's Brood

If Theodore Roosevelt could not fight overseas, his four sons could, and one by one he had secured places for them that would nudge them as close as possible to danger. "I should be ashamed of my sons if they shirked war," he wrote, "just as I should be ashamed of my daughters if they shirked motherhood." The memory of his father's failure to fight in the Civil War still haunted him: "I have always explained to my four sons that if there is a war during their lifetime, I wish them to be in a position to explain to their children, why they did go to it, and not why they did not go to it."

Besides, he wanted his boys to experience what he had famously called the "supreme triumphs of war" as he had in Cuba. "You and your brothers," he told Ted Jr., "are playing your parts in the greatest of the world's great days, and what man of gallant spirit does not envy you? You are having your crowded hours of glorious life; you have seized the great chance, as it was seized by those who fought at Gettysburg and Waterloo, and Agincourt and Arbela and Marathon."

He was sitting in his study at Sagamore Hill on July 16, 1918, attending to his correspondence, when Phil Thompson of the Associated Press knocked at the door. He said that the *New York Sun* had just received a curious telegram: all it said was, "WATCH SAGAMORE HILL IN EVENT OF [DELETED BY CENSOR]." Roosevelt understood immediately. "One of my boys is in trouble."

Two had already been in trouble.

First, Archie's knee and elbow had been shattered by German shells, and he had been awarded the French Croix de Guerre. Then, Ted had been gassed leading his men on the front lines in one battle and been awarded the Silver Star for his gallantry in another. Kermit was unhurt, but he had survived several close calls fighting with the British army in Mesopotamia, and he, too, had been decorated for his bravery.

Quentin, the youngest and perhaps the best loved of the Roosevelt boys, had joined the army's fledgling Air Service. He was engaged to Miss Flora Payne Whitney, but forbidden by her parents to marry until the war was over. When a visitor told Quentin how proud the country was to see all the Roosevelt sons in uniform, he just grinned. "Well," he said, "you know it's rather up to us to practice what father preaches."

Quentin's fellow flyers in the 95th "Kicking Mule" Aero Squadron called him the "Go and Get 'Em Man" because of his eagerness for combat. On July 5, 1918, he'd survived his first dogfight. "You get so excited that you forget everything except getting the other fellow," he wrote to his mother.

On the 10th, he'd shot down a German plane. "The last of the lion's brood has been blooded!" his father said when he heard the news.

ABOVE Quentin Roosevelt sprawls dead next to his broken aircraft in a battered photograph taken by a German soldier. Copies of the picture eventually made their way to all the Roosevelts. "Two bullet holes in the head," Eleanor told a friend, "so he did not suffer and it is a glorious way to die."

OPPOSITE Theodore Roosevelt, grieving for his lost son and wracked with pain from the inflammatory rheumatism that made it agony to walk and would drive him to the hospital for a time, clings to his seventh grandchild, Edie Derby. When a friend expressed her sympathy, he replied, "Do not sympathize with me. Have you ever known any man who has gotten so much out of life as I have? . . . I have made the very most out of my life."

On the 14th, Quentin had gone up again with his comrades. A stiff wind blew them dangerously deep into Germany. An enemy formation rose to meet them. Fourteen planes mixed in a "general melee," one American pilot remembered, "rolling and circling and diving . . . [with] the continuous tat, tat, tat, tat of the machine guns." The Americans flew separately back to their base. Quentin never got there: bullets had riddled his cockpit; his plane plunged into a rutted field.

At dawn the next morning, Thompson again climbed the piazza steps at Sagamore Hill. He said further dispatches confirmed that Quentin had been killed. Roosevelt hesitated, pacing up and down. "But—Mrs. Roosevelt? How am I going to break it to her?"

He went inside and half an hour later returned with a formal statement: "Quentin's mother and I are very glad that he got to the Front and had a chance to render some service to his country, and to show the stuff there was in him before his fate befell him."

Roosevelt remained stoical in public, but he was privately anguished. "To feel that one has inspired a boy to conduct that has resulted in his death, has a pretty serious side for a father—and at the same time I would not have cared for my boys and they would not have cared for me if our relations had not been just along that line."

His coachman came upon him in the stable, his face buried in the mane of his son's pony, murmuring, "Poor Quentyquee, poor Quentyquee."

RIGHT Franklin enjoys the sea air aboard the USS *Dyer,* on his way to the war at last. Halfway across the Atlantic, he noted in his journal that "ten miles ahead of this Floating City of Souls a torpedo may be waiting to start on its quick run." No enemy torpedo ever materialized, but a German submarine was spotted several miles away—and over the years, in his retelling, the American destroyer and the German submarine grew closer and closer until he was claiming that the sub had come up first on one side of his ship and then the other.

OPPOSITE, TOP Roosevelt, wearing his distinctive inspection outfit, visits a massive naval gun emplacement on the Western Front. Behind him, in the cloth cap, is his good-time companion, Livingston Davis.

OPPOSITE, BOTTOM Franklin samples some of the "sublime Scotch" that kept him and his party warm while fishing in the rain in Scotland.

A Man Must Be What He Is

That same summer, Franklin Roosevelt had finally persuaded his chief to let him sail for Europe on an inspection tour. He had the time of his life. In London, he bought himself three pairs of silk pajamas, praised the heroism of the men he called "my" Marines at the Battle of Belleau Wood, chatted with King George V, who told him he'd "never seen a German gentleman"— and, at a dinner at Grey's Inn, had a brief encounter with Winston Churchill, the man with whom he would one day direct a far bigger war. Churchill, then the First Lord of the Admiralty, took no notice of him, a fact which did not please FDR when he learned it many years later.

In France, Franklin visited his wounded cousins, Ted and Archie, accompanied a drunken congressional delegation to the Folies Bergère, and toured the battlefields in a special costume he'd designed for himself. At one battered village, he was allowed to fire an artillery shell into the German lines, seven miles away, and at a crossroads called "the Angle of Death" he stood in the open snapping photographs long enough for the Germans to call in artillery. He and his party had to drive off so fast he left his suitcase behind.

"The more I think of it," he wrote Eleanor, "the more I feel that being only thirty-six my place is not at a Washington desk, even a Navy desk. I know you will understand." He now hoped to get himself a navy commission and join a naval battery on the Western Front. But first he traveled to Scotland to inspect the North Sea mines and spent a couple of days salmon fishing in a cold rain before sailing home. Once aboard the USS *Leviathan,* he collapsed in his cabin with double pneumonia. When the ship docked in New York, orderlies had to carry him ashore. An ambulance brought him to his mother's house. He was carried to a guest room upstairs.

Eleanor unpacked her husband's luggage and came upon a bundle of letters addressed to him and written by her own onetime social secretary, Lucy Mercer. At that moment, she remembered later, "the bottom fell out of my own particular world," and she was forced, she said, to "face myself, my surroundings, my world, honestly for the first time."

Lucy Mercer was beautiful, cultured, and soft-spoken. She came from an old Maryland Catholic family that had fallen on hard times. Bamie Roosevelt had recommended her not long after the young Roosevelts arrived in Washington five years before, and Eleanor had been pleased with the way she had helped steer her through the shoals of society in the nation's capital.

Lucy had been part of the Roosevelt household for three years. The children liked her. So did Sara: "She is so sweet and attractive," she wrote, "and she loves you, Eleanor." But she also came to love Franklin—"his ringing laugh," Lucy remembered, "all the ridiculous things he used to say . . . his extraordinarily beautiful head."

When Eleanor and the children were away at Campobello, Lucy and Franklin had spent time together, dining at the homes of discreet friends, sailing and picnicking along the Potomac. Alice Longworth had seen them driving around Washington together and teased Franklin about Miss Mercer. "Isn't she lovely?" was all he would say.

Rumors may have reached Eleanor. She had let her secretary go in June of 1917, but within two weeks Lucy enlisted in the navy—and then was conveniently assigned to Franklin's office at the Navy Department. At Campobello that summer, Eleanor worried about where her husband was and what he was up to. In October, Franklin's boss Josephus Daniels dismissed Miss Mercer from the service. The threat to the Roosevelt marriage seemed to have been lifted.

But now, more than a year later, it was clear that Lucy Mercer was still an important part of her husband's life. Lucy's relationship with Franklin confirmed every fear Eleanor Roosevelt had ever harbored about herself: no one would ever love her for long.

According to family tradition, she offered her husband his "freedom." His mother was said to have told her son she would not stand in his way if he wanted to leave his wife and five children—but she also would not provide him with another penny, and would make sure he did not inherit his beloved Springwood. Louis Howe weighed in, too: a divorce, he said, would end Franklin's political career.

Franklin promised never to see Lucy again. Eleanor agreed to remain with him. But the experience taught her, she would write many years later, "that practically no one is entirely bad or entirely good . . . that a man must be what he is." She neither forgot nor forgave her husband's transgression: it became almost a measure of one's intimacy with her to have been quietly told what he had done and how she had dealt with it. But the bitter memory of her husband's betrayal would not prevent her from forming with him one of the most powerful political partnerships in American history.

OPPOSITE Lucy Mercer, shortly before she joined the Roosevelt household in 1913 as Eleanor's social secretary. A cousin remembered that "every man who ever knew her fell in love with her."

ABOVE Lucy and Winthrop Rutherfurd, the elderly widower she married in 1920. He was twenty-nine years her senior, and when Franklin overheard the news, a member of the Roosevelt family remembered, he "started like a horse in fear of a hornet."

The Old Lion

When the Great War ended in Allied victory on November 11, 1918, Theodore Roosevelt was fifty-nine years old but felt and looked far older. On the evening of January 5, 1919, he sat reading in his children's empty nursery. He'd recently been hospitalized, and was still weak, weary, oddly short of breath. But he'd long since made his peace with the Republican Party and was determined to make one more run at the presidency. "I cannot go without having done something to that old gray skunk in the White House," he'd told a recent visitor. He dismissed the "Fourteen Points" upon which Wilson hoped to build a lasting peace as just "fourteen scraps of paper," and opposed American participation in the proposed League of Nations: "Let each nation reserve the right to itself for its own decisions, and . . . make it perfectly clear that we do not intend to take a position of an international Meddlesome Mattie."

The year 1920 would bring him back to power. He was sure of it. So were many political leaders on both sides of the aisle.

Meanwhile, he needed rest. As he closed his book and got ready for bed that evening he said to Edith, "I wonder if you will ever know how I love Sagamore Hill."

During the night he suffered a pulmonary embolism—a fatal blood clot in the lung.

Archie cabled his brothers: "The old lion is dead." "I have never known another person so vital," William Allen White wrote, "nor another man so dear." "Death had to take him sleeping," Vice President Thomas Marshall told the press, "for if Roosevelt had been awake, there would have been a fight."

Two days later, as pallbearers prepared to carry his coffin to a hilltop grave at Oyster Bay, a New York police captain said to Roosevelt's sister Corinne, "Do you remember the fun of him . . . ? It was not only that he was a great man, but, oh, there was such fun in being led by him."

Franklin and Eleanor Roosevelt had been unable to attend the funeral. They were at sea, on their way to Europe. He was going back to dismantle naval installations. She insisted she go along, too, to look after him, she said: his health was still fragile. So was their marriage. Theodore Roosevelt's death stunned them both. He had been Franklin's hero all his life—"the greatest man I ever knew," he said. He had been a hero to Eleanor, too, and a vivid link to her beloved father. But Theodore Roosevelt's death was about to provide Franklin Roosevelt with a great opportunity.

ABOVE Edith and Theodore Roosevelt toward the end of their lives together. "My sorrow is so keen for the young who die," he wrote in 1918, "that the edge of my grief is blunted when death comes to the old, of my own generation; for in the nature of things we must soon die anyhow—and we have warmed both hands before the fire of life."

OPPOSITE Theodore Roosevelt's casket being carried to his grave at Oyster Bay. "I don't feel sorry for him," Kermit wrote his grieving mother from France. "He wouldn't want it, that would be the last thing. There never was anyone like him, and there won't be."

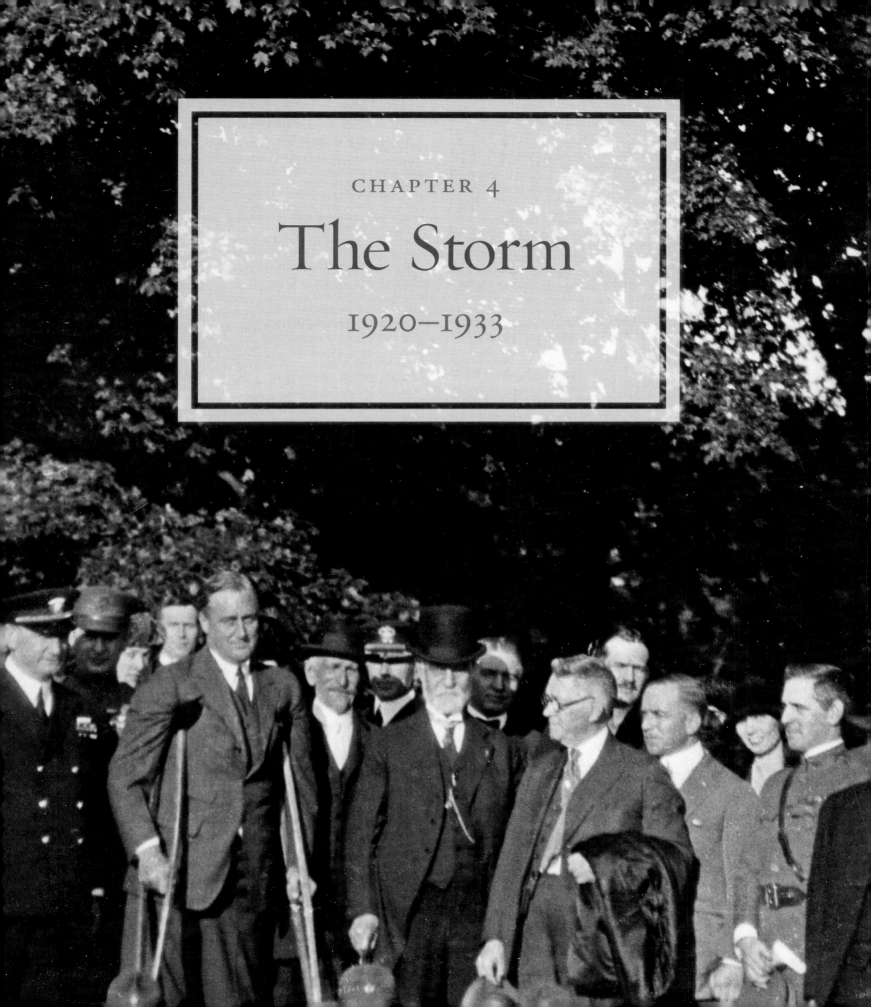

CHAPTER 4

The Storm

1920–1933

Breaking the Heart of the World

PRECEDING PAGES Franklin Roosevelt, leaning heavily on his crutches, manages to attend a Pittsburgh meeting of the National Executive Conference of the Boy Scouts in 1924, the year he had once hoped to run for president. Polio kept him out of politics, but he did his best to keep his name alive by other means.

ABOVE British schoolgirls strew roses in Woodrow Wilson's path as he arrives at Dover, on his way to the Paris Peace Talks in January 1919. "It is marvelous indeed how all the world is turning to the President!" wrote one of his aides. Wilson himself was more realistic; unless he could engineer a just peace he feared people would "turn about and hiss me."

The Paris Peace Talks were already under way when Franklin and Eleanor Roosevelt arrived in the French capital in January 1919. They had no direct involvement; Franklin was abroad on Navy Department business. But it was impossible not to be swept up in the excitement. "I never saw anything like Paris," Eleanor reported to her mother-in-law. "It is full beyond belief and one sees many celebrities and all one's friends! People wander the streets unable to find a bed and the prices are worse than New York for everything."

Much of the world hoped that Woodrow Wilson would succeed at Versailles in helping to build a postwar world based on the lofty principles of his Fourteen Points, that the Great War might really have been what he had once called it—"the war to end all wars." To achieve that noble goal, he insisted upon the creation of the League of Nations. Without such an organization, he told his fellow delegates, "no arrangement that you can make would either set up or steady the peace of the world."

Other Allied leaders proved less interested in Wilson's postwar vision than in obtaining reparations from the defeated enemy. United States senators, who would be required to ratify any treaty, were not invited to Paris, even as observers.

In February, Wilson sailed home to sign bills passed in his absence before returning to Versailles for more weeks of negotiation. The Roosevelts boarded the same warship and lunched with the president. "The United States must go into [the League]," he told them, "or it will break the heart of the world for she is the only nation that all feel is disinterested."

In the end, it was Woodrow Wilson's heart that would be broken. He returned to the United States in July and personally delivered the treaty to the Senate for its approval, saying it had "come about by no plan of our conceiving, but by the hand of God," but his political enemies, led by Theodore Roosevelt's old friend Henry Cabot Lodge, and his own stubborn refusal to compromise with others in the Senate who would have agreed to membership with reservations, combined to keep America out of the League. The president himself became a virtual prisoner in the White House, partially paralyzed by strokes, unwilling to be seen or heard in public.

ABOVE Eleanor (her back turned) and FDR chat with President Wilson aboard the *George Washington*, the ship that carried him home from Europe in February. The uniformed young man behind the president is W. Sheffield Cowles Jr., the son of Theodore Roosevelt's sister Bamie.

LEFT Wilson rides through San Francisco on September 18, 1919, part of his cross-country campaign to rally support for the League of Nations. Seven days later at Pueblo, Colorado, he would suffer the first of the series of strokes that crippled him and destroyed the last hope of American participation in the international organization.

That Fight Can Still Be Won

By the summer of 1920, things looked very bad for the Democratic Party in the upcoming presidential election. The U.S. Senate had refused to ratify the Treaty of Versailles and rejected membership in the League of Nations. Wilson's dream, said a triumphant Henry Cabot Lodge, "is as dead as Marley's ghost." American voters, plagued by soaring postwar prices and alarmed by labor strife, were weary of reform and increasingly uninterested in events overseas.

At Chicago in June, the Republicans nominated for president an amiable but undistinguished compromise candidate, Ohio Senator Warren G. Harding, who promised "not heroism but healing, not nostrums but normalcy."

To run against him, the Democrats, meeting in San Francisco, settled on another Ohioan, Governor James M. Cox.

Cox then picked thirty-eight-year-old Franklin Roosevelt to balance the ticket: he was an easterner with an independent reputation, had a good record in wartime Washington, and—most important—bore a last name the party hoped would appeal to independent voters who had planned to cast their ballots for Theodore Roosevelt that year. "Franklin's nomination . . . really didn't require much shoving," a friend wrote from San Francisco. "He had played a fine part all through the convention and when Cox was nominated . . . sublime availability geographically as well as from every standpoint was so apparent . . . he went through in quick time."

Franklin professed to be surprised. When called to the telephone to hear the news, his mother, working in the garden of her father's old house overlooking the Hudson at Newburgh, New York, did not. She had taught her boy that nothing he ever really wanted was beyond his grasp. She wrote him right away, sending her regards to the son she now believed would be "our future President." "All my love and interest goes to you," she said, "and as always is centered in you."

The Democratic candidates traveled to Washington and went to the White House to get the ailing president's blessing. Wilson was wheeled onto the South Portico, a woolen shawl around his shoulders despite the summer heat, his useless left arm dangling. In a voice that could barely be heard, he thanked them for coming.

Cox told the president how much he admired the battle he'd waged for the League.

"Mr. Cox," Wilson said, "that fight can still be won."

Cox promised to make the League the central issue of his campaign.

Wilson said he was very grateful, before being wheeled back inside.

"His utter weakness was startling," FDR told reporters afterward, "and I noticed tears in the eyes of Cox. . . . It was one of the most impressive scenes I have ever witnessed."

Franklin Roosevelt would never forget the sight of the president he'd served for seven years, defeated and helpless.

Published 3 times a week.
Illustrated Current News, Inc., 982 Chapel Street, New Haven, Conn.

ILLUSTRATED CURRENT NEWS

Entered as second class matter October 26, 1915, at the Post Office at New Haven, Connecticut, under Act of March 3, 1879.

Wednesday, August 18, 1920
Vol. 1   No. 1075

VICE PRESIDENT FRANKLIN ROOSEVELT ONE OF THE YOUNGEST OF CANDIDATES

The Democrats nominated Franklin D. Roosevelt who is shown above "accepting" his nomination at Hyde Park, New York for vice president. He is under 40, a live wire and has had loads of political experience and was formerly Assistant Secretary of the Navy.

We Must Go Forward or Flounder

The formal ceremony at which Franklin was to accept the vice presidential nomination was held a few weeks later at Springwood. Five thousand people turned out to hear him speak, ruining his mother's lawn and trooping through her house, where, as Eleanor wrote, "for so many years only family and friends were received."

Franklin spoke for nearly an hour. He gamely denied that Americans had tired of reform or had lost interest in the world beyond their borders. To reject the League of Nations would betray the cause of peace for which Americans had gone to war and sacrificed so much, he said. "We cannot anchor our ship of state in this world tempest, nor can we return to the placid harbor of long years ago. We must go forward or flounder."

The odds against victory were high, but Franklin hurled himself into the campaign, traveling by train all across the country, sometimes delivering thirteen speeches a day.

"During three months in the year 1920," he remembered, "I got to know the country as only a candidate—or a traveling salesman—can get to know it."

Theodore Roosevelt had always encouraged his young cousin's political career, even though Franklin was a Democrat. But in the years after his death,

OPPOSITE Sara Delano Roosevelt greets her boy on the Springwood portico while in the background local Democrats march up the driveway to see FDR formally accept his nomination for vice president. "I kept wishing for your father," Sara told him later, "but I believe he knew and was with us."

TOP The *Illustrated Current News* introduces Franklin, the "live wire," to its national readership. Eleanor and two of the Roosevelt sons can be seen in the crowd, just above his extended arm; his proud mother looks on from behind.

ABOVE The Republican ticket of Warren G. Harding and Calvin Coolidge

friends and business associates, politicians and well-wishers, all the tensions in the crowded household, were bad for her boy. As soon as it could be arranged, she believed, he should return to the quiet of Hyde Park, where she could care for him, at least for a time, just as she and Franklin had once cared for his ailing father.

"My mother-in-law thought we were tiring my husband and that he should be kept completely quiet which made our discussions . . . somewhat acrimonious," Eleanor remembered. "She always thought she understood what was best, particularly where her child was concerned, regardless of what any doctor might say."

Eleanor was sure she knew what was best for Franklin, too. She was a stern taskmaster, reminding him to do his painful exercises on time and for as long as his doctors decreed. He resented her intrusion and found himself again trapped between the two most important women in his life: his wife urging him to greater effort; his mother urging him to rest and relax. His doctors eventually insisted that he had to get away from what one of them called "the intense and devastating influence of the interplay of these high-voltage personalities."

In late spring he went home to Hyde Park.

ABOVE, LEFT Sara Delano Roosevelt in her New York City living room. When a book about her son suggested she had sought to make a permanent invalid of him by taking him to Springwood in the spring of 1922, she indignantly denied it in a private letter to him: "All I did was say that if the doctors thought it best for you to have for some months a quiet life, I would keep Hyde Park open & live there for a time."

ABOVE FDR's first pair of braces, fitted out with a pelvic band that provided enough extra strength and stability to allow him finally to stand. Later, enough strength would return to the muscles of his stomach and lower back to allow him to use shorter and less cumbersome braces.

ABOVE Daisy Suckley's signed Christmas portrait, 1921, the year before she was first called to Franklin's side

RIGHT In order to achieve this apparently relaxed pose on the south porch at Springwood in the late spring of 1922, FDR had to lift his unbraced right leg into place with his hands.

My God, He Was Brave

In Hyde Park, without his wife and children present, the constant stress eased, but the routine set by his solicitous mother was as rigid as it had been when he was a little boy: breakfast on a bed tray, up and dressed by ten, lunch with his mother at one, followed by a nap, tea at four, dinner at seven, put to bed by eleven—with physical therapy and sedentary hobbies like building toy boats and stamp collecting to fill the long hours in between.

One day that spring, Sara made a telephone call to Wilderstein, the home of the Suckley family, distant cousins of the Roosevelts, just up the Hudson in Rhinebeck. She asked to speak to Margaret, known to friends and family as "Daisy." Her son was lonely, she said, and needed company. Would Miss Suckley come to tea?

She would. Ten years younger than Franklin and unmarried, she had been dazzled by him ever since she'd seen him at a party, laughing as he whirled one partner after another around the dance floor.

Now, she found him immobilized. Daisy felt privileged to sit with him several times that spring and summer on the Springwood lawn as he pulled himself around a set of exercise bars telling extravagant stories about himself to keep her entertained and as unaware as possible of his helplessness. "I'm not going to be conquered by a childish disease," he told her again and again.

"My God, he was brave," she remembered.

He'd been fitted out with steel braces. They weighed fourteen pounds and ran from above his waist all the way to his heels. Once the catches at his knees were locked to keep his legs from buckling, it took two people to haul him to his feet and a third to slide crutches under his arms.

At first, he simply hung from his crutches, then managed to drag his legs across a room, and finally began to try to make his painful way alone down the drive that led from Springwood to the Albany Post Road. It was a perilous, exhausting business, swinging his rigid braced legs through the crutches with each step, trying not to topple forward.

He made it only once and never tried again.

ABOVE The quarter-mile-long driveway between Springwood and the Albany Post Road down which FDR struggled on crutches. "It's a bit traumatic when you're fifteen," Anna remembered, "to see your father, whom you've regarded as a wonderful playmate, who took long walks with you, . . . could out-jump you, . . . walking on crutches . . . struggling in heavy steel braces. And you see the sweat pouring down his face, and you hear him saying, 'I must get down the driveway today—all the way down the driveway.'"

Becoming an Individual

One day that June, Eleanor received a phone call from a stranger, a lively sounding woman named Nancy Cook who said she was the executive secretary of the new Women's Division of the state Democratic Party. Would Mrs. Franklin D. Roosevelt be willing to speak at a fund-raising luncheon? Eleanor hesitated; she dreaded speaking in public. But Louis Howe and her husband insisted she do it. It would help her to resume the independent life that meant so much to her—and it would keep the Roosevelt name before the public, something Howe and his boss were always eager to do.

The speech went well, and she got to know Nancy Cook and Cook's partner, Marion Dickerman, a reformer and educator who in 1919 had been the first woman ever to run for the New York State Legislature. For some fifteen years they would be among Eleanor's closest friends.

With their encouragement, Eleanor began organizing the Democratic women of Dutchess County and got her first real taste of raw politics on elec-

ABOVE Eleanor Roosevelt (right) and Esther Lape stride into the U.S. Capitol Building, where Lape would defend their work on the American Peace Award before the Senate Special Committee on Propaganda, 1924.

ABOVE, RIGHT Eleanor Roosevelt, 1924

tion day. Some of the Democrats she drove to the polls in Poughkeepsie had been paid for their votes. She was appalled by the bribery—but delighted by the outcome: Al Smith, Franklin's old political ally and sometime critic, easily beat his Republican opponent for governor.

Over the months that followed, she would join the Women's City Club of New York and the Women's Trade Union League, making more new friends, and taking on new causes and responsibilities.

None meant more to her than serving under her friend Esther Lape on the committee to choose the winner of the American Peace Award. It offered $100,000 to the author of the "best practicable plan by which the United States may co-operate with other nations for . . . world peace." More than 22,000 submissions were received, including one from Franklin. The winner called for adherence to the Permanent Court of International Justice and cooperation with—but not membership in—the League of Nations.

Senate isolationists charged that the prize was secretly sponsored by foreign interests seeking to undermine U.S. sovereignty. The Federal Bureau of Investigation looked into the matter and found no evidence to back the senators' charge, but during the probe Eleanor Roosevelt's name made the first of countless appearances in its files.

She had no regrets. "I was thinking things out," she remembered of those days, "and becoming an individual. Had I never done this, perhaps I might have been saved some difficult experiences, but I have never regretted even my mistakes. They all added to my understanding of other human beings."

ABOVE, LEFT Nancy Cook, Marion Dickerman, and Eleanor during a summer visit to Campobello in 1926. To some on the Oyster Bay side of the family, Eleanor's new friends were "she-males," "female impersonators." But Franklin saw how important they were to his wife—and to the work he and Eleanor hoped would keep his political hopes alive. The women, in turn, admired his courage and appreciated his shrewd political counsel. He called them part of "our gang."

ABOVE Louis Howe, who was nearly as important to Eleanor Roosevelt's development as he was to Franklin's. He worked with her to overcome a nervous tendency to giggle while speaking to an audience. "Have something to say," he told her, "say it, and sit down." He also sometimes acted as a sounding board, encouraged her to become a public figure in her own right, and, much later, would tell her he would like to make her president of the United States.

The Grand and Glorious Occasion

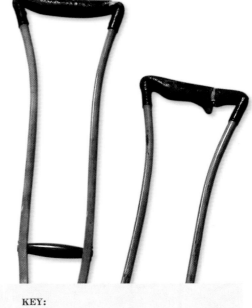

On the morning of October 9, 1922, a little over a year after FDR was stricken, he determined to make an appearance at his Fidelity & Deposit office in the Equitable Building. His secretary, Missy LeHand, had planned a welcome-back banquet.

The Roosevelt family Buick pulled up in front of 120 Broadway. The chauffeur opened the back door. Franklin heaved himself onto the jump seat and extended his legs so that the chauffeur could pull them straight and lock his braces in place. An impatient driver began honking. The chauffeur left Roosevelt with his stiff legs protruding in the air to have words with him. A crowd gathered to see how the big cripple in the shiny car would manage to get out.

The chauffeur returned, hauled his employer to his feet, and placed his crutches beneath his arms. FDR's hat fell off. A stranger picked it up and put it back on his head. Roosevelt laughed and thanked him, then started, slowly, cautiously for the door, trying not to notice the gawkers standing nearby. Someone held the door open for him and he stumped inside and started for the elevators.

The gleaming lobby floor was slippery. The chauffeur was supposed to wedge his foot against the tip of the left crutch to keep him from falling. Somehow, his foot failed to hold, and Roosevelt went down.

Men and women watched, not sure what to do.

Franklin pulled himself up to a sitting position, his legs straight out in front of him. His chauffeur alone wasn't able to get him to his feet. Laughing and acting as if his fall had been the funniest thing in the world, that it happened all the time and needn't worry anyone, Roosevelt asked two young men in the crowd to help him up.

He finally reached the elevators and attended the luncheon.

Afterward, he told friends he'd had "a Grand Reception," and that it had been a "grand & glorious occasion." But he did not return for two more months.

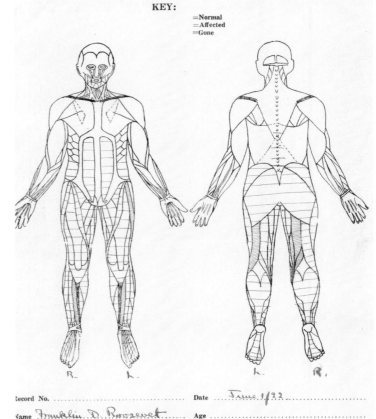

OPPOSITE The gleaming, polished lobby floor of the Equitable Building, onto which FDR fell in full view of a crowd of curious office-goers

ABOVE On June 1, 1922, Dr. Robert Lovett of Harvard—the leading American authority on infantile paralysis, who had first diagnosed Roosevelt roughly nine months earlier—examined FDR and then drew up this muscle chart, delineating in horizontal red lines all the muscles that had suffered damage. Behind it are the battered crutches that betrayed him.

Sunburned and in Fine Shape

I n February of 1923, Franklin and Eleanor, Franklin's valet, LeRoy Jones, and his secretary, Missy LeHand, all traveled south to the Florida Keys, where he and a friend named John Lawrence had bought a dilapidated seventy-one-foot houseboat, hoping that several weeks at sea in the sun might help rebuild his legs. They christened her the *Larooco,* a combination of their last names.

Eleanor did not stay aboard for long. She found the days boring and the nights along the coast "eerie and menacing." With Eleanor away, Missy LeHand served as Franklin's hostess and companion, setting a pattern they would follow for the next twenty years. She was Catholic, unmarried, half his age, and more than half in love with the boss she called "FD"—"EffDee" in her letters.

He was fond of her, as well, and some who knew them would always wonder about the nature of their relationship.

Missy seemed to understand his slightest shift of mood. "She knows when he is bored before he realizes it himself," one visitor remembered. "She can tell when he is really listening and when he is merely being polite—which no one else can." Her devotion was complete. Suitors would come and go over the years, some genuinely interested in her, some hoping to gain access to her

ABOVE FDR aboard the houseboat *Larooco* with (left to right) his valet, LeRoy Jones, sailing master Robert S. Morris and his wife, Dora, who did the cooking, a young mechanic who kept the ancient motor running—and a prize grouper. The ship's name was a combination of "Roosevelt" and "Lawrence," for its co-owner, John Lawrence.

boss through her. None could compare with him in her eyes. Sara called her son's secretary "nice little 'Missy,'" but worried that people would talk about his spending so much time alone with a woman not his wife. Eleanor seems never to have objected, even to have been grateful to know that her husband had the sort of admiring companionship he always craved and which she could not provide. Her friend Marion Dickerman believed that she avoided the "belittling emotion of jealousy" when it came to Missy largely because she could not bring herself to believe that any woman—and especially any secretary—could replace Lucy Mercer in her husband's affections.

Franklin loved everything about life aboard the houseboat: fishing, crawling from deck to deck out of sight of curious strangers, defying Prohibition by sharing rum drinks in the evenings with old friends who found the time to come down and be with him, and being lifted in and out of the water with a pulley arrangement of his own devising. "The West Coast [of Florida] is wholly wild and tropical," he wrote his mother that spring. "I have been in swimming . . . and it goes better and better. I'm sure this warmth and exercise is doing lots of good. . . . I am sunburned and in fine shape."

ABOVE Franklin, an old friend Frances De Rahm, and Missy LeHand with their lines in the water, somewhere off the Florida coast. When his mother saw this photograph and noticed the sideburns her son had grown she burst into tears because it reminded her so much of his late father.

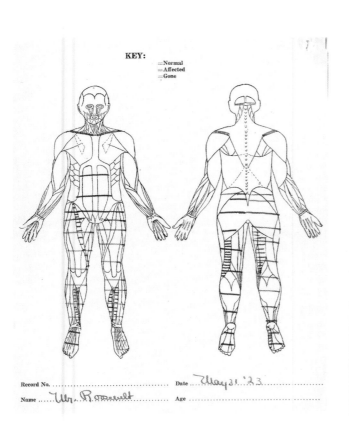

KEY:
=Normal
=Affected
=Gone

Record No. .... Date *May 31 '23* ....
Name ...... *Mr. Roosevelt* .... Age ....

Name *Mr. Roosevelt* Date *May 31 1923* Record No.
Characteristic gait

Left		Right
	Facial	
	Neck	
	Sternomastoid	
	Suprahyoid	
	Infrahyoid	
fair Anterior	Back	
poor Lateral	Abdominal	Anterior *fair*
		Lateral
	Legs	
	Measurements	
	Calf	
	Thigh	
	Length	
poor	Gluteus maximus	*poor*
fair	Ilio psoas	*poor*
poor	Sartorius	
trace	Tensor fasciae latae	*poor*
poor	Hip abductors	*trace*
poor	Hip adductors	*trace*
poor	Quadriceps	*trace*
fair Inner		Inner 0
0 Outer	Hamstrings	Outer *poor*
poor	Gastrocnemius	*poor*
0	Anterior tibial	0
0	Posterior tibial	*fair*
poor	Peroneus longus	*fair*
poor	Peroneus brevis	*fair*
	Extensor longus digitorum	*poor*
fair	Extensor brevis digitorum	*trace*
poor	Extensor proprius hallucis	*fair*
fair	Flexor longus digitorum	*poor*
fair	Flexor brevis digitorum	*poor*
poor	Flexors of the proximal phalanges	*poor*
fair	Flexor longus hallucis	0
fair	Flexor brevis hallucis	*poor*

He was still hoping somehow to walk on what one physician called "flail legs." But no real progress could be discerned. "I am very much disheartened about [Mr. Roosevelt's] ultimate recovery," one physician wrote. "I cannot help feeling that he has almost reached the limits of his possibilities. I only hope I may be wrong in this." Roosevelt was sometimes privately disheartened, too; Missy LeHand remembered days when it was noon before he could bring himself to leave his cabin and "greet his guest wearing his lighthearted façade."

When his doctors finally told him that further progress was unlikely he refused to accept their verdict. Rules that applied to others did not apply to him. He was certain he would walk again. One after another, he would try and abandon supposed "cures"—sun lamps, a special electrified belt called the "I-on-a-co," an oversized motorized tricycle. There were two more cruises on the *Larooco,* as well, and he spent several weeks working at Marion, Massachusetts, with an eccentric neurosurgeon named William McDonald who promised Roosevelt he would soon be able to walk without braces provided he underwent strenuous exercise in the bay followed by still more arduous workouts on land.

Nothing worked. "Polio was a storm," one of Roosevelt's physiotherapists taught her patients. "You were what remained when [the storm] had passed."

It was once part of the Roosevelt legend that polio somehow brought the

Roosevelts closer together. It did not. Between 1925 and 1928, Franklin would spend more than half his time—116 of 208 weeks—away from home, struggling to find a way to regain his feet. Eleanor was with him just 4 of those 116 weeks, and his mother was with him for only 2. His children hardly saw him.

"Those were the lonely years," James remembered. "For a long while during this time of illness . . . we had no tangible father, no father-in-being, whom we could touch and talk to at will—only an abstract symbol, a cheery letter written from off somewhere on a houseboat. . . . Neither Anna, nor I, nor my brothers had the guidance and training that I think Father would have given us had he not been involved in his own struggle to re-establish a useful life for himself."

OPPOSITE, LEFT, TOP AND BOTTOM On May 31, 1923, just a day short of a year after Dr. Robert Lovett first diagrammed Roosevelt's muscle loss, he did it again and made detailed notes: of the forty-four muscles whose strength he had measured in 1921, seven showed very slight improvement but seven had deteriorated. Twelve months of lonely work had yielded no measurable overall improvement at all.

OPPOSITE, RIGHT In this photograph, taken at the home of Dr. William McDonald at Marion, Massachusetts, in the summer of 1925, Roosevelt appears to be standing without braces. But LeRoy Jones and Dr. McDonald are actually holding him upright and the wheelchair into which he will shortly sink is just behind him.

ABOVE After a swim, FDR and Missy LeHand huddle together in a dinghy, photographed from the deck of the *Larooco* drifting somewhere off the coast of Florida.

Not a Thing to Lose

Eleanor, not Franklin, went to political war that spring—against Charles Murphy, the Tammany Hall boss who had outmaneuvered her husband during his first term as a state senator thirteen years before.

"I have wanted you home the last few days," she wrote Franklin, "to advise me on the fight I'm putting up. . . . Mr. Murphy and I disagree. . . . I imagine it is just a question of what he dislikes most, giving me my way or having me give the papers a grand chance for a story. . . . There's one thing I'm thankful for. I haven't a thing to lose and for the moment you haven't, either."

She and her new friends had already driven all over the state, organizing Democratic women. The issue now was who would pick two woman delegates and two delegates-at-large to the national convention in July—men like Murphy, who had always run things, or the growing number of women Eleanor had been recruiting for the party.

When Murphy insisted on remaining in charge, she publicly warned him at a Democratic women's dinner of what would happen if he failed to share power fairly. "It is always disagreeable to take stands," she said. "It is always easier to compromise, always easier to let things go. To many women, and I am one of them, it is extraordinarily difficult to care about anything enough to cause disagreement or unpleasant feeling, but I have come to the conclusion this must be done for a time until we can prove our strength and demand respect for our wishes."

When Murphy still refused to change his ways, Eleanor appealed directly to Governor Al Smith. He overruled Murphy. Thanks to Eleanor, the women, not the boss, would pick their own delegates-at-large.

Franklin wrote her to tell her how proud he was.

"You need not be proud of me dear," she answered. "I'm only being active till you can be again—it isn't such a great desire on my part to serve the world and I'll fall back into habits of sloth quite easily. Hurry up, for as you know, my ever-present sense of the uselessness of things will overwhelm me sooner or later."

ABOVE Tammany Hall, hung with flags and bunting in readiness for the Democratic national convention in July 1924

OPPOSITE Eleanor Roosevelt demonstrates a new voting machine. It was important for women to go to the polls, she wrote in 1924, but "if they expect to gain the ends for which they fought they must [also] gain for themselves a place of real equality and the respect of the men."

tunity to instill in her students some of the qualities her own beloved school-mistress, Mademoiselle Souvestre, had instilled in her: open-mindedness, independent thinking, social consciousness. "I teach because I love it," she explained. "I cannot give it up."

She organized the household in Albany, assigning Missy LeHand a bedroom larger than hers, found space for her circle of friends as well as Franklin's, and toured prisons and hospitals on her husband's behalf, remembering his exhortation to lift the lids on cooking pots to check whether people were getting the quality of food they were supposed to get.

And she sometimes stood in for him at political events, as well. "Dear Franklin," she wrote after attending a Staten Island Democratic Club luncheon: "Arrived at [12:30], stood and shook hands till 1:30; ate till 3:30; talked till 5:20; home here at 6:40 nearly dead! . . . You are the finest Governor ever and I have all the Virtues and would gladly have dispensed with half [of them] could I have left at four!"

ABOVE Eleanor Roosevelt meets with students at the Todhunter School, which she, Marion Dickerman, and Nancy Cook had purchased together just a year before her husband ran for governor. She enjoyed the classroom but loved even more shepherding her wealthy charges through courtrooms and settlement houses and past the same crowded tenements that had opened her eyes to the plight of the less fortunate when she was young.

ABOVE Earl Miller and Eleanor during a trip to
Chazy Lake, New York

RIGHT Eleanor and Earl Miller, in his uniform as a
state trooper, look on as Governor Roosevelt confers
a medal on the explorer Admiral Richard E. Byrd
after his return from the South Pole in 1929.

The Pirate and the Lady

Early in his first term as governor, Franklin began to worry that his wife, who insisted on driving her own automobile when undertaking inspection tours for him and who wanted the least possible fuss made over her wherever she went, might someday get into trouble without someone to protect her. Finally, he assigned one of his own bodyguards to remain at her side wherever she went.

Corporal Earl Miller of the New York State Police had been Al Smith's bodyguard, as well as a navy boxing champion, judo instructor, trick rider, and circus acrobat. He was handsome and high-spirited—Marion Dickerman called him "brazen"—and quickly became devoted to his new charge, whom he called "the Lady." He taught her to shoot, gave her tennis lessons, bought her a horse, encouraged her to "try to smile" whenever photographers came near. She was flattered by his attention, grateful for the appreciation her husband and four sons only rarely expressed for her. When the Roosevelts were at home in the Governor's Mansion, she saw to it that Miller was seated at the family dinner table. She sometimes cooked for him, visited his mother, and was pleased to be asked for advice about his many girlfriends. (He would be married three times.)

Invariably, just as there were rumors about the governor and Missy LeHand, there were whispers concerning the governor's wife and her strapping companion. Nancy Cook and Marion Dickerman worried that he sometimes seemed to "manhandle" their friend. Louis Howe fretted because there was already talk.

Miller always denied that he had ever had a romantic relationship with Mrs. Roosevelt. And in 1949, when the last of Miller's wives threatened to sue Eleanor for alienation of affection, her son, Franklin Jr.—who had agreed to defend his mother if the case ever got to court—asked her to tell him everything. Of course, she had loved Earl, she said, but "in the sense you mean there was nothing."

RIGHT In three frames from "The Pirate and the Lady," a home movie made at Chazy Lake in 1934 by Marion Dickerman, Earl Miller, costumed like the film star Douglas Fairbanks, kidnaps a giggling Eleanor Roosevelt—who was by then the first lady of the United States.

A Matter of Social Duty

Al Smith had been a great governor of New York. FDR was merely a good one, at least at first. He provided help for small farmers, expanded the work begun by his predecessor in conservation and public power—and learned how to use the radio in an informal way to explain to voters all that he was doing. His admiring cousin the journalist Joseph Alsop once summed up his early governorship this way: "[H]e poked no political hornet's nest for ideological reasons, yet was humane, liberal, efficient and . . . popular."

When he opened his *New York Times* on Friday morning, October 25, 1929, he was no better prepared than any other governor to understand what was about to happen to his state, his country, and much of the world, as well. "The most disastrous decline in the biggest and broadest stock market of history rocked the financial district yesterday," the paper reported. "It car-

ried down with it speculators, big and little in every part of the country. . . . Losses were tremendous and thousands of prosperous brokerage and bank accounts, sound and healthy a week ago, were completely wrecked in the strange debacle due to a combination of circumstances, but accelerated into a crash by fear." Investors called it "Black Thursday," but its losses would be eclipsed four days later by "Black Tuesday," October 29, the worst day in Wall Street history.

The next day, President Hoover assured the country of the soundness of the economy. Like many people in both parties, Roosevelt initially believed that what he privately joked was "the little tussle downtown" was simply a painful but necessary correction to a wildly overvalued stock market. But as the weeks went by it was clear that something else was happening: the economy steadily spiraled downward, banks collapsed, homes were foreclosed, millions lost their jobs. The Great Depression had begun.

Everyone seemed to feel its impact. FDR's own son-in-law, Curtis Dall,

ABOVE Just a few blocks west of the Roosevelts' Manhattan home, an American flag flies bravely over a cluster of wood-and-tar-paper shacks built by homeless men in the heart of Central Park. Like hundreds of thousands of desperate people all across the country, they named their temporary village "Hooverville," after the president whom they had come to blame for everything that was happening to them.

would lose his job and the home he had bought in Westchester County and have to move with Anna and FDR's first two grandchildren into the Roosevelt house on East Sixty-fifth Street.

In early 1930, while the White House was still insisting that employment was rebounding, Roosevelt resolved to act. "The situation is serious," he said, "and the time has come to face this unpleasant fact dispassionately." FDR came out publicly for unemployment insurance—then still a radical notion—and established the country's first state commission to establish reliable jobless figures and stabilize employment.

Americans differed—and still differ—over what caused the Depression and what should have been done to end it. But Herbert Hoover's grim personality, his repeated unconvincing promises that recovery was just months away, and his fondness for appointing commissions—sixty-two of them in all—to study the problem without any seeming outcome combined to persuade a growing majority of Americans that new leadership was needed.

And FDR, working with his three closest advisers—Louis Howe; James A. Farley, the chairman of the state Democratic Party; and Ed Flynn, the Democratic boss of the Bronx—sought to make sure he would be the man chosen to bring it about. With his advisers' help—and his wife's seasoned skill at rallying Democratic women—he was reelected governor in 1930 by almost three-quarters of a million votes. "I do not see how Mr. Roosevelt can escape becoming the next presidential nominee of his party," Farley told the press the next morning, "even if no one should raise a finger to bring it about."

"This country needs, and unless I mistake its temper, this country demands bold, persistent experimentation," FDR told a Georgia audience—and he set about to provide it. He created the Temporary Emergency Relief Administration—TERA—the first state agency in the country to provide public relief for the jobless, and he named as its executive director a dynamic young social worker from Iowa named Harry Hopkins. (In the six years that followed, TERA would assist some five million people—40 percent of the state's populace, most of whom would eventually return to the workforce.) "I assert," Roosevelt said, "that modern society, acting through its government, owes the definite obligation to prevent the starvation or dire want of any of its fellow men and women who try to maintain themselves but cannot. . . . To these unfortunate citizens aid must be extended by government—not as a matter of charity but as a matter of social duty."

That basic belief would animate Roosevelt's New Deal.

OPPOSITE A big county fair crowd turns out to hear FDR campaign for reelection in 1930. Upstate New York had traditionally been Republican territory, but by providing help to small farmers and arguing that "if the farmer starves today, we will all starve tomorrow," Roosevelt persuaded many rural voters to change their allegiance—and impressed Democratic leaders in rural states with his vote-getting ability among people like theirs.

ABOVE Governor Roosevelt enjoys his big victory on the morning after election day, 1930. "Well, as far as I can see, the Republican ship went down with all on board," Theodore Roosevelt Jr. wrote to his mother that day. "Cousin Franklin now, I suppose, will run for the presidency and I am already beginning to think of nasty things to say concerning him."

Is *Franklin D. Roosevelt* Physically Fit *to be* PRESIDENT?

By EARLE LOOKER

A Man to Man Answer to a Nation-Wide Challenge

GOVERNOR *and Mrs. Franklin D. Roosevelt, from recent photographs.*

To Meet Any Demand

The most serious hindrance to FDR's winning the nomination was the persistent rumors about his health. People whispered that infantile paralysis had affected his mind, even that he was suffering from syphilis.

To offset those rumors, Roosevelt obtained a $500,000 life insurance policy and then secretly encouraged a freelance journalist named Earle Looker to "challenge" him to prove his fitness for office, and to write up the results in *Liberty* magazine, then the nation's most widely read magazine.

Then, also behind the scenes, Roosevelt provided the money to pay three leading diagnosticians to look him over. The examination itself was wholly legitimate. All three doctors signed a statement declaring, "[W]e believe his powers of endurance are such as to allow him to meet all the demands of public or private life"—though one of them, an unshakable Republican, privately told his colleagues that he wanted it understood that "so far as I'm concerned this doesn't go for above the neck."

Earle Looker expressed his relief to the potential presidential candidate: "Well sir, we got away with the *Liberty* article despite all obstacles. . . . I think we can be sure that at least seven and a half million readers are sure you are physically fit!"

FDR would never again feel the need to speak in detail about his health to any journalist.

ABOVE The telegram sent to Earle Looker attesting to FDR's "health and powers of endurance," and Looker's *Liberty* magazine article, meant to put permanently to rest any questions about Roosevelt's fitness to serve as president.

OPPOSITE Propped against his car door but otherwise the picture of smiling good health, Franklin Roosevelt returns to Groton School to visit his son FDR Jr., 1932.

An Unprecedented and Unusual Time

As the 1932 Democratic convention opened in Chicago, Roosevelt was the clear front-runner, with a reputation as the most activist and effective governor in the country. Still, he had nine rivals, including his embittered old ally, Al Smith, and the conservative Speaker of the House, John Nance Garner of Texas. It took four ballots—and the second place on the ticket for Garner—for Roosevelt to secure the nomination.

Custom still required the candidate to wait weeks to be formally notified of his nomination. With the country in such a desperate condition and communications so much more immediate than they once had been, that delay struck Roosevelt as pointlessly anachronistic. He decided to board a small Ford Tri-Motor and fly from Albany to Chicago to accept the nomination right away.

It was a stormy flight through dense clouds with three refueling stops,

ABOVE FDR, about to take off from Albany for Chicago to accept his party's nomination for president. "We have a perfect day for this trip," he shouted to reporters over the sound of the tiny plane's engines. "I'm very happy to be going out to Chicago, and everybody knows the reason why I'm so happy."

but FDR slept serenely through much of it while Sam Rosenman, his chief speechwriter, put the final touches on what he should say to the convention. When they arrived in Chicago, Louis Howe—who had looked forward to this day almost as eagerly as had the candidate himself—handed FDR a wholly different speech. Rather than wound his most cherished adviser, Roosevelt used Howe's opening page when he reached Chicago Stadium and began to speak:

> My friends of the Democratic national convention of 1932, I appreciate your willingness after these six arduous days to remain here, for I know well the sleepless hours which you and I have had. . . . The appearance before a national convention of its nominee for president to be formally notified of his selection is unprecedented and unusual, but these are unprecedented and unusual times.

Twenty-nine years earlier, Theodore Roosevelt had promised the American people a "Square Deal." Now, eleven years after polio seemed to many to have crushed his political hopes forever, Franklin Roosevelt went on to make a promise of his own.

> Never before in modern history have the essential differences between the two major parties stood out in such striking contrast as they do today. Republican leaders have not only failed in material things, they have failed in national vision. . . . Throughout the nation, men and women, forgotten in the political philosophy of these last years, look to us for guidance and for a more equitable opportunity to share in the distribution of national wealth. . . . Those millions cannot and shall not hope in vain.
>
> I pledge you—I pledge myself, to a New Deal for the American people.

TOP A 1932 license plate urges motorists to vote for the national Democratic ticket: Franklin D. Roosevelt for president, John Nance "Cactus Jack" Garner for vice president—and a swift end to Prohibition. Roosevelt, like a generation of national politicians before him in both parties, had hoped to avoid taking sides in the ongoing debate between "wets" and "drys." But Al Smith's forces at the convention pushed him into standing four-square for repeal of the 18th Amendment.

ABOVE Gripping James's arm, FDR acknowledges the cheers of the delegates at Chicago Stadium, July 2, 1932. "This is more than a political campaign," he told them, "it is a call to arms. Give me your help, not to win votes alone, but to win in this crusade to restore America to its own people."

President Hoover had grown so unpopular that one of Roosevelt's defeated rivals for the nomination told FDR all he had to do to win was to stay alive till November.

With the Depression deepening, a double line of policemen armed with rifles now ringed the U.S. Capitol to keep out demonstrators. When seventeen thousand mostly jobless veterans of the Great War and their families descended on Washington to demand immediate payment of a bonus not officially due for several years, Hoover called out the army. The veterans were brutally driven from the capital. Roosevelt told an aide, "This will elect me."

Still, he took no chances. With the bold but sometimes contradictory counsel of three Columbia University professors—Raymond Moley, Rexford Tugwell, and Adolph Berle Jr.—whom the press called his "brains trust,"

he campaigned hard all across the country, promising help for "the forgotten man at the bottom of the economic pyramid," attacking Hoover for inaction—and simultaneously pledging to slash the federal budget by 25 percent. Hoover denounced him as "a chameleon on . . . plaid."

TOP, LEFT AND OPPOSITE FDR campaigns at the Hollywood Bowl. In full view of bystanders and at least one photographer, aides help Roosevelt snap his braces into place so that he can stand, grasp James's arm and his cane, and then begin to make his cautious, awkward way through the enthusiastic throng waiting inside. Once FDR was elected, the Secret Service had orders to discourage photographers from taking pictures like these and to keep crowds at a distance so that he would not be knocked down in the crush.

TOP, RIGHT Army troops use tear gas and fixed bayonets to rout unemployed veterans from their temporary shelters in Washington, D.C.

RIGHT Hoosiers mob Roosevelt in Indianapolis.

The Out-of-Season Roosevelts

ABOVE At Madison Square Garden, Theodore Roosevelt's widow makes clear to New York Republicans that she is one of them, that she will enthusiastically vote for Herbert Hoover, not her late husband's distant cousin. "These are trying times for us," she told a friend that fall, "and the confusion of names does not help. Continually, letters [arrive] congratulating me on my distinguished son the Democratic nominee. His line parted six generations ago from my husband's."

ABOVE, RIGHT Ted Jr. and Alice Roosevelt Longworth, who shared her brother's belief that he, not Franklin, should be running for president. FDR, she said, was "ninety percent mush and ten percent Eleanor."

OPPOSITE Theodore Roosevelt Jr., his wife, Eleanor, and their two sons, Theodore Roosevelt III (left) and Cornelius Van Schaack Roosevelt, at home in the Malacanang Palace, the residence of the governor-general of the Philippines in Manila. President Hoover had appointed the late president's son to the post, and as election day approached he identified himself to a reporter as Franklin Roosevelt's "fifth cousin, about to be removed."

Now, when Americans spoke of "Roosevelt," they meant Franklin, not Theodore. "The Oyster Bay Roosevelts," Alexander Wolcott wrote, "have become the 'out-of-season' Roosevelts."

When Theodore Roosevelt's younger sister, Corinne Roosevelt Robinson, crossed party lines to vote for FDR that fall, her old friend Sara Delano Roosevelt thanked her: "I never expected it, dear. . . . Some people have fine minds, others have warm hearts, but you have both."

But Alice Roosevelt Longworth campaigned hard against him aboard President Hoover's train. "There we were—the Roosevelts—hubris up to the eyebrows, beyond the eyebrows," she recalled, "and then who should come sailing down the river but Nemesis in the person of Franklin."

And at Sagamore Hill, Theodore Roosevelt's widow, Edith, was so infuriated at receiving some three hundred congratulatory messages from people who mistakenly thought Franklin was one of her sons that she made an unprecedented appearance at a Republican rally in Manhattan to introduce the Republican incumbent, just to make it clear that this Oyster Bay Roosevelt would also be voting for Herbert Hoover.

Someone once asked Sara Delano Roosevelt why so many of the Roosevelts of Oyster Bay seemed so hostile to her branch of the family. She didn't know, she said. But "perhaps it's because we're so much better-looking than they are."

All Light and No Darkness

On election night, November 8, 1932, Franklin Delano Roosevelt won the presidency by seven million votes and carried forty-two of the forty-eight states. His party took control of both chambers of Congress. It was the greatest Democratic victory in more than three-quarters of a century and, as FDR told his proud mother when he got home to East Sixty-fifth Street, "the greatest night of my life."

During the four long months between Roosevelt's election and his inauguration, the Depression steadily deepened. Stocks, bonds, farm prices—everything continued to spiral downward. Nearly four hundred banks failed in January and February alone. At least fifteen million Americans were without work.

They wanted to know what their president-elect was going to do to help them. He did not tell them. President Hoover called repeatedly upon Roosevelt to join him in what he called "co-operative action" to end the crisis, but FDR refused, wary of being trapped into supporting

ABOVE On the morning after election day, Roosevelt's broad grin was featured on the front page of nearly every newspaper in the country. Many readers were heartened by his apparent optimism, but some echoed the question of a Presbyterian minister in Pennsylvania: "What's he smiling about? Doesn't he understand how serious the crisis is?"

RIGHT The president-elect with some of his advisers, aboard a train that took him from New York to Washington and a fruitless meeting with Herbert Hoover. *Left to right:* Admiral Gary Crayson, physician to Presidents Theodore Roosevelt, Wilson, and Taft; veteran diplomat Norman H. Brown; "brains trusters" Raymond Moley and Rexford Tugwell; and William H. Woodin, who would become Roosevelt's first secretary of the treasury.

orthodox policies of which he did not approve. Off the record, the president-elect told a reporter that the country's troubles were not yet "my baby."

Hoover privately denounced him as a "madman," a "gibbering idiot."

"When I talk to [Roosevelt] he says 'Fine! Fine! Fine!'," Louisiana Senator Huey Long complained. "But [Senate Majority Leader] Joe Robinson goes to see him the next day and again he says, 'Fine! Fine! Fine!' Maybe he says 'Fine' to everybody."

Roosevelt spent the rest of the fall at Hyde Park, rested at Warm Springs for a time, then went to sea for twelve days, fishing in the Caribbean aboard the *Nourmahal,* a palatial yacht owned by an old Hudson River neighbor, Vincent Astor. To some it seemed in poor taste for the president-elect to be vacationing in such ostentatious luxury and such privileged company in the midst of so great a crisis. FDR enjoyed himself. "I didn't even open the brief-case," he told the press.

"To certain people," wrote Milton MacKaye in the *New Yorker,* "Roosevelt must always be a little less than glamorous. The reason is that his outlook on life is perennially optimistic, that he pushes ahead with full speed, always with a confidence that every story has a happy ending. They believe that he is, in short, something of a grown-up Boy Scout. He is all light and no dark-ness; all faith and no skepticism; all bright hope and no despair. One expects shadow and depth in a great man."

ABOVE FDR sets sail aboard the *Nourmahal.* Vincent Astor is at the president-elect's right. To his left are his son James and TR's son Kermit, who remained friendly with the Hyde Park branch of the family. Later, when a reporter asked Ted Roosevelt to explain how his brother could have gone fishing with FDR, Edith Roosevelt answered for him. "Because his mother was not there."

The Turmoil in My Heart

Eleanor was as ambivalent about her husband's latest victory as she had been when he was elected governor. "I was happy for Franklin, of course, because I knew that in many ways it would make up for the blow that fate had dealt him. . . . But for myself I was . . . deeply troubled. As I saw it, this meant the end of any personal life of my own. . . . I had watched Mrs. Theodore Roosevelt and had seen what it meant to be the wife of the president. . . . The turmoil in my heart was rather great that night and the next few months were not to make any clearer what the road ahead would be."

Her life changed forever the morning after election day when she emerged from the East Sixty-fifth Street house to walk the family's Scottish terrier and found herself surrounded by a beefed-up New York police detail and reporters who dogged her every step.

In an effort to find something more meaningful to do than "stand in line and receive visitors and preside over official dinners" when the Roosevelts moved to the White House, she asked Franklin if she might handle some of his mail. He looked at her "quizzically," she remembered, and gently turned her down: Missy LeHand would see it as interference. "I knew he was right and that it would not work," she recalled, "but it was a last effort to keep in close touch and to feel that I had a real job to do."

She would have to work out what she called "my own salvation" by herself.

In late January she accepted an invitation from Mrs. Herbert Hoover to come to Washington and look over the White House. She agreed to come but refused to be met at Union Station by a White House car. She would take a taxi to the Mayflower Hotel, instead, spend the night, and then walk to and from 1600 Pennsylvania Avenue. The next morning, Warren Delano Robbins, her husband's cousin and the chief of protocol at the State Department, turned up at the Mayflower in a limousine, anyway.

Eleanor politely told him she'd rather walk.

"But Eleanor, darling, you can't do that," he said. "People will recognize you! You'll be mobbed."

She walked.

Eleanor Roosevelt was determined to be a different kind of first lady. She knew she would be criticized, she told a friend, "but I can't help it."

ABOVE Aboard a commercial airplane shortly after election day, the copilot points out landmarks to the future first lady on a flight from New York to Cleveland, where she had a speaking engagement—the kind of independent travel she feared life in the White House would make impossible.

OPPOSITE Eleanor leaves the White House on foot after calling upon Mrs. Herbert Hoover, January 28, 1933. Walking at her side is Ike Hoover (no relation to the outgoing president), who had been chief usher since her uncle Theodore's time, and who had greeted her at the door as "Miss Eleanor," just as he had done twenty-nine years earlier. He marveled at the inauguration-day plans she'd already made: which houseguests would stay in what rooms; what the family liked for breakfast, lunch, and dinner; what servants would be needed—"everything the Chief Usher could wish to know except what the weather might be on March fourth."

These Things Are to Be Expected

The president-elect's fishing trip ended in Miami, Florida, on the evening of February 15, 1933. Some 25,000 people gathered in Bayfront Park to greet him. His open touring car inched its way into the middle of the crowd and stopped so that he could say a few words. A spotlight was trained on him. He pulled himself up onto the top of the backseat and was handed a microphone. He was no stranger to Florida waters, he reminded the crowd, and he hoped to come back soon to enjoy some more wonderful fishing. The people cheered.

In the darkness less than thirty feet behind the car was an Italian-born bricklayer named Giuseppe Zangara. He hated "all presidents," he said later, and "everybody who is rich." He had hoped to shoot President Hoover; now, he wanted to kill Roosevelt. He stood just a little over five feet tall and had to climb onto a wobbly folding chair to see his intended target. By the time he'd done so FDR had finished his remarks and slid back down into his seat. Only the top of his head was visible. Zangara missed Roosevelt but managed to get

off five shots before bystanders tackled him. Five people were hit, including Anton Cermak, the mayor of Chicago, who had been standing next to the president-elect's car.

FDR never flinched. He refused to take cover, ordered the Secret Service to lift the wounded mayor into his car, and held him during the race to the nearest hospital. "Tony, keep quiet," he said again and again. "Don't move. It won't hurt you if you keep quiet." Doctors credited Roosevelt with keeping the mayor from going into shock.

Eleanor was in New York. Franklin called to reassure her. "He's all right," she said afterward. "He's not the least bit excited. These things are to be expected."

Like Theodore Roosevelt nearly twenty-one years earlier, Franklin seemed unaffected by coming so close to death. "There was nothing," an aide who spent that evening with him remembered, "not so much as the twitching of a muscle, the mopping of a brow, or even the hint of a false gaiety—to indicate that it wasn't any evening in any other place. I have never seen anything in my life more magnificent."

ABOVE, LEFT Mayor Cermak, seconds after he was hit, blood already beginning to spread across his shirtfront. The bullet collapsed half of his lung, and may have clipped his colon. He would die of septicemia on March 6, 1933, two days after FDR's inauguration.

ABOVE The would-be assassin enjoys press coverage of the Miami incident and its aftermath. He was tried for attempted murder and sentenced to eighty years in prison. After Cermak died, he was retried for murder in the first degree, found guilty, and electrocuted—all within five weeks of the shootings.

LEFT Roosevelt visits the wounded in Jackson Memorial Hospital the morning after his close call.

The Only Thing We Have to Fear

At his inauguration seventeen days later, gripping James's arm, Roosevelt would demonstrate another kind of courage, making his slow, careful, rocking way out of the Capitol Building and onto the inaugural platform in full view of tens of thousands of anxious onlookers waiting under a gray sky for some hint of hope from the new president.

The banks were closed in forty of the forty-eight states. The Stock Exchange had suspended trading. Industrial production had been cut almost in half. Nearly half of all American farmers faced foreclosure. Almost one out of three wage earners was without work, and when their families were included in the grim tally at least forty million people were without a reliable source of income. No one who was still employed felt their job was safe. No one knew what would happen to their savings.

Eleanor remembered the mood of the throng. "It was very, very solemn and a little terrifying. . . . You felt [people] would do anything—if only someone would tell them what to do. . . . One has the feeling of going it blindly because we're in a tremendous stream and none of us know where we are going to land."

"This nation is asking for action, and action now," Roosevelt said. "Our greatest primary task is to put people to work."

That was what Americans had been waiting to hear. A roar of applause swept across Capitol Plaza. Roosevelt was prepared, he said, under his "constitutional duty, to recommend the measures that a stricken nation in the midst of a stricken world may require," but if that were not enough to meet the crisis then he would ask Congress to grant him "broad executive powers to wage a war against the emergency, as great as the power that would be given to me if we were in fact invaded by a foreign foe."

It was FDR's bold pledge to act that resonated most powerfully with his frightened fellow citizens that morning—but looking back, it was an earlier passage of his speech that Americans would remember best. It echoed hard-earned lessons that had informed the lives of first Theodore and then Eleanor Roosevelt—and now informed Franklin's life, as well.

So, first of all, let me assert my firm belief that the only thing we have to fear is fear itself—nameless, unreasoning, unjustified terror which paralyzes needed efforts to convert retreat into advance.

OPPOSITE FDR takes the oath of office from Chief Justice Charles Evans Hughes, March 4, 1933.

ABOVE AND TOP Weeks before the inauguration, the cartoonist Peter Arno created this *New Yorker* cover featuring a dour Herbert Hoover and an ebullient Roosevelt riding to the Capitol together, but it never ran because, in light of FDR's close call in Miami, the editor thought it would have been in bad taste. In this case, life imitated art: Hoover really did remain silent all the way. When the car passed a construction site FDR, desperate to make conversation, found himself saying, "Lovely steel!" The outgoing president did not respond.

CHAPTER 5

The Rising Road

1933–1939

Franklin Is a Man

Among the friends and family members invited to watch Franklin Roosevelt's inaugural parade from the reviewing stand was his forty-two-year-old sixth cousin, Daisy Suckley. She was quiet, good-humored, unmarried—and already deeply devoted to Franklin Roosevelt. His invitation had been so exciting, she told a relative, that when the weekend was over she thought she'd have to enter a convent.

"My seat," she noted that evening, "was on the President's stand, section B, top row, from where I saw the White House grounds, the parade, & the President's head throughout the afternoon. He had a high chair to sit on, which gave the *effect* of his standing. . . . The first part [of the parade] was dignified, the last part a sort of circus—Tom Mix cavorting in white on a black horse—Movie actresses on a float—Bands in fantastic feather costumes, etc. Democracy!"

For many Americans, democracy itself seemed under siege that morning. They were in the third year of a great worldwide Depression so crippling that it seemed that unless the new president acted with unprecedented boldness, the American experiment itself might be at an end. Self-government seemed to be failing in much of the larger world: Mussolini's fascists already controlled Italy; Adolf Hitler was poised to become Germany's dictator; a new military government in Japan had seized the Chinese province of Manchuria.

And there were many who feared that the magnetic but essentially untried man in the reviewing stand could not possibly be equal to the task.

Still, eleven years earlier, Daisy had witnessed firsthand Roosevelt's gallant struggle against the ravages of polio. "Franklin is a man—mentally, physically and spiritually," she confided to her diary. "What more can I say?"

The rest of the country could only hope that she was right.

PRECEDING PAGES Roosevelts return to the White House in the spring of 1933. Eleanor holds her first grandson, Curtis Dall (dubbed "Buzzie" by the newspapers). His sister, Eleanor (known as "Sistie"), peeks through the iron railing. FDR and the children's mother, Anna, are at the right; she had recently separated from her husband and moved with her parents into their new home.

ABOVE An exultant FDR spots an old friend in the crowd that lined the street from the Capitol to the White House.

OPPOSITE Holding on to a specially built railing and perched on a high stool hidden from the crowd so that he appears to be standing, the new president reviews his inaugural parade.

LEFT Daisy Suckley's invitation to the inauguration, treasured by her all her life, even though the inaugural committee misspelled her name

Take a Method and Try It

A president could never be judged great, Theodore Roosevelt once explained, unless he had faced and overcome a great crisis. Franklin Roosevelt would find himself confronted by the two greatest crises since the Civil War.

He had been taught since boyhood to believe himself capable of succeeding at anything to which he put his mind and hand—and in part because of that belief, he proved to have the power to make a majority of his fellow citizens believe it, too. "I have never known a man who gave one a greater sense of security," Eleanor Roosevelt recalled. "I never heard him say [that] there was a problem that he thought it was impossible for human beings to solve. . . . I never knew him to face life or any problem that came up with fear."

HE'S A ROOSEVELT ALL RIGHT.

For all his ebullience and high spirits, FDR was essentially a lonely man. No one was allowed to know all that was going on within what one aide called his "thickly forested interior." Ideology did not interest him. Once, asked for his "philosophy," he said he was a Christian and a Democrat and that was all. He was steeped in tradition and conservative by instinct, but he was also utterly unafraid of experimentation. "It is common sense to take a method and try it," he said. "If it fails, admit it frankly and try another. But above all, try something."

Roosevelt moved fast. He had his entire cabinet sworn in at once, something that had never been done before. It included Harold Ickes, an old Progressive Party follower of the president's cousin Theodore, as interior secretary, and southern democrats like Senator Cordell Hull from Tennessee, who became secretary of state. Henry Wallace, the Republican editor of a farm journal from Iowa, was named secretary of agriculture; and Frances Perkins took the oath of office as secretary of labor, the first woman ever to serve in any cabinet. Over the next dozen years, the ranks of government would for the first time come to include more talented women—as well as Catholics, Jews, and African Americans.

Within forty-eight hours, Roosevelt called a special session of Congress, proclaimed a national "bank holiday," and ordered his secretary of the treasury to draw up a bill aimed at providing government help to private bankers to reopen their institutions. Meanwhile, Americans would have to get along with whatever cash they had in their pockets.

TOP FDR meets with his first cabinet in the Oval Office, its walls hung with his own nineteenth-century prints of life along the Hudson. Interior Secretary Harold Ickes is second from the left. Postmaster General James A. Farley, who had helped guide FDR's presidential campaign, sits to Ickes's left. Secretary of State Cordell Hull is at the president's right. Labor Secretary Frances Perkins is at the far right, next to Secretary of Agriculture Henry A. Wallace.

ABOVE "He's a Roosevelt All Right": On March 14, just ten days after FDR's inauguration, the speed and vigor with which he had already taken charge reminded a cartoonist for the *Kansas City* (Missouri) *Star* of the first President Roosevelt.

My Friends

"I want to be a preaching president," FDR said, "like my cousin Theodore." He believed, just as TR had believed, that the presidency was "pre-eminently a place of moral leadership."

From the moment he took office, FDR understood that no program—and no presidency—could work unless the president communicated effectively with the voters. To do that, he welcomed the press into his office twice a week. Except for Theodore Roosevelt, most presidents before him had treated reporters as little better than spies. FDR called them by their first names, claimed to be a newspaperman himself because he'd once edited the *Harvard Crimson*, and would provide a constant stream of copy that kept him always at the center of events.

Then, on Sunday evening, March 12, just four days after his first press conference, eight days after his inauguration, Roosevelt asked the radio networks for time to address the people of the country. The CBS announcer introducing him said, "The President wants to come into your home and sit at your fireside for a little fireside chat."

The new medium baffled most politicians; they still orated into the microphone, as if trying to reach the farthest edges of a crowd. Roosevelt had already mastered radio while governor of New York: he was warm, reassuring, intimate.

Some sixty million Americans gathered around their radios to hear him. He began by calling them all "my friends."

> I want to talk for a few minutes with the people of the United States about banking. . . . To talk with the comparatively few who understand the mechanics of banking, but more particularly with the overwhelming majority of you who use banks for the making of deposits and the drawing of checks.

In fourteen and a half minutes, he explained how the banking system was supposed to work and how it had failed, and what he and Congress had done together to remedy the situation. The banks were to reopen the following morning and some feared that so many panicked depositors would withdraw their savings that it would bring about the total collapse of the banking system. And so he ended by appealing for calm. "I can assure you, my friends, that it is safer to keep your money in a reopened bank than it is to keep it under the mattress. . . . Let us unite in banishing fear. It is your problem, my friends—your problem, no less than it is mine. Together we cannot fail."

The people believed him. The following morning, when banks reopened more people deposited money than withdrew it. The immediate crisis was over. "Capitalism," one of Roosevelt's advisers remembered, "was saved in eight days."

ABOVE FDR welcomes reporters to the Oval Office for the first of the 998 press conferences he would hold as president, March 8, 1933. "I am told that what I am about to do will become impossible," he told them, "but . . . we are not going to have any more written questions." Some answers would have to be off the record, he added, and he would not answer what he called "iffy" questions, but everything else was fair game. The gaunt man behind the president is Marvin McIntyre, an original member of the Cuff-Links Gang, who would become appointments secretary. Seated at the president's desk is his stenographer, Henry M. Kannee, whose job it was to make sure his boss was not misquoted.

OPPOSITE When the grossly mismanaged—and misleadingly named—Bank of the United States failed in New York in 1930, terrified depositors lined up through the night at all fifty-seven branches, hoping to withdraw their money. Tens of thousands of people, most of them of modest means, lost their savings. New Deal legislation would stabilize the banking system; during the 1920s some five hundred banks had failed every year, but fewer than ten would go under annually after 1933.

The First One Hundred Days

ABOVE FDR surrounded by CCC youths in Shenandoah National Park, one of four camps he visited on the same day in August 1933. The CCC, he would later boast, "has probably been the most successful of anything we have done." Louis Howe and Harold Ickes are seated second and third from left; to the president's left are Henry Wallace and one of Roosevelt's original "brains trusters," Rexford Tugwell.

The first one hundred days of the Roosevelt administration were without precedent. Never in American history had so much transformative legislation been passed by Congress in so little time. Republicans as well as Democrats voted for it. During the first hundred days, fifteen major bills granted the federal government the power to decide which banks should reopen and which should be allowed to fail; to guarantee depositors' bank deposits and to definitively separate commercial and investment banking activities, in the Glass-Steagall Act; to demand greater transparency in the selling of stocks and dictate the gold value of the dollar; to make loans to homeowners to save them from foreclosure and keep farm income high by paying farmers *not* to

JUS' MINDIN' HIS BUSINESS AND GOIN' ALONG!

produce; to provide public jobs for those who needed work; and to provide public power and flood control to the vast Tennessee River basin that sprawled across six states, through the federal Tennessee Valley Authority, or TVA.

No New Deal program created to stimulate the economy and combat unemployment was dearer to the president's heart than the Civilian Conservation Corps, the CCC. Pushed through Congress in less than a week after Roosevelt's inauguration, it eventually put more than three million jobless young men to work preserving the American landscape—controlling erosion, developing national parks, planting hundreds of millions of trees. The men earned thirty dollars a month, and sent twenty-five of it home to help their families.

TOP, LEFT "A Young Man's Opportunity," a recruitment poster for the Illinois branch of the CCC, the most popular of all New Deal programs: by 1936, 82 percent of those responding to a national poll approved of it, including nearly two-thirds of all Republicans, and most Americans shared FDR's hope that it would become a permanent agency.

TOP In the oppressive heat of Washington in June, exhausted, shirt-sleeved members of the joint Senate and Congressional Finance Committees struggle to wind up their work at the end of the first hundred days.

ABOVE An elderly, out-of-breath Congress struggles to keep up with the fast-moving new president in Clifford Berryman's cartoon "Jus' Mindin' His Business and Goin' Along," which appeared in the *Washington Star*, March 25, 1933. "Congress doesn't pass legislation anymore," Will Rogers said. "They just wave at the bills as they go by." Throughout his administration, Roosevelt's vigorous leadership would cause cartoonists to ignore his handicap and show him walking, leaping, running.

ABOVE, RIGHT In 1933, the blue eagle NRA
sticker, meant to show a business's adherence to
codes set by the National Recovery Administration,
seemed to be everywhere—including on the door of
Val-Kill Industries, the furniture shop that Nancy
Cook (left) and Eleanor Roosevelt had started to
aid local craftsmen.

ABOVE Enthusiasm for the NRA was not universal.
Here, a communist cartoonist takes literally the
words of Earl Browder, the party general secretary:
"For the working class, the [National Recovery Act]
is truly an Industrial Slavery Act, . . . a forerunner
of American fascism."

OPPOSITE New Yorkers crowd rooftops along
Fifth Avenue to watch the mammoth National
Recovery Act parade, September 13, 1933. A quarter
of a million marchers passed by in a procession that
lasted from early afternoon to well past midnight.

FDR's most ambitious—and daring—program was the National Recovery Administration, which set prices and wages in 541 industries. Roosevelt was asking businesses to keep wages up and simultaneously keep prices down. Two million employers signed up.

The NRA was initially so popular that when a parade it sponsored marched down Fifth Avenue, more than two million New Yorkers came out to cheer. "There is a unity in this country," FDR said, "which I have not seen since we went to war in 1917."

Some of the legislation enacted during the first hundred days would eventually be overturned by the courts. Other laws would turn out to have been counterproductive. But in just a little over three months, the federal government that had been a mostly passive observer of the people's problems had become an active force in trying to solve them. "It's more than a New Deal," Harold Ickes noted in his diary. "It's a new world. People feel free again. They can breathe naturally. It's like quitting a morgue for the open woods."

A Working Woman

Traditionally, first ladies were often seen but rarely heard; Mrs. Hoover, for example, had confined her public remarks largely to her enthusiasm for the Girl Scouts. That sort of life would have smothered Eleanor Roosevelt. She had been an important person in her own right before her husband's election, and refused to become a mere appendage now.

She organized family life in the White House and took seriously her ceremonial role—she once shook the hands of 3,100 guests in 90 minutes—though she had little patience with formalities; the chief usher was appalled when she insisted on running the elevator herself and asked to have a swing for her grandchildren hung from a tree on the White House lawn.

Behind the scenes, she lobbied her husband hard on issues important to her—the creation of at least one CCC camp for women; the appointment of more women to government positions; the assurance that labor would not suffer under the NRA.

OPPOSITE An official portrait of the new first lady, made in the White House by the fashionable firm of Harris & Ewing in 1933. Posing for photographs was always an ordeal for Eleanor Roosevelt.

ABOVE In 1933, the Roosevelt children pooled their resources and commissioned the artist Otto Schmidt to paint this portrait of their mother as a surprise birthday gift for their father. According to her son Elliott, when it was unveiled at dinner on January 30, 1933, its subject burst into tears and left the room. "It's hateful," she said; she would never be able to live up to such a prettified portrayal of herself. But FDR liked it so much he had it hung above the door in his second-floor Oval Study, where it remained throughout his presidency.

But she swiftly began to assert herself in public, as well. She announced that she would hold weekly press conferences of her own. Since only men could attend her husband's meetings with the press, she allowed only female reporters to attend hers. When a reporter warned her to be careful what she said for fear of embarrassing her husband, Eleanor explained that when she said things that caused criticism she would often do so deliberately—to "arouse controversy" and to "get the topics talked about and so get people to thinking about them." "At the President's press conferences all the world's a stage," Bess Furman of the Associated Press wrote; "at Mrs. Roosevelt's all the world's a school."

She also signed on to speak over the radio, agreed to write regularly for the *Woman's Home Companion* and the North American Newspaper Alliance, and began work on her first book, *It's Up to the Women*, in which she argued that the modern woman was "a working woman who wanted to be able to do something which expresses her own personality, even though she may be a wife and mother."

And she insisted on being allowed to travel as she always had, on her own. Despite her uncle Theodore's wounding in 1912, despite her husband's brush with death in Miami just a few weeks earlier, Eleanor refused Secret Service or police protection. The American people are "wonderful," she explained. "I simply can't be afraid of going among them." Her aunt Corinne, Theodore Roosevelt's younger sister, told a friend that Eleanor was more like her brother "than any of his [own] children."

By the end of the first hundred days, a friend remembered, "Eleanor as much as her husband had come to personify the Roosevelt era."

OPPOSITE Newspaperwomen surround Eleanor Roosevelt in the Monroe Room on the second floor of the White House living quarters, at the second press conference ever held by a first lady, March 13, 1933. Scornful male reporters dismissed their female rivals as worshipful "incense-burners" because some were seen seated at the first lady's feet in this photograph, and editors muttered that no real news would ever emerge from such a meeting—until early the following month, when Mrs. Roosevelt announced that, while she did not drink alcohol herself, once Prohibition had formally ended, first beer and then wine would be served again in the White House. It made headlines across the country.

ABOVE Mrs. Roosevelt speaks to bonus marchers during an unannounced visit to their encampment at Fort Hunt, Virginia, May 16, 1933. Some three thousand of the disgruntled jobless veterans whom Herbert Hoover had driven from Washington returned to the area that spring, still determined immediately to obtain the bonus that had been promised to them. FDR was not willing to provide it, but he did offer them places in the CCC and, unlike his predecessor, supplied food, medical care, even concerts by the navy band. And, at Louis Howe's urging, Eleanor inspected the camp without an escort, shared coffee with the men, and later assured her press conference that she'd been in no danger from such "remarkably clean and orderly-looking, grand-looking boys." "Hoover sent the army," a bonus marcher told a reporter. "Roosevelt sent his wife."

A World of Love

Lorena Hickok—"Hick" to Eleanor Roosevelt—had been one of America's top newspaperwomen in 1932, when she was assigned by the Associated Press to cover the Democratic candidate's wife—and soon found herself so in love with her subject that she quit her job with the Associated Press because she felt she could no longer be objective. The result was one of the most intense friendships of Eleanor Roosevelt's life. When apart, the two women wrote one another daily.

> *Hick dearest,*
>
> *It was good to talk to you. . . . The one thing which reconciles me to this job is the fact that . . . I begin to think there may be ways in which I can be useful. I am getting some ideas which I want to talk over with you. . . .*
> *A world of love to you & good night & God bless you, "light of my life."*

In July of 1933, the two friends quietly took off alone together in Eleanor's blue Buick convertible for a sixteen-day vacation on the back roads of New England and the Gaspé Peninsula in Canada. The Secret Service wanted to send an escort; the first lady refused to have one, but she did agree to carry a revolver in her glove compartment—though she carried no ammunition with which to load it.

When one man in Canada heard Eleanor give her last name he asked if she happened to be any relation to the late Theodore Roosevelt, whom he had greatly admired. Yes, she answered, "I am his niece." They had tea together without his ever figuring out that she was married to the current president of the United States. That kind of anonymity would not last long. Eleanor Roosevelt's frequent travels would soon help make her the best-known woman in the world.

The nature of her relationship with Lorena Hickok was a subject of controversy among some of their friends during their lifetimes and has been debated among historians and biographers ever since. There is no question of Hickok's feelings for Mrs. Roosevelt and also no question that Eleanor felt strongly about her. But a letter from Eleanor to Hick, written in 1935, offers a possible clue: "I know you often have a feeling for me which for one reason or another I may not return in kind but I feel I love you just the same & so often we entirely satisfy each other that I feel there is a fundamental basis on which our relationship stands."

TOP AND ABOVE A favorite portrait of Lorena Hickok in 1932, when she first fell in love with Eleanor Roosevelt, and a fragment from one of Eleanor's letters to her, written from the White House. It was Hickok's idea to have the first lady hold her own press conferences.

ABOVE AND LEFT Amateur snapshots of Lorena Hickok and the first lady during the trip they took together in the summer of 1933 without security of any kind: driving virtually unrecognized down a street on the Gaspé Peninsula in Quebec, and arriving at the Richmond Hotel in Lawrence, Massachusetts. "It has been a wonderful trip," Eleanor wrote Franklin afterward from Campobello, "& Hick is grand to travel with. Nothing bothers her. She isn't afraid. She doesn't get tired and she's always interested."

Arthurdale

ABOVE Harry Hopkins. "I am for experiment-ing . . . in various parts of the country," he said, "trying out schemes which are supported by reasonable people [to] see if they work. If they do not work, the world will not come to an end."

ABOVE, RIGHT A coal miner's daughter fetches kerosene for her family's lamps in Scotts Run, West Virginia, in the middle of the region Lorena Hickok called "the damndest cesspool of human misery in America."

OPPOSITE, TOP Project manager Bushrod Grimes explains to Eleanor Roosevelt and Nancy Cook, whom she had appointed as an adviser on housing, how the new community of Arthurdale is to be laid out.

OPPOSITE, BOTTOM A Scotts Run coal miner at his woodstove. "Some of the older miners still could speak only enough English to understand the orders given by the mine boss," Eleanor recalled. "Nobody had taken the trouble to help the adults who were going to live and work in this country, learn English and understand our government."

When Eleanor Roosevelt and Lorena Hickok ended their vacation in the summer of 1933, Hickok moved into her own room at the White House and then went to work traveling the country as chief investigator for Harry Hopkins, the head of the Federal Emergency Relief Administration.

Able and impatient, fueled by cigarettes and black coffee, Hopkins combined the hard-eyed sensibilities of a seasoned political operative with the conscience of a committed social worker. Told a new federal program was likely to succeed in the long run, he answered that wasn't good enough. "People don't eat in the long run," he said. Hopkins would remain one of Roosevelt's most effective and devoted advisers throughout his presidency, eager always to know from Hickok what was really happening outside Washington. His instruction to her couldn't have been more direct:

What I want you to do is to go out around the country and look this thing over. . . . Go talk with preachers and teachers, businessmen, work-ers, farmers. Go talk with the unemployed, those who are on relief and those who aren't. And when you talk with them don't ever forget that but for the Grace of God, you, I or any of our friends might be in their shoes.

Eleanor read every one of the reports Hickok wrote and made sure they were among the papers she left on FDR's bedside table each evening so that he could read them, too.

In late August, Hickok telephoned Eleanor at the White House. If she wanted to see for herself how bad things were, she should come to the company town of Scotts Run, West Virginia.

"[It was] the worst place I'd ever seen," Hickok remembered. "In a gutter, along the main street . . . , there was stagnant, filthy water, which the inhabitants used for drinking, cooking, washing, and everything else imaginable. On either side of the street were ramshackle houses, black with coal dust, which most Americans would not have considered fit for pigs. And in those houses every night children went to sleep hungry, on piles of bug-infested rags, spread out on the floor."

The first lady of the United States came, driving alone in her Buick. The American Friends Service Committee had been working in the region to help unemployed coal miners and their families. Some men, blackballed for daring to protest conditions, had been without work for eight years. There was already a plan by West Virginia University to shift some families to a big plot of gently rolling land nearby owned by a family named Arthur.

Eleanor returned to Washington, committed to taking over the project and making "Arthurdale" a model community.

FDR shared Eleanor's enthusiasm. So did Louis Howe. All three believed that the lives of the rural poor should be improved so that they would not be tempted to move to the already overcrowded industrial cities. Roosevelt had

long hoped to resettle as many as a million families into planned rural communities. Arthurdale seemed a good place to start.

One hundred and sixty-five families were eventually chosen. Each was to be given a furnished home—complete with electricity, indoor plumbing, and a refrigerator, all rarities then in much of rural America—as well as a plot of land, farm equipment, and livestock, with thirty years to pay the government back for its investment.

The project was troubled from the beginning. The first prefabricated houses did not fit their foundations. The finished homes cost four times what had been budgeted. When Interior Secretary Ickes complained to FDR, the president just shrugged. "My Missus," he said, "unlike most women, hasn't any sense about money at all."

When Eleanor tried to attract small-scale industries to the area, congressional opponents refused to provide any funds. A vacuum cleaner plant failed. So did a shirtmaker and a tractor manufacturer.

Eleanor refused to give up. She was as dedicated to Arthurdale as her husband was to Warm Springs. When federal funds proved insufficient, she contributed nearly all her earned income and canvassed wealthy friends to underwrite projects, including a progressive high school that allowed miners' children to get advanced schooling that their parents could not have imagined.

To its critics, Arthurdale came to symbolize everything that was wrong with the New Deal. They charged that it was wasteful, overambitious, socialistic, and, like most of the hundred or so other rural communities built by the New Deal, unlikely to survive for long.

But for those who lived there, Eleanor Roosevelt was a godsend and Arthurdale was a triumph. "We woke up in hell," one of the first homesteaders remembered, "and went to bed the next night in heaven."

TOP, LEFT Rapt Arthurdale residents listen to Mrs. Roosevelt: "I want you to succeed," she told them, "not only for yourselves, but for what it will mean to people everywhere . . . who are starting similar projects. You are the first and your success will hearten [them]."

ABOVE AND TOP, RIGHT Arthurdale, not long after its first residents moved in, 1934

OPPOSITE Eleanor talks with reporters on an Arthurdale construction site. "The homestead projects were attacked in Congress, for the most part," she said, "by men who had never seen for themselves the plight of the miners or what we were trying to do for them."

SECOND ANNUAL BIRTHDAY BALL
OF
PRESIDENT ROOSEVELT
BENEFIT of SUFFERERS of INFANTILE PARALYSIS
AT HIGHLAND PARK CASINO
WEDNESDAY EVE. JANUARY 30, 1935
MUSIC BY TWO ORCHESTRAS
RESERVATIONS 25c COUPLE   LADIES 25c
CALL 3749-J

Happy Birthday, Mr. President

January 30, 1934, was Franklin Roosevelt's fifty-second birthday. Ever since the vice presidential campaign of 1920, the Cuff-Links Gang had gathered on or about his birthday to reminisce and celebrate with toasts, speeches, and elaborate costumed skits organized by Louis Howe. This time, Howe suggested that since the Republican opposition had begun to denounce FDR as a Caesar—dictatorial and answerable to no one—they make the Roman imperial court their theme. Photographs of the memorable tableau that resulted, staged at one end of the hallway in the White House living quarters, were distributed among the guests—who managed to keep them private for nearly three decades.

On that same evening, a more serious Roosevelt tradition was born: the president's Birthday Balls, arranged annually all across the country to raise money for the Warm Springs Foundation and, after 1938, the National Foundation for Infantile Paralysis—better known as the March of Dimes.

TOP Looking uncannily like her son, the president's mother acknowledges applause at one of the first Birthday Balls, held at New York's Astor Hotel in 1934. The ticket entitled the bearer to dance at a less glittering version at the Highland Park Casino in Quincy, Illinois, the following year.

ABOVE Gold cuff links belonging to Charles H. McCarthy, FDR's secretary during the 1920 campaign and one of the seven original members of the Cuff-Links Gang

FAR LEFT Emperor Roosevelt and his court: Eleanor and Anna flank the throne; Irvin McDuffie, FDR's White House valet, stands behind it. Missy LeHand and Eleanor's longtime secretary, Malvina Thompson, are seated at the lower left. The master of the revels, Louis Howe, is the helmeted figure at the right, just above the president's press secretary, Stephen Early.

ABOVE Mary McLeod Bethune, director of Negro Activities for the National Youth Administration, Eleanor Roosevelt, and Aubrey Williams, executive director of the NYA

TOP Twenty of the forty-five members of Roosevelt's so-called "black cabinet"—African American officials whom FDR had appointed to positions in the executive branch. Mrs. Bethune is at the center. The third man from the left in the front row is Robert C. Weaver, who began his public career in 1933 as an assistant to Harold Ickes. Thirty-three years later, President Lyndon Johnson would appoint him as secretary of housing and urban affairs, the first African American ever to serve in the cabinet.

A New Deal for Black Americans

Most Americans suffered during the Depression, but African Americans suffered most. Three out of four still lived in the Jim Crow South. More than half of them were without work—and federal relief almost always went to needy whites first. Some 400,000 desperate people migrated north during the 1930s only to discover that, in many big cities, there was no work to be had.

Theodore Roosevelt had once sought to deal with African American citizens through a single representative: Booker T. Washington.

Franklin and Eleanor Roosevelt understood that the world had changed, and FDR's administration would prove more sympathetic to African American aspirations than any of its predecessors.

Eleanor Roosevelt obtained several posts within the administration for her friend the educator Mary McLeod Bethune. When Bethune came to the White House for dinner for the first time, so the story goes, a gardener stopped her. "Hey there, Auntie," he said, "where y'all think you're going?" She looked him up and down, then asked, "Which one of my sister's children are you?" No one ever tried to stop her again.

Following the advice of Bethune and others, FDR appointed an informal network of second-level officials who came to be called his "black cabinet," and Harold Ickes and Harry Hopkins struggled to ensure that New Deal relief programs did not discriminate.

By 1935, one-third of all black Americans would be receiving federal help of some kind—and African Americans all over the country were shifting

their allegiance from the party of Abraham Lincoln to the party of Franklin Roosevelt.

Local prejudice persisted in federal programs. Most CCC camps were segregated. The coal miners of Arthurdale voted to keep out black homesteaders. Black reporters were barred from the president's press conferences. Still, as Mrs. Bethune wrote, African Americans, "for the first time in their history," felt their grievances would be heard with "sympathetic understanding and interpretation" during the Roosevelt administration.

ABOVE Gordon Parks captured this portrait of a Washington, D.C., domestic worker with a photograph of the president on whom she and many other African Americans now pinned their hopes.

LEFT African Americans at work on the Fort Loudon Dam, the uppermost of nine dams on the Tennessee River, built by the Tennessee Valley Authority to provide the region with electricity and flood control.

Here's Mr. Roosevelt's Message on Lynching

In His Annual Speech to Congress on Jan. 4 the President Said *This* on Mob Murder

WASHINGTON, Jan. 10.—In his annual message to Congress last Friday President Roosevelt had the following to say about lynching:

A Vile Form of Collective Murder

The shame of lynching persisted. In 1933, twenty-six Americans died at the hands of mobs, three times as many as had been lynched the year before. New York Senator Robert Wagner and Senator Edward Costigan of Colorado introduced a bill to make any local official who failed to protect his prisoners against a mob subject to prosecution in the federal courts. Southern politicians denounced it as an assault on states' rights.

FDR had declared lynching a "vile form of collective murder" and was willing to sign the bill—if it was passed. But he felt he could not back it in public. On April 26, 1935, southern senators, vowing "the bill shall not pass," began a filibuster.

Walter White of the National Association for the Advancement of Colored People asked to see the president, hoping he would intercede. His appointments secretary said the boss was far too busy. Eleanor intervened and invited White to tea on the South Portico with the president and the president's mother.

There was really nothing he could do, FDR said. Eleanor persisted. So did Sara Delano Roosevelt.

FDR was immovable. Seniority had given southern Democratic senators and congressmen more than their share of chairmanships. "I did not choose the tools with which I must work," he told White. If he came out for the anti-lynching bill, he would be unable to pass legislation the whole country needed—including African Americans. The bill died on May 1st. The president liked to remind critics who thought him too cautious that "you have to wait, even for the best things, until the right time comes." Although bills to end lynching would be revived again and again during his administration, that time would never come.

But Eleanor Roosevelt argued for all of them, at the risk of irritating her husband. "He might have been happier with a wife who was completely uncritical," she wrote. "That I was never able to be, and he had to find it in other people. Nevertheless, I think I sometimes acted as a spur, even though the spurring was not always wanted or welcome. I was one of those who served his purposes."

"This is her first lynching."

OPPOSITE, TOP Pickets march outside Washington's Constitution Hall, where a National Crime Conference was getting under way whose agenda did not so much as mention lynching, December 1934. Civil rights groups were then still hopeful the president would lead the fight to end lynching.

OPPOSITE, BOTTOM LEFT Curiosity seekers, including small children, gather around the body of a young man named Rubin Stacy, lynched near Fort Lauderdale, Florida, in July 1935, a little over two months after the anti-lynching bill died in Congress. Murdered for "frightening" a white woman, he had actually been guilty only of knocking on her door and asking her for a little food.

OPPOSITE, BOTTOM RIGHT "Here's Mr. Roosevelt's Message on Lynching," the *Amsterdam News*'s bitter front-page comment on the president's silence on the subject

ABOVE "This is her first lynching," drawn for the *New Yorker* by Reginald Marsh after seeing photographs like the one on the opposite page

"Rosy" Returns to Warm Springs

To most Americans FDR was always "President Roosevelt." But to his fellow polios at Warm Springs, he was simply "Rosy," and whenever he could manage it during the White House years he fled Washington to be among them. A few days in Georgia always restored his energy—and lifted the spirits of all the patients struggling to regain their feet.

During his early days at Warm Springs, FDR had lifted his own spirits by fitting out a farmer's old Model T with hand controls and setting out alone along the slithery red-clay back roads of Meriwether County. He continued that tradition during his presidency, insisting that the Secret Service stay well behind his car, stopping in front of the drugstore to honk and shout, "Let's have a Coke!" so that the soda jerk would run out and bring him one.

"He just dearly loved to leave the road and weave in and out among the long-leaf pines," Henry Wallace remembered. "He wanted to show that he could go faster than anybody, when he had the right kind of motor behind

ABOVE Arriving at the Warm Springs depot and surrounded by admirers, the president prepares to make his way down the ramp kept aboard his specially equipped railroad car. Whenever he was scheduled to visit, people from all over Meriwether County came to town to get a glimpse of him. Roosevelt carried Warm Springs—and Meriwether County—all four times he ran for president, by victory margins that ranged from 12 to 1 to 50 to 1.

him." But he also took the time to stop and talk with people. "He had sense enough to talk to a man who didn't have any education," a farmer remembered, "and he had sense enough to talk to the best educated man in the world. . . . He could talk about *anything*."

"I want to farm just like the local farmers do," he told the county agent. "The only difference is, I want to make a profit." He never did, though he bought 1,750 acres of land and tried growing nearly everything on it—pine trees, beef cattle, apples, peaches, grapes. The farm "seemed always to require expenditure for wages, for upkeep, for improvements and for extensions," Rexford Tugwell remembered. "But it was a delight [to FDR] nevertheless. It pleased him so much because it offered a challenge. He always tended to believe that something could be done with apparently hopeless enterprises. . . . All his efforts would come to very little in the end; but he had not yet . . . accepted the inevitable. He was still hopeful."

ABOVE Around Thanksgiving, Roosevelt loved to preside over "Founder's Day" at Warm Springs, carving an oversized turkey with a theatrical flourish. In 1939, when this picture was taken, a little patient named Suzanne Pike got to occupy the seat next to him because she had just stood up in her braces for the first time. After the banquet, he always stood in the doorway and shook the hand of every patient.

LEFT FDR, at the hand controls of his automobile, stops to chat with patients wheeled out onto the lawn in front of a newly dedicated infirmary to see him. "His greatest contribution was himself," one polio recalled, "the apparent ease with which he handled himself. His example proved to us that 'A polio could do *anything*'—even be President of the United States."

Putting Americans to Work

By the spring of 1935, the panic that had gripped America on inauguration day had largely subsided. And Roosevelt had launched three sweeping new programs: the National Youth Administration to provide training for young people without work; the Rural Electrification Administration, which would light up much of the American countryside; and the Works Progress Administration, which would change the face of much of the American landscape. The WPA built or rebuilt 2,500 hospitals, 6,000 public schools, 10,000 airport landing fields, and enough miles of roadway to pave the continent from coast to coast more than 200 times.

Jobless artists, writers, composers, and musicians benefited from the WPA as well—Saul Bellow and Thomas Hart Benton, Ralph Ellison and Orson Welles, Berenice Abbott and Alan Lomax, and hundreds of others. It turned out nearly a thousand publications, including guides to all forty-eight states, staged plays and performed symphonies in small towns that had never seen a live performance, revived the art of mural painting on the walls of schools and post offices, commissioned photographers to chronicle the human cost of the Depression, transcribed the memories of American slaves and collected the folk songs all kinds of Americans sang. "Whatever form this [art] took," the critic Alfred Kazin remembered, "it testified to an extraordinary self-scrutinizing. . . . Never before did a nation seem so hungry for news of itself."

New Deal critics charged that the WPA was a giant boondoggle intended only to benefit the Democrats. FDR was unrepentant. "I realize," he told an Atlanta audience, "that gentlemen in well-warmed and well-stocked clubs will discourse . . . on the suffering that they are going through . . . because their government is spending money on work relief. Some of these gentlemen tell me that a dole would be more economical. That is true. But the men who tell me that have, unfortunately, too little contact with the true American to realize that . . . most Americans want to give something for what they get . . . which is in this case honest work."

TOP Working for the WPA, the artist William Gropper painted this dam-building mural for the lobby of the Department of the Interior, 1938.

ABOVE AND OPPOSITE PAGE Posters for New Deal programs, commissioned by administrators convinced both that art should be a part of the lives of all Americans and that out-of-work artists deserved employment just as much as farmers or factory workers did. Eventually, there were poster divisions in eighteen states as well as the District of Columbia.

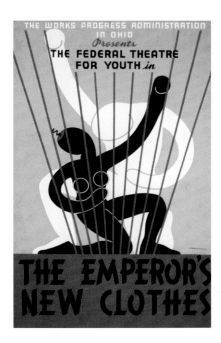

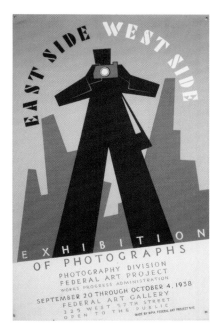

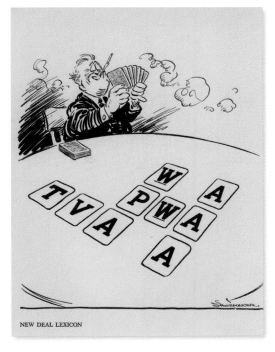

ABOVE "New Deal Lexicon," *Chicago Daily News* cartoonist Vaughn Shoemaker's take on the New Deal's fondness for bewildering acronyms.

The Rising Road • 323

Trouble, Left and Right

I n 1935, the United States was in its fifth year of Depression. Two and a half million Americans had returned to work, but more than ten million remained jobless.

A drought afflicted forty-six of the forty-eight states. The topsoil of the southern plains was being blown away, and hundreds of thousands of Americans were on the move toward California in search of work. People everywhere were growing impatient.

On the right, the American Liberty League, organized by some of America's most powerful industrialists, charged that the New Deal was only making things worse, that Roosevelt had become a dictator, defying the Constitution, encouraging "class warfare." Their most celebrated spokesman was FDR's old ally Al Smith, the former Democratic governor of New York. The New Dealers, he said, were hell-bent on socialism. "There can only be one capital," Smith said, "Washington or Moscow. There can be only one flag, the Stars and Stripes or the flag of the godless Soviets."

On the left, socialists and a handful of communists took to the streets, denouncing Roosevelt as a captive of capitalism, incapable of bringing about real change. Other men were peddling other schemes. Dr. Francis Townsend, an elderly California physician, promised to grant a monthly pension to every worker over sixty who was willing to retire and spend the money within thirty days.

Father Charles Coughlin, the Detroit radio priest, preached in favor of inflated currency and against Wall Street and international bankers.

ABOVE By 1935, when the humor magazine *Life* published this caricature of Al Smith, the progressive Democratic candidate for president just seven years earlier had become the best-known voice of the conservative Liberty League.

TOP FDR greets a farmer's son near Julesburg, Colorado, where there had been no rain for months and the soil itself was blowing away. "YOU GAVE US BEER," read a placard along his route, "NOW GIVE US WATER." Roosevelt answered, "That beer part was easy."

INDUSTRIAL SLAVERY–

Roosevelt's "New Deal"

By I. AMTER

Price 1c.

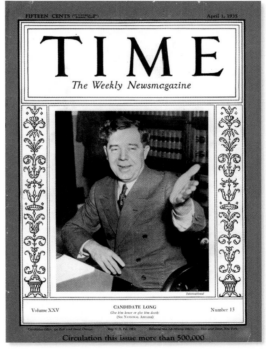

FIFTEEN CENTS

April 1, 1935

TIME

The Weekly Newsmagazine

Volume XXV

CANDIDATE LONG

Number 13

Circulation this issue more than 500,000

CLOCKWISE FROM LOWER LEFT Voices of the opposition: a Communist Party pamphlet charges that the New Deal is merely a cleverly disguised capitalist assault on the working class; Dr. Francis Townsend spells out his plan to provide jobs for young people by paying older workers to give up theirs; Rev. Charles E. Coughlin, America's most popular radio performer, who had once told his listeners "the New Deal is Christ's Deal," has now decided Roosevelt is "anti-God"; and Louisiana Senator Huey P. Long, whose promises of shared wealth and talk of leading a third party make some Roosevelt advisers nervous about the president's prospects for reelection in 1936

But the biggest threat to FDR's reelection chances in 1936 came from the South. There was widespread speculation that Senator Huey P. Long, the flamboyant, populist ex-governor of Louisiana, planned to lead a third party coalition against him. Long called his program "Share Our Wealth," and hundreds of thousands of voters signed up all across the country. Democratic National Committee chairman Jim Farley feared Long would start out with at least 12 percent of the vote, enough to deny FDR several important states—and, perhaps, bring about a Republican victory.

On Monday, May 27, 1935, things got even worse. The United States Supreme Court handed down a unanimous decision, in a case brought by a kosher chicken producer from Brooklyn, which invalidated the National Recovery Administration on the grounds that the NRA had unconstitutionally delegated legislative power. The NRA was already understood to be a failure. It had only *raised* prices and *lowered* wages—exactly the opposite of what it was supposed to do. But the grounds on which the NRA decision was made—including a narrow interpretation of the interstate commerce clause—seemed to suggest that other New Deal programs might also be swept away.

Roosevelt was stunned at first, and denounced the Court for relegating the country to "the horse-and-buggy definition of interstate commerce." But in early June, just as congressmen were preparing to leave town for the summer, Roosevelt seized back the initiative, calling upon them to enact five major pieces of legislation by autumn.

In part to steal a little of what FDR called "Huey's thunder," he proposed new taxes on the wealthiest Americans.

He also wanted the Federal Reserve System strengthened and a new law to break up monopolistic holding companies.

And, in the interest of achieving for ordinary Americans something of the sense of security that had been his since boyhood, Roosevelt threw himself behind two bills initially championed by the Democratic senator from

New York, Robert F. Wagner. They would turn out to be two of the most momentous pieces of legislation in American history.

The first, called the Wagner Act, created the National Labor Relations Board and for the first time provided a federal guarantee of labor's right to organize and bargain collectively.

But the second, the Social Security Act, would prove the most far-reaching. It would provide old-age insurance paid for by taxes on employees and their employers, share with the states responsibility for insuring the unemployed, and provide federal aid to the states to help care for dependent mothers and children, the handicapped and the blind.

There was a sweltering, bruising, summer-long struggle on Capitol Hill. Compromises reduced the impact of some of the legislation. But newspapermen called it the "Second Hundred Days"—and the beginning of a Second New Deal.

And then, in September, Huey Long was cut down by an assassin's bullet. The road to Roosevelt's reelection now seemed wide open.

A Never-Ending Voyage

In public, Franklin Roosevelt always projected cheerful optimism. Even in private, he rarely let anyone know how he really felt. But beginning in the late summer of 1935, he began making an exception for his admiring distant cousin, Daisy Suckley.

One afternoon that month in Hyde Park, he took her for a drive in his hand-controlled car to a favorite picnic spot, the crest of a forested ridge on the Roosevelt property he and Daisy had named "Our Hill."

There, they began what they both called their "voyage," confessing to one another the loneliness each sometimes felt, speaking of a special bond of friendship, agreeing to share confidences by letter and long-distance telephone.

"Do you know that you alone have known that I was a bit 'cast down' these past weeks," he wrote to her. "I couldn't let anyone else know it—but, somehow, I seem to tell you all those things and what I don't happen to tell you, you seem to know, anyway!"

He even spoke to her of the pain his braces sometimes caused, something he never mentioned to his wife.

Franklin addressed her as "M.M." for "My Margaret," and carried her letters with him wherever he went. She sometimes signed her letters "Y.M."— "Your Margaret." They sent one another long-distance mental messages.

She once tried to summarize their relationship:

TOP AND ABOVE Daisy Suckley and three of her Scotties on the lawn of Wilderstein, her family home at Rhinebeck, New York, and a 1935 letter to FDR that includes her drawing of the hilltop structure she hoped to share with him and liked to call "O.H"—"Our House."

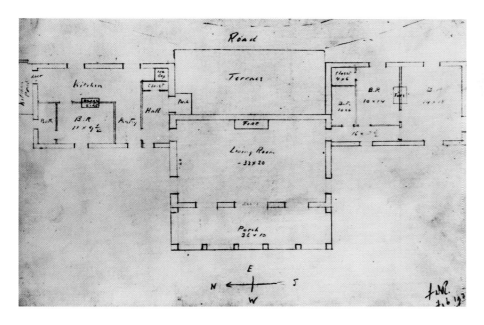

Dear F. Do you mind if I do a little thinking aloud . . . ? The subject is friendships and the way they start *and grow—an introduction, a shake of the hand, a few casual words to begin . . . and the friendship . . . usually finds very definite limits not so far from the surface.*

On rare occasions, however, it seems to start in the deepest depths—a never-ending voyage of discovery . . . with never a feeling of fear because of the safe and solid ship one is underfoot.

They planned together a stone cottage to be built on their hilltop where she began to hope, after he had finished the traditional two terms, she might live with him as his nurse and companion. Daisy often appeared at FDR's side throughout the remainder of his presidency, so quiet and unassuming and discreet that his own secretaries, puzzled by her presence, dismissed her as "the little mud wren."

TOP, LEFT The president visits the construction site with New York's mayor Fiorello H. La Guardia and Congresswoman Caroline O'Day, one of Eleanor's closest allies. Top Cottage was not completed until 1939.

ABOVE, LEFT FDR's own plans for his cottage, 1938. When they were published with his initials in the corner, licensed architects denounced him for claiming to be an architect when he had no license.

ABOVE Daisy Suckley took this snapshot of her great friend at a hilltop picnic in Dutchess County. FDR occupies a car seat, pulled out of his automobile by the Secret Service. The Scottie in his lap was Daisy's gift to him. Roosevelt's original name for his new pet was "Murray the Outlaw of Falahill," after a sixteenth-century Scottish ancestor, John Murray of Falahill, but it was quickly shortened to "Fala."

That Man in the White House

To his admirers, FDR could do no wrong. "Every house I visited," the journalist Martha Gellhorn marveled after a visit to the southern textile region, "millworker or unemployed, had a picture of the President. These ranged from newspaper clippings (in destitute homes) to large colored prints, framed in gilt cardboard. . . . And the feelings of these people for the President is one of the most remarkable phenomena I have ever met. He is at once God and their intimate friend; he knows them all by name, knows their little town and mill, their little lives and problems. And, though everything else fails, he is there, and will not let them down."

A southern millworker was asked why he so admired FDR: "Because," he said, "Mr. Roosevelt is the only man we ever had in the White House who would understand that my boss is a sonofabitch."

Roosevelt's enemies felt just as strongly as his admirers. Some called him "That man in the White House" because they could not bear even to say his name. Many of those among whom he'd grown up or gone to school denounced him as "a traitor to his class." When someone unwisely mentioned FDR in the presence of J. P. Morgan Jr., whose father had earlier done battle with the president's cousin Theodore, Morgan is said to have exploded, "God damn all Roosevelts."

Whether Americans were for Roosevelt or couldn't stand him, they were fascinated by him and by his family and by the life they led at 1600 Pennsylvania Avenue and beyond it. "You know how it was when Uncle Ted was [in the White House?]—how gay and homelike," FDR had remarked to a relative not long after he moved in. "Well, that's how we mean to have it!"

OPPOSITE In early 1935, photographer Thomas McAvoy, working for *Time* magazine, obtained permission to take pictures of FDR in the Oval Office using a brand-new Leica camera that required no flash. The result was the first set of candid photographs ever taken of a president at work. In them, Roosevelt reads and reacts to correspondence, signs a law, confers with Marvin McIntyre and Missy LeHand, pauses to drink a glass of water, then goes back at it.

TOP, LEFT AND RIGHT Roosevelt's portrait hangs in the kitchen of a Portuguese American family in Falmouth, Massachusetts, and a millworker's living room in Greensboro, Georgia.

ABOVE *Time* profiles four White House insiders: Louis Howe, Stephen Early, Missy LeHand, and Marvin McIntyre. The public seemed almost as interested in Roosevelt's inner circle as it was in the president himself.

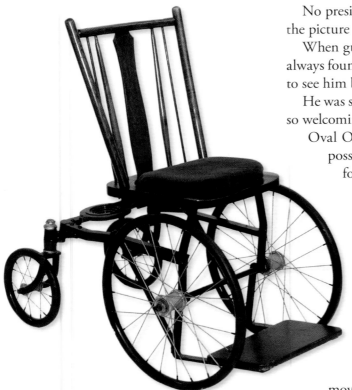

No president's family had ever received such incessant coverage—though the picture it presented was always incomplete.

When guests filed into the formal dining room at the White House, they always found the president already seated at the head of the table. No one was to see him being wheeled down the hall.

He was so skilled at drawing a visitor's attention away from his immobility, so welcoming and so vigorous in his gestures, that some came away from the Oval Office convinced that he'd risen to greet them when he could not possibly have done so. Even some of those who knew him best were fooled, convinced by his ability to appear unruffled by his handicap that his crippling really did not affect him—and therefore need not alarm them. Rex Tugwell, for one, wrote that FDR was "never bothered by polio."

To ensure that the public at large was not alarmed either, the Secret Service became expert at installing and removing special ramps to allow the president to enter a building without anyone seeing him being carried. And when the White House imposed rules on how he could be filmed and photographed, few complained, at least at first: no images of FDR in his wheelchair or getting in or out of cars were permitted; no visual record was to be made of the arduous effort it took him to move just a few feet. Photographers who defied the rules—including ordinary tourists—had their film confiscated by the Secret Service.

Most Americans understood that their president was "lame." His battle with polio—a battle he was often said to have "won"—was known to nearly everyone. But the extent of his disability came as a revelation to newspaper correspondents newly assigned to the White House, who saw the president wheeled into a room for the first time.

ABOVE One of Roosevelt's self-designed wheelchairs: the wheels were fitted to an ordinary armless kitchen chair so that FDR could use his powerful arms to shift to conventional seating without help. He used the wheelchair only to move from place to place and rarely stayed in it long. When a newspaper suggested that he was "confined" to a wheelchair he denied it: "As a matter of fact, I don't use a wheelchair at all except a little kitchen chair on wheels . . . and solely for the purposes of saving time." An ashtray slid out from the back for easy access.

RIGHT A sailor snapped this rare image of FDR in his wheelchair aboard the USS *Indianapolis* in 1933.

OPPOSITE Military guards watch as FDR is wheeled into a back entrance at the Bethesda Naval Hospital on his way to visit Interior Secretary Harold Ickes, who was recuperating from a heart attack, June 15, 1937. When this photograph, taken by Carl Mydans, appeared in *Life*, White House press secretary Stephen Early demanded that the navy bar photographers from its premises during presidential visits.

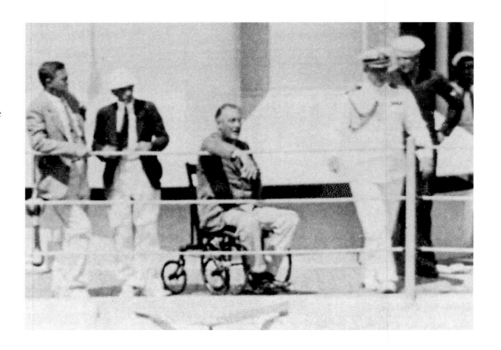

See ROOSEVELT Page 2

Amateur Pictures Permitted

Amateur photographers along the route of the Presidential procession will be allowed to take pictures of the President as long as they stay out of the street.

The only restrictions in pictures are when the President is walking.

When the President is seated in his automobile, or after he starts speaking in Ellwood Park, photographers can take as many pictures as they want to, said secret service men.

The journalist John Gunther remembered the "shock" he felt at once seeing the president carried in the arms of two burly aides: "he seemed, for one thing, very small."

Stephen Early, the president's press secretary, had orders to turn away all reporters' questions about the president's disability. "It's not a story," he'd say, and that was supposed to be that.

In part because of White House reluctance to comment about the president's paralysis, rumors about his health proliferated, including one persistent story that polio had somehow left him deranged so that he had to be institutionalized from time to time at Warm Springs. Once, after Mrs. Roosevelt had finished a speech in Akron, Ohio, a woman in the audience asked, "Do you think your husband's illness has affected your husband's mentality?"

"I am glad that question was asked," the first lady said. "The answer is yes. Anyone who has gone through great suffering is bound to have a greater sympathy and understanding of the problems of mankind."

OPPOSITE, TOP Trapped in his chair in full view of hundreds of spectators, unable to take shelter from a cold, steady rain, FDR endures an outdoor ceremony at the 300th anniversary of Harvard's founding, 1936.

OPPOSITE, BOTTOM LEFT AND RIGHT A temporary ramp constructed by the Secret Service so that the president's car could drive up to the raised doorway for the funeral of House Speaker William B. Bankhead in 1940, and a permanent one, installed in the White House living quarters to accommodate the president's wheelchair

TOP H. A. Lucas, the porter aboard the president's special railroad car, arranges the day's newspapers in FDR's paneled compartment for the run from Warm Springs back to Washington, 1938. Because the president had difficulty keeping his balance at high speeds, the engineer had orders never to exceed thirty-five miles an hour for fear of hurling him from his seat. Lost time was made up at night, when FDR was safely in his berth.

LEFT The Secret Service explains the ground rules for amateur photographers in advance of a presidential visit to Amarillo, Texas, in 1938.

On December 31, 1935, Eleanor Roosevelt began a newspaper column called "My Day." It appeared six times a week in newspapers all across the country and provided a forum for her political views and an almost hour-by-hour account of all the things she was doing. Readers wrote that it made her seem like a family friend who lived next door.

But she made little mention of the domestic difficulties of her five children. There would eventually be nineteen marriages among them.

James served for a time as his father's assistant, despite charges that he was using his position to further his own business interests; stress-related ulcers eventually forced him out of the West Wing.

Anna, who had married early to get away from the tensions within her family, divorced Curtis Dall in order to marry John Boettiger, a newspaperman covering the White House.

Elliott, named for Eleanor's troubled father, was troubled as well: he refused to attend college, rarely stayed in one place for long, and used his famous name to get ahead in a series of speculative businesses.

Franklin Jr., who inherited his father's looks and charm, earned a reputation at Harvard as a playboy.

And John—who had only been five when his father developed polio and virtually vanished from his life—did what he could to avoid the spotlight, working quietly for a time as a clerk at Filene's Basement in Boston.

"One of the worst things in the world is being the child of a President," FDR once said. "It's a terrible life they lead."

Her children's troubles often enveloped Eleanor in the depression that haunted her all her life. "If anyone looks at me I want to weep," she told Lorena Hickok after one of her children made unwanted headlines. "I get like this sometimes. It makes me feel like a dead weight and my mind goes round and round like a squirrel in a cage. I want to run and I can't and I despise myself." Her frequent travel made headlines, inspired cartoons, and benefited a host of causes, but it proceeded in part from a need to outpace despair, just as her uncle Theodore had sought to outpace his own demons. "When one isn't happy," she told a close friend, "it's hard not to live at high speed."

OPPOSITE The L. C. Smith Super Speed typewriter on which Malvina Thompson, Eleanor Roosevelt's secretary, typed her boss's columns and correspondence at Val-Kill

OPPOSITE, TOP LEFT The first lady, eager to get a firsthand look at underground working conditions in a coal mine, Bellaire, Ohio, 1935

OPPOSITE, TOP RIGHT The Roosevelts in a rare moment together on the lawn behind Springwood early in the administration

TOP, LEFT FDR and Anna Roosevelt Boettiger enjoy a softball game between White House newspapermen and a team fielded by the broadcaster Lowell Thomas, near Pawling, New York, 1935.

ABOVE, LEFT Franklin Roosevelt Jr. with the movie star Errol Flynn and his wife, Lily Damita, at a Washington hotel

ABOVE Elliott Roosevelt and his mother at the Los Angeles airport, moments after she completed her first transcontinental flight, 1933. He had recently left his first wife and baby and was now intent on marrying again.

Clash of the Clans

On Sunday, January 19, 1936, a major snowstorm blocked Manhattan streets and blanketed Central Park, but the president and his wife were determined to make it to the Museum of Natural History, where FDR was officially to open the new Theodore Roosevelt Memorial.

The museum had been synonymous with the Roosevelt family since 1869, when Theodore Roosevelt Sr. helped raise the first funds for its construction. As boys, both Theodore and Franklin Roosevelt had contributed birds and birds' eggs to its collections, and TR had donated hundreds of additional scientific specimens gathered during his hunting and exploring expeditions on three continents.

Both branches of the family were invited to share the platform.

The White House had recently tried to tighten restrictions on newspaper photographers. All candid shots were now outlawed; only pictures of the president at the podium made from a tripod were to be permitted. In protest, New York cameramen refused to click the shutter, so the ceremony itself went unphotographed.

It was an awkward occasion. The Oyster Bay Roosevelts sat on one side. The Hyde Park clan sat on the other, their smaller numbers supplemented by Daisy Suckley and a sprinkling of Delanos.

FDR confined his remarks to praise for what he called his boyhood hero's "spirit of vital activity," his lifelong battle to "transform politics from a cor-

rupt traffic to a public service." But New York's mayor, Fiorello La Guardia, a voluble Independent who supported the New Deal, used the occasion to go after the Supreme Court, which had just declared the Agricultural Adjustment Administration unconstitutional and now seemed bent on demolishing everything the New Deal had done. If Theodore Roosevelt were still alive, La Guardia said, he would share Franklin Roosevelt's frustration at the Court's apparently unshakable conservatism.

It was all too much for Theodore Roosevelt Jr., who spoke last, on behalf of Oyster Bay. He refused even to acknowledge the presence of his cousin, the president of the United States, and added to his prepared remarks about his father's love of nature the charge that most of the eminent "gentlemen" who had just spoken so warmly of his father "had never fought alongside him but against him during his lifetime."

"The young Theodore showed who he is by making a very stupid speech," Daisy Suckley wrote that evening, "and by not knowing enough to open it by addressing himself to the President and the other important people there. He almost certainly did it on purpose to avoid addressing his cousin Frank."

As the 1936 election year began, relations between Hyde Park and Oyster Bay were as frigid as the winter weather.

OPPOSITE, TOP LEFT Roosevelt, in a top hat, makes his careful way out of New York's Episcopal Church of the Incarnation on the snowy morning of January 19, 1936. Because of the treacherous footing, a Secret Serviceman precedes him down the ramp in case he falls forward. When this picture was published in the New York *Daily News*, the caption explained that it had to be "snapped from half a block away"; photographers were allowed no closer, a stricture that led New York press photographers to refuse to cover the rest of the president's visit to the city.

OPPOSITE, LEFT AND TOP RIGHT Invitation to the dedication of the Theodore Roosevelt Memorial Hall at the American Museum of Natural History, at which the Hyde Park and Oyster Bay Roosevelts were to appear together; and the facade of the memorial itself. Six years later, an equestrian statue of TR, flanked by an American Indian and an African gun bearer, would be put in place at the foot of the stairs.

ABOVE, LEFT Theodore Roosevelt Jr. speaking at his inauguration as president of the National Republican Club in New York City two years before the museum ceremony. When this picture was first published, the caption writer for the Associated Press felt it necessary to identify its subject as "a distant cousin of President Franklin D. Roosevelt," a fact that cannot have pleased the man who had hoped one day to succeed his father in the White House.

ABOVE New York schoolchildren surround a portrait of the man for whom the Theodore Roosevelt Memorial was named, 1936

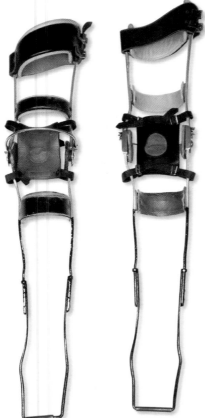

A Rendezvous with Destiny

On Saturday evening, June 27, 1936, FDR was driven onto the University of Pennsylvania's Franklin Field in Philadelphia to accept his party's nomination for a second term as president. More than 100,000 Democrats cheered as his car circled the field and stopped near the platform from which he was to speak. He was helped out of his car, grasped James's arm, and started up the aisle. He spotted the aged poet Edward Markham in the crowd and stopped to shake his hand. Somehow, he lost his delicate balance and twisted. The knee lock on his left brace snapped open under the extra pressure. His leg collapsed. His bodyguard, Gus Gennerich, and Secret Serviceman Mike Reilly kept him from going all the way down, but James dropped his father's speech, which scattered across the floor. Jim Farley and other aides did their best to block the crowd's view.

"There I was hanging in the air, like a goose about to be plucked but I kept on waving and smiling, and smiling and waving," Roosevelt remembered. "I called to Jimmy out of the corner of my mouth to fix the pin."

" 'Dad,' Jimmy called up. 'I'm trying to pick up the speech.'

" 'To hell with the speech,' I said. . . . 'Fix the god-damned brace. If it can't be fixed there won't be any speech.'

"By this time I was mad clear through. . . .

"I could feel Jimmy fumbling and then I heard the pin snap back into place. My balance was restored and my weight was lifted from poor Gus."

"Clean me up, damn it," Roosevelt said.

James gathered up the scattered pages, and the president resumed his rocking gait toward the podium, continuing to smile as if nothing had happened.

By the time he got there, James had managed to put the pages of the speech back into the right order.

"I was still mad when I began . . . ," Roosevelt said. "It wasn't until I reached the line about 'economic royalists' that I knew I had them, and then I gave it to them."

These economic royalists complain that we seek to overthrow the institutions of America. What they really complain of is that we seek to take away their power. . . .

Governments can err. Presidents do make mistakes. But the immortal Dante tells us that divine justice weighs the sins of the cold-blooded and the sins of the warm-hearted in different scales.

Better the occasional faults of a Government that lives in a spirit of charity than the consistent omissions of a Government frozen in the ice of its own indifference.

There is a mysterious cycle in human events. To some generations much is given. Of other generations much is expected. This generation of Americans has a rendezvous with destiny.

OPPOSITE, TOP Lit by floodlights and waving his hat, FDR—accompanied by a phalanx of Secret Servicemen—rolls into Philadelphia's Franklin Field past cheering Democratic convention delegates, eager to hear him rally them for the fall campaign. Moments later, out of sight of the camera but in full view of part of the crowd, his left leg collapsed beneath him.

OPPOSITE, LEFT By 1936, FDR was dependent on far less cumbersome braces than he once had been, but unless the two locks on either side of each knee were snapped solidly in place, he ran the risk of falling.

ABOVE, LEFT AND RIGHT Dusted off after his near fall, Roosevelt waves at the huge, enthusiastic crowd. The United States was engaged in a war, he said, "a war for the survival of democracy . . . for ourselves and for the world. I accept the commission you have tendered me. I join with you. I am enlisted for the duration of the war."

Roosevelt's Republican opponent was Alf Landon, the able but unassuming governor of Kansas, who had enlisted in Theodore Roosevelt's Bull Moose crusade in 1912. When Landon promised to retain useful elements of the New Deal, FDR summarized the Republican message in a speech laced with sarcasm.

> We *believe* in Social Security; we *believe* in work for the unemployed; we *believe* in saving homes. Cross our hearts and hope to die, we believe in all these things; but we do not like the way the present Administration is doing them. Just turn them over to us. We will do all of them—we will do more of them—we will do them better; and, most important of all, the doing of them will not cost *anybody anything*.

Frustrated, the Republicans changed tactics, accusing FDR of being a socialist in disguise. The Oyster Bay Roosevelts joined the attack. Theodore Roosevelt Jr. addressed the president himself in a Pennsylvania speech. "You have been faithless," he said. "You have urged Congress to pass laws you knew were unconstitutional. . . . You have broken your sacred oath taken on the Bible."

Alice Roosevelt Longworth went still further. Her father had conquered *his* illness—childhood asthma—and therefore had championed the "strenuous life," she said. But because Franklin remained in a wheelchair, he had become a "mollycoddle," peddling a "mollycoddle philosophy."

TOP, RIGHT Alf Landon button, featuring the sunflower symbol of his state of Kansas. Landon's radio addresses were so uninspiring, Harold Ickes said, that "the Democratic Campaign Committee ought to spend all the money it can raise to send him out and make speeches."

ABOVE With a Secret Serviceman standing on the running board of his automobile, FDR leaves the Knoxville, Tennessee, railroad station for a campaign appearance, September 9, 1936. "Four years ago," one passenger aboard the president's train wrote, "the people were quiet and undemonstrative," hopeful but unsure anyone could help them. "This year, the crowds were larger . . . and . . . passed any bounds for enthusiasm—really wild enthusiasm."

RIGHT There can have been few more ardent FDR admirers than the enthusiast who produced this crowded 1936 campaign placard. Perhaps he had admired TR as well, since he credits Theodore's pledge of a "Square Deal," not Franklin's promise of a "New" one.

Eleanor Roosevelt rarely responded to criticism of herself, but this attack on her husband's character was more than she could bear. "No one who really knew both men could make that contrast," she wrote in her column. "No man who has brought himself back from what might have been an entire life of invalidism to physical, mental and spiritual strength . . . can ever be accused of preaching or exemplifying a mollycoddle philosophy."

Nothing any critic said seemed to matter. "The forces of organized money are unanimous in their hatred for me," he told a cheering New York crowd, "and I *welcome* their hatred." Wherever FDR went, he asked the crowds if they were better off than they had been when he took office. They were: national income had now more than doubled; unemployment had nearly been cut in half.

Voices called out, "Thank you, Mr. President!" and "You saved my home!" Some people bowed their heads in prayer as his train rattled past. In Denver, someone scrawled in chalk on a boxcar "Roosevelt is my friend."

Eleanor found it all overwhelming, as she said in a letter to Lorena Hickok: "I have never seen on any trip such crowds or enthusiasm," she wrote. "If they really have all this faith I hope he can do a good job for them. . . . I realize more and more that F.D.R. is a great man, and he is nice to me, but as a person I'm a stranger and I don't want to be anything else! P.S. How I hate being a show, but I'm doing it so nicely!"

At Springwood on the evening of election day, as the returns began coming in, FDR blew a big smoke ring and murmured, "Wow." He would win 60.8 percent of the popular vote, the largest percentage anyone had ever won, and this time carried forty-six of the forty-eight states. FDR had forged a new Democratic Party—a "Roosevelt coalition"—that brought together western farmers and big-city industrial workers, immigrants and African Americans and the Solid South.

TOP, LEFT An electric mantelpiece clock in the form of a ship's wheel, made by the Gibraltar Electric Clock Company of Jersey City, depicts Roosevelt "AT THE WHEEL FOR A NEW DEAL," 1936.

TOP, RIGHT Election night, Manhattan: New Yorkers gather at Rockefeller Center to watch returns come in on an electric map. By evening's end, forty-six of the forty-eight states would light up for Roosevelt.

ABOVE Election night, Hyde Park: The Roosevelts greet their neighbors after the extent of his victory is clear. *Left to right:* Anna, John, the president's mother, FDR, Franklin Jr., and Eleanor

The Nine Old Men and the Roosevelt Recession

At Roosevelt's second inaugural, held on January 20, 1937, under the brand-new Twentieth Amendment, he promised to finish the job he'd started. "I see one-third of a nation ill-housed, ill-clad, ill-nourished," he said.

> But it is not in despair that I paint that picture for you. I paint it for you in hope—because the Nation, seeing and understanding the injustice of it, proposes to paint it out. . . . The test of our progress is not whether we add more to the abundance of those who have much; it is whether we provide enough for those who have too little.

The Supreme Court seemed determined to block that progress. It had continued on its conservative course, overturning a number of New Deal statutes, including the NRA and the AAA. It seemed only a matter of time before it moved against the National Labor Relations and Social Security Acts. Future reforms seemed to be in jeopardy, as well.

Buoyed by his big victory, Roosevelt resolved to act. He had been reelected without the help of his old friend and closest adviser, Louis Howe, who had

ABOVE, RIGHT FDR delivers his second inaugural address in the face of a cold, steady winter rain, January 20, 1937.

ABOVE "Qualifying Test for Supreme Court Jobs," Edward S. Brown's reaction to Roosevelt's Court plan, ran in the *New York Herald Tribune* on February 12, 1937. "This is a bloodless *coup d'état*," Walter Lippmann wrote in the same newspaper. "No issue so great or so deep has been raised since secession."

recently died. Howe's political duties had been taken over by others, but no one had replaced him as the man who had felt free to tell FDR when he was about to be a "damned fool."

The plan the president sent to Capitol Hill without any warning to the leadership stunned friends and enemies alike: he asked for the power to name a new justice for every sitting member of the Court who did not resign six months after reaching the age of seventy. Roosevelt claimed the retirement of elderly judges would improve the Court's "efficiency." Almost no one believed that was his real purpose.

Daisy Suckley asked the president to explain the plan during a weekend visit to Hyde Park. He did his high-minded best. When he was finished, she asked, "Don't you mean that you are packing the Court?"

FDR roared, "I suppose you're right, Daisy! I suppose you're right!"

Many in Congress saw it that way, too. The Senate Judiciary Committee called for the plan to be "so emphatically rejected that its parallel will never again be presented to the free representatives of the free people of America." Arkansas Senator Joseph Robinson, the majority leader who had reluctantly agreed to try to shepherd it through the Senate, suffered a fatal heart attack.

But then the Court itself began suddenly to shift, upholding a series of laws most observers had expected it to overturn. In the end, Roosevelt's bill was allowed to die. Over the coming years, the president would be given the opportunity to replace eight members of the Court. He may have lost the battle, Roosevelt liked to say, but he had won the war.

ABOVE, LEFT The "nine old men" of the Supreme Court whose power Roosevelt hoped to dilute. Chief Justice Charles Evans Hughes sits at the center. His was the oldest Court in history; the average age of the justices was seventy-one; five of the nine were seventy-four or older. The columnists Drew Pearson and Robert S. Allen, who coined the phrase, described them as "aloof from all reality, meting out a law as inflexible as the massive blocks of marble that surround them in their mausoleum of justice."

ABOVE "I Did Not Vote For That!" appeared in the *Brooklyn Daily Eagle* a few days after the president's proposal for expanding the Court was made public. "The people are with me," the president assured James Farley, but as it became clear that FDR was seeking a fundamental change in the constitutional order, even many of his most enthusiastic supporters would have second thoughts.

Still, his Court-packing plan had made him a host of enemies within his own party, and strengthened a growing conservative congressional coalition that would make substantive new legislation far more difficult to pass.

In August of 1937, there was still more trouble. The economy had been steadily improving since 1933, so steadily that American output had finally begun to outpace 1929 levels. FDR and some of his advisers started to worry about inflation. In response, the president slashed funds for relief and public works, in the interest, he said, of balancing the budget. The result was a sudden, precipitous economic decline that continued for nine frightening months. Republicans called it the "Roosevelt Recession." Industrial production fell again by more than a third. So did wages. Widespread strikes by workers demanding union recognition slowed factories still further. Four million additional Americans found themselves out of work. The president, Harold Ickes confided to his diary, "is [getting] punch drunk from the punishment that he has suffered."

FDR's own advisers were divided as to what he should do. Some urged him to continue to hold the line on spending. Other, more left-leaning New Dealers, including his wife, wanted him to return to the stimulus programs that had seemed to be working earlier. "Like almost every woman I know of moderate means," Eleanor wrote, "I am always terribly nervous until all my bills are paid and I know I still have a balance in the bank. . . . I do hope, however, that in this budget-balancing business we make our economies without making people suffer who are in need of help. There are wise and unwise economies, as every housewife knows."

In the end, FDR sided with the liberals, persuading Congress to pump billions of dollars more into public works and public housing.

The decline halted. "We are on our way again," Roosevelt said. And he won passage of the Fair Labor Standards Act, which for the first time set federal minimum wages and maximum hours.

Meanwhile, the midterm elections were approaching. Furious at the conservative members of his own party who had joined forces with Republicans on Capitol Hill, the president barnstormed the South during the primaries, championing liberal challengers and urging voters to oust the conservative incumbents he called "copperheads."

The "purge" proved an embarrassment. Voters still admired Roosevelt but resented his intrusion into local races. All but one of his targets survived his assault.

"Roosevelt is his own worst enemy," one triumphant southern senator said.

"Not," said another, "so long as I am alive."

Before Franklin Delano Roosevelt, there had been no unemployment compensation or Social Security; no regulation of the stock market; no federal guarantee of bank deposits or labor's right to bargain; no national minimum wage or maximum hours; no federal commitment to high employment; and no price supports for farmers or federal funds for electric power with which to light their homes. But for all the New Deal's achievements, the American

ABOVE, LEFT A seemingly chastened president leaves church the Sunday after four of his liberal Senate primary candidates were thrashed by senior conservative Democrats. In the elections that followed in November, the Republicans would pick up eighty-one House seats, eight more in the Senate, and thirteen governorships, as well. The Democrats still controlled Congress: "We have a large majority," Vice President Garner said, "but it is not a *New Deal* majority."

ABOVE Democratic Senators Millard Tydings of Maryland and Walter George of Georgia congratulate one another after easily winning primary victories over the president's nominees.

OPPOSITE On the evening of January 7, 1939, photographer Thomas McAvoy captured the embattled president's shifting moods as he presided over the annual Jefferson-Jackson Day dinner at the Mayflower hotel, just a few blocks from the White House.

ABOVE Sharing the dais, Vice President Jack Garner and Postmaster General Farley join FDR in enthusiastic applause. Since neither man thought FDR would run for a third term in 1940, each hoped to succeed him as president.

ABOVE, RIGHT Eleanor Roosevelt attended the dinner, too, and approved of her husband's speech: "I'm not sure it was wise," she wrote to a friend, "but it was honest & certainly fearless."

economy was still struggling. Many of those who most needed help were still not getting it, and Congress was increasingly unwilling to follow Roosevelt's lead—and seemed intent, in fact, on dismantling much that he had done. It blocked appointments, slashed relief appropriations, and over the coming months would force him to end some of the least popular New Deal experiments.

FDR's "iridescent dream of a perfectly pure liberal party untainted by conservatism and reaction," wrote William Allen White, "has been knocked into a cocked hat." Walter Lippmann predicted a Republican landslide in 1940.

Editorialists began writing that FDR was finished as an effective leader and had become a lame duck whose last two years as president were likely to be without real achievement. "President Roosevelt could not run for a third term," one wrote, "even if he so desired."

FDR did not then intend to run again, but he refused to say so, for fear of further undermining his own position, and at the Jefferson-Jackson Day dinner in January 1939 he delivered a fighting speech. Recent Republican victories, he said, must serve to "bring us real Democrats together" with all those who "preach the liberal gospel" to defeat "the enemies of the American people—inertia, greed, ignorance, shortsightedness, vanity, opportunism." Otherwise, he said, any Democrat who ran for president in 1940 was sure to lose.

The president concentrated on domestic politics that evening, but privately his attention was already beginning to turn away from reform toward readying a reluctant country for a new crisis that now threatened to engulf the world.

A Terrible Thing

Adolf Hitler had come to power in Germany at almost precisely the same moment Franklin Roosevelt first became president. Americans had looked on with horror as he crushed his domestic opposition, persecuted German Jews, supported a fascist uprising in Spain, reclaimed the Rhineland from France in 1936, and annexed Austria two years later. Americans also deplored the Italian fascist Benito Mussolini's brutal attack on Ethiopia and sympathized with China in her struggle against invasion by imperial Japan.

But most Americans also continued to see events overseas as none of their business. More than 116,000 American lives had been lost in the Great War, and few thought it had been worth it. In the intervening years, their representatives on Capitol Hill had worked to ensure that the United States would not again become entangled in events overseas. They shrank the army, kept America out of international organizations, limited immigration, and enacted three Neutrality Acts barring arms sales to either side in any future war.

Franklin Roosevelt believed, as Theodore Roosevelt had believed, that the United States had an important role to play overseas. But he had been consumed with the economic crisis during his first years as president, needed the support in Congress of progressive Republicans who were also implacable isolationists, and for the most part had been willing to go along with public sentiment.

"What worries me," he had told a friend as the violence increased overseas, "is that public opinion over here is patting itself on the back every morning thanking God for the Atlantic and Pacific Oceans."

At first, his efforts at informing the American public of the dangers it faced did not go well. When the president compared fascist aggression to a spreading disease that needed to be quarantined, pacifists charged that Roosevelt was starting America down the slope to war and isolationist congressmen threatened to impeach him. The leaders of his own party remained silent. The president offered no concrete proposal. "It is a terrible thing," he told an aide, "to look over your shoulder when you are trying to lead—and find no one there."

OPPOSITE Members of the Women's International League for Peace and Freedom, in Washington to present a petition to FDR calling for universal disarmament, cluster around a statue of Admiral David Farragut in the heart of the Capitol, May 30, 1933.

TOP, LEFT In Chicago on October 5, 1937, Roosevelt calls for an international "quarantine of the aggressor nations." When he realized there was little American sympathy for any kind of collective action overseas, he dropped the subject.

TOP, RIGHT AND ABOVE Adolf Hitler in 1925, eight years before assuming power in Germany, and the Italian fascist dictator Benito Mussolini parading in Rome in the spring of 1938. Together, Mussolini said, Nazi Germany and fascist Italy would form the "axis" around which Europe was destined to revolve.

ABOVE In 1938, peace advocates like this protester still greeted even the most tentative White House moves toward strengthening America's defenses with hostility and derision.

RIGHT In the aftermath of *Kristallnacht*, Austrian Jews crowd a passport office in Vienna seeking visas to escape Nazi rule.

OPPOSITE, TOP LEFT AND RIGHT A Berlin synagogue gutted on *Kristallnacht*, and the official White House statement deploring the Nazi assault on the Jews, amended by the president's strong personal reaction in his own hand

OPPOSITE, BOTTOM One of many telegrams and letters from American anti-Semites received by the White House after Roosevelt's denunciation of Nazi thuggery. It accuses the president of being a "catspaw" for "International Jew war mongers."

By September of 1938, Hitler was demanding to annex the German-speaking portion of Czechoslovakia known as the Sudetenland. At Munich, at the end of that month, the British prime minister, Neville Chamberlain, agreed not to oppose him—in exchange for a promise of what Chamberlain called "peace in our time."

Then, on the evening of November 9, Hitler's paramilitary thugs looted Jewish homes all over Germany, smashed Jewish shops, and burned synagogues. Scores of Jews died, and thousands were imprisoned. The rest were required to pay what the Nazis called an "atonement fine" of 20 percent of their assets to the state. It was remembered as *Kristallnacht*—the "Night of Broken Glass."

FDR told a press conference he could "scarcely believe . . . such things could occur in a twentieth century civilization." He ordered the visas of fifteen thousand German and Austrian resident aliens extended so that they

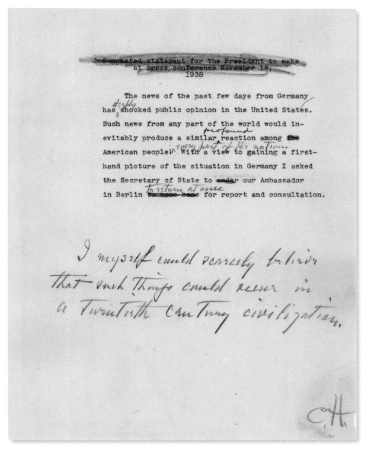

would not be forced to return to Nazi rule—and he recalled his ambassador from Berlin, something neither Britain nor France dared do.

But a Gallup poll taken in early 1939 would show that 85 percent of American Protestants and 84 percent of Catholics opposed offering sanctuary to European refugees. So did more than one-quarter of American Jews. "What has happened to us in this country?" Eleanor Roosevelt wrote. "If we study our own history we find that we have always been ready to receive the unfortunate from other countries, and though this may seem a generous gesture on our part, we have profited a thousand-fold by what they have brought us."

In March of 1939, Hitler sent his armies into what remained of Czechoslovakia. Poland looked to be next, and Britain pledged to go to war if Germany invaded her.

Roosevelt begged Congress to allow arms sales to Britain and France. The House watered down his proposal, and it never even reached the Senate floor.

That spring, FDR sent a list of thirty-one sovereign nations to Hitler, asking the dictator to pledge that he had no plans to attack any of them. Hitler did not bother to reply. Instead he launched a two-hour tirade of contempt directed at Roosevelt personally. It was clear that the Führer of Germany believed he had nothing to fear from the president of the United States.

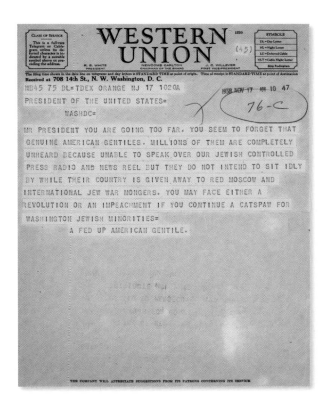

All the Luck in the World!

When FDR learned that King George VI and Queen Elizabeth of England were to visit Canada in the spring of 1939, he invited them to extend their trip to include Washington, New York, and his own home at Hyde Park, where, he said, "the simplicity and naturalness of such a visit would produce a most excellent effect" on American public opinion. Both he and the British government wanted to do all they could to bring their two peoples together in the face of Hitler's growing threat. The royals agreed to come, even though a previous British ambassador's wife objected that Springwood was unsuitable for the king and queen—"a dismal, small house, extremely badly run and most uncomfortable."

Roosevelt was sure that the royal presence would "be an excellent thing for Anglo-American relations," and he was right; some 750,000 people turned out to see them in Washington, almost twice the city's population; three and a half million more cheered them in New York, many shouting, "Hiya King!"

The royal couple spent two days at Springwood. They attended the Roosevelt family church, swam in the pool at Val-Kill, and attended a picnic at the president's new hilltop cottage, where much was made in the newspapers of the fact that the king had enjoyed a hot dog and even asked for a second.

On the evening of June 11, as the royals' train started to pull out of Hyde Park, beginning their journey home to what seemed more and more like war, FDR called out, "Good luck to you. All the luck in the world." At the same time, Eleanor remembered, "the people who were gathered everywhere on the banks of the Hudson . . . began to sing 'Auld Lang Syne.' There was something incredibly moving about this scene—the river in the evening light, the voices of many people singing this old song . . . the train slowly pulling out with the young couple waving good-bye. One thought of the clouds that hung over them and the worries they were going to face and turned away from the scene with a heavy heart."

OPPOSITE "Well, at last I greet you!" FDR focuses his charm on Queen Elizabeth of England as she and King George VI arrive at Union Station in Washington, D.C., June 8, 1939. The president grips the arm of his military aide, Major General Edwin "Pa" Watson.

ABOVE With FDR at the wheel, the royal couple and James Roosevelt's wife, Betsey Cushing Roosevelt, drive to Top Cottage for a picnic. "Motorcycle police cleared the road ahead of us," the queen remembered sixty years later, "but the president pointed out sights, waved his cigarette holder about, . . . was conversing more than watching the road. . . . There were several times when I thought we would go right off the road and tumble down the hills. . . . It was a relief to get to the picnic."

LEFT AND BELOW The Roosevelts and the royal couple wave goodbye as the train carrying the king and queen leaves Hyde Park.

CHAPTER 6

The Common Cause

1939–1944

The Sphinx

In the summer of 1939, Franklin Roosevelt was more than halfway through his second four years as president. None of his predecessors had dared defy the precedent set by George Washington and run for a third term. At first, FDR did not expect to do so either, though he continued to maintain his silence on the subject. Work was beginning on a presidential library at Hyde Park, where he planned to store his papers and write his memoirs, and he had built himself a hilltop cottage nearby where he could get away from visitors and where both his close personal secretary Missy LeHand and his devoted distant cousin Daisy Suckley separately hoped to live with him. He told another relative, "I am a tired and weary man."

PRECEDING PAGES British Prime Minister Winston Churchill, FDR, and Allied brass at the Casablanca Conference, January 1943

OPPOSITE FDR gazes fondly into Daisy Suckley's camera on the porch at Top Cottage. "I had a lovely time alone with the P[resident]," she wrote after one of their visits to the hilltop. "You can say anything & ask any questions of him when alone, but when others are there I am always afraid of saying something I shouldn't or asking what he doesn't want to answer."

ABOVE The president spars with the press at a Val-Kill picnic, July 4, 1939. "It is a game with me," Roosevelt once told a friend. "They ask me a lot of questions and I really enjoy trying to avoid them." The man in the dark suit behind FDR is William D. Hassett, assistant secretary to the president. The woman in the polka-dot dress is Grace Tully, the assistant—and eventual successor—to Missy LeHand, who sits facing her.

BURCK
(CHICAGO TIMES)

To Mrs. Eleanor Roosevelt — with admiration and good wishes — J. Burck May 1940,

"BUT IT WOULD MAKE SUCH A NICE SCOOP IF YOU'D ONLY TELL ME, FRANKLIN."

Eleanor Roosevelt was weary, too. "There is no end to the appointments, teas, social obligations," she wrote. That year alone, she would entertain 323 overnight guests, oversee dinner for 4,729 more visitors, preside over tea for over 9,000—and shake hands with another 14,000—all while dictating a daily column, delivering 45 lectures, conducting a weekly radio program, and trying to focus on the host of social issues that took her all over the country.

She did not want four more years of it, she told an old friend, and couldn't wait for the day when she could at long last "take on a job and see it through to a conclusion" on her own. If FDR didn't leave the White House in 1941, she had warned her daughter, Anna, she would.

Then everything began to change.

OPPOSITE This eight-foot-tall papier-maché sculpture was the centerpiece of a satirical review at the annual Gridiron Club dinner in 1939. It portrays Roosevelt as the Sphinx because he remained so maddeningly silent about whether or not he planned to run for a third term. FDR attended the dinner and was so amused by the statue that he asked that it be sent to the "Oddities Room" in his new library and museum at Hyde Park. When it got there, an unwise aide asked the president's mother if she didn't think it was a pretty good caricature of her son. It was *not*, she said; her jaw was identical to his. Did she think this grotesque object looked *anything* like her?

ABOVE "But It Would Make Such a Nice Scoop if You'd Only Tell Me, Franklin." Of all the caricatures of her that appeared over the years, its subject said, it was this one, by Jacob Burck of the *Chicago Daily Times*, "that amused me most." The president did, in fact, keep her in the dark about his plans, along with the rest of the country.

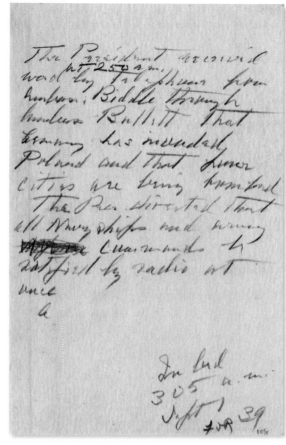

I Can Feel Little Pity

In the early-morning hours of September 1, 1939, Eleanor Roosevelt was asleep at Val-Kill when the telephone rang: "It was my husband in Washington," she reported the next day, "to tell me the sad news that Germany had invaded Poland and that her planes were bombing Polish cities. . . . I feel no bitterness against the German people. I am deeply sorry for them, as I am for the people of all other European nations facing this horrible crisis. But for [Hitler], the man who has taken this responsibility on his shoulders, I can feel little pity. It is hard to see how he can sleep at night and think of the many people in many nations whom he may send to their deaths."

When the Great War broke out in 1914, Woodrow Wilson had called upon all Americans to remain neutral "in thought as well as deed." As the Second World War began, FDR was careful not to make the same request. "This nation will remain a neutral nation," he said, "but I cannot ask that every American remain neutral in thought as well. Even a neutral has a right to take account of facts. Even a neutral cannot be asked to close his mind or close his conscience."

Roosevelt and most of his fellow citizens sympathized with Hitler's victims—and with France and England when they went to war to stop him. But an even bigger majority was still opposed to any American involvement overseas, for fear that the Allies would pull the United States into another war.

ABOVE FDR's notes on the early-morning telephone call to the White House during which he learned that the Second World War had begun, dated, initialed, and carefully preserved by him: "The President received word at 2:50 a.m. by telephone from Ambass. [Anthony Drexel] Biddle through Ambass. [William] Bullitt that Germany has invaded Poland and that four cities are being bombed. The Pres. directed that all Navy ships and army commands be notified by radio at once. In bed 3:05 a.m. Sept. 1, 39. FDR." Biddle was the ambassador to Poland, Bullitt to France.

ABOVE, LEFT A Polish girl grieves for her sister, killed by German strafing during the first hours of the German attack. "Well, it's come at last," Roosevelt said when he was first told of the invasion. "God help us all."

OPPOSITE German troops parade through Warsaw, September 28, 1939. Half the city's buildings had been destroyed or heavily damaged; forty thousand civilian city dwellers had died. "Take a look around Warsaw," Hitler told reporters. "That is how I can deal with any European city."

ARMY'S MARSHALL.
No other General ever faced the problem: operations on six continents.

The Scene Has Darkened

The United States was poorly prepared for conflict. The army was smaller than that of Romania: fewer than 174,000 men were in uniform, fitted out with tin hats and leggings issued during the Great War and carrying rifles designed in 1903. The army still owned tens of thousands of cavalry horses. Even Roosevelt's beloved navy was only marginally bigger than it had been when he took office.

The question became how far Roosevelt dared go to help the Allies. According to one poll, roughly one-third of all Americans wanted nothing to do with the warring nations; another third was willing to sell arms to the belligerents as long as the United States would "take no sides and stay out of the war entirely." "I am almost literally walking on eggs," Roosevelt told a visitor.

Three weeks after Hitler invaded Poland, FDR called upon Congress to revise the Neutrality Act and end the embargo on the sale of arms to belligerents—but only by arguing that the stronger the Allies got the less likely it was that the United States would ever have to go to war. After six

bitter weeks of debate, Congress did lift the ban, but insisted that arms could be shipped only on American vessels and sold only on a "cash and carry basis."

Most of the progressive midwestern Republicans, who had once supported New Deal legislation, were isolationists opposed to any aid to the Allies. Roosevelt found himself more dependent than ever before on the conservative southern Democrats he'd once tried to purge from his party.

After the Nazis devastated Poland, a shadowy seven-month lull settled over Europe. Senator William Borah, an isolationist from Idaho and the former lover of Alice Roosevelt Longworth, dubbed it the "Phony War."

Then, in the spring of 1940, the Phony War became real again. In April, the Nazis invaded Denmark and Norway. On May 10, German bombers filled the skies over Brussels, Amsterdam, and Rotterdam; German troops invaded the Netherlands, Luxembourg, Belgium, and France.

"VERY WELL, ALONE"

ABOVE Winston Churchill in the study at his country home, Chartwell. Many of his messages to FDR were written in the quiet of this room.

OPPOSITE Disaster at Dunkirk: Allied troops huddle together on the beach, vulnerable to attack from the air and hoping to be rescued by one or another of the nine hundred military and civilian vessels that made up a motley armada plying back and forth across the English Channel. Reporting the evacuation to Parliament on June 4, Churchill vowed that if, as now seemed likely, Germany sought next to invade Britain, "We shall fight them on the beaches, we shall fight on the landing grounds, we shall fight in the fields and in the streets, we shall fight in the hills, we shall never surrender."

The following day, Winston Churchill, who had warned for years of the Nazi threat to Britain, became prime minister. By early June, the Germans would force 338,000 British, French, and Belgian troops to flee across the English Channel, leaving behind at Dunkirk hundreds of thousands of tons of armaments and heavy equipment.

"The scene has darkened swiftly," Churchill told Roosevelt in the first of a series of nearly two thousand secret wartime messages between the prime minister and the president. "The small countries are simply smashed up, one by one, like matchwood," he said. "We expect to be attacked here ourselves. . . . If necessary we shall continue the war alone, and we are not afraid of that." But unless the United States would sell Britain several hundred aircraft and lend her forty to fifty destroyers, he could not promise to hold out for long.

Roosevelt had been corresponding quietly with Churchill for almost a year. Churchill had been first lord of the admiralty then, but Roosevelt had understood that he might well be prime minister one day.

FDR did all that he felt he could to help. "These are ominous days," he told Congress, and asked for half a million more men for the army and called for the building of fifty thousand warplanes within the next twelve months— enough planes to outstrip the German air force in a single year—and to provide sufficient additional aircraft for sale to Britain. Fifty thousand planes was ten times the country's current capacity. Critics thought he was delusional. "This seemed at first like an impossible goal," a close adviser wrote, "but it caught the imagination of the Americans, who have always believed they could accomplish the impossible."

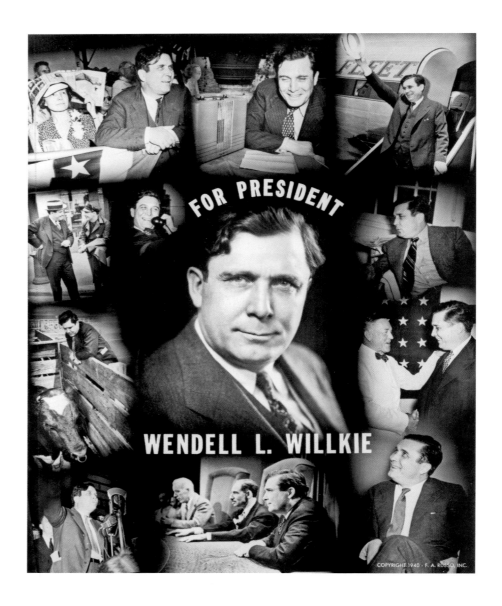

Two Times Is Enough for Any Man

Two days after France surrendered to the Nazis, the Republicans met in Philadelphia to choose their presidential nominee. The front-runners were mostly isolationists. But recent events in Europe had shaken the delegates, and in the end they chose an unlikely but remarkable dark horse: a big, rumpled, corporate attorney from the Midwest who had once been a Democrat and who, like FDR, believed that the United States had a crucial role to play abroad: Wendell Willkie.

FDR believed him "the most formidable candidate" the Republicans could possibly have chosen.

A few days later, Eleanor expressed her concerns to her daughter:

Anna Darling:

The Republican convention seems so "usual" and the times so "unusual" that I find it hard to reconcile the two. . . . France is crushed. . . . What will be Hitler's next move? South America or the U.S.A.? And will Japan be acting with them in a concerted plan? It looks that way just now. What a sad world.

Roosevelt continued to remain silent about whether or not he would break with tradition and run for a third term. He did nothing to discourage others from announcing their candidacies, including his own former campaign manager, James Farley. And he refused to attend the upcoming Democratic convention in Chicago, claiming that the international situation was far too grave. Instead, he dispatched his close adviser Harry Hopkins to try to organize a supposedly spontaneous "draft." Many delegates—southern conservatives, Farley advocates, and those opposed to a third term for any man—felt used and angry.

Labor Secretary Frances Perkins called FDR from Chicago, pleading with him to appear personally at the convention and calm things down. If he didn't, she said, he wouldn't have the party behind him in the fall. He refused to come, but suggested she ask his wife if she would appear on his behalf.

Eleanor Roosevelt was at Val-Kill, listening to the convention on the radio. There had been changes in her inner circle. Her friendship with Nancy Cook and Marion Dickerman, with whom she'd built her cottage, had cooled. She saw less of Lorena Hickok and Earl Miller, too. But with her this evening was a new friend and confidant, a former youth leader named Joseph P. Lash who had become a sort of surrogate son. The Democrats were in trouble, she told him. They hadn't ended unemployment. They now seemed about to break the no-third-term ban, which she believed was "a very great tradition." And she felt that her husband had already served his purpose in history.

The phone rang. It was Frances Perkins. Would she go to Chicago? Only if the president asked her himself, Eleanor answered. She wanted to be coaxed—and she wanted Franklin to do the coaxing.

She spoke to FDR.

"Well, would you like to go?" he asked.

"No, I wouldn't like to go. I'm very busy. . . . Do you really want me to go?"

Yes, he finally answered. "Perhaps it would be a good idea."

She boarded a plane and headed for Chicago.

Meanwhile, as the nominations began, Senator Alben Barkley of Kentucky, the convention chairman, told the delegates that he had a message for them from FDR: "The President has never had, and has not today, any desire or purpose to continue in the office of President, to be a candidate for that office, or to be nominated by the Convention for that office. He wishes, he wishes in all earnestness and sincerity to make it clear that all of the delegates to this Convention are free to vote for any candidate."

As Barkley finished, a single disembodied voice began a chant. Delegates

OPPOSITE, LEFT AND ABOVE, TOP The Republican case against the Roosevelts; and the Democratic response

OPPOSITE, RIGHT A Willkie poster, 1940. Although the Republican nominee had made his name and fortune on Wall Street, Republican publicists made much of his Indiana boyhood and supposed closeness to everyday people. When the newspaperman Joseph Alsop, a Roosevelt cousin, said that the Willkie-for-president fervor came "from the grassroots," Alice Roosevelt Longworth answered, "Yes, from the grassroots of 10,000 country clubs."

ABOVE Eleanor Roosevelt and her new friend, Joseph Lash. As with so many in her closest circle, her relationship with him was initially built on how she could be useful. "She had a compelling emotional need to have people who were close, who in a sense were hers," Lash remembered, "and upon whom she could lavish help, attention, tenderness."

joined in. It was later discovered that the chanting was led by the Chicago superintendent of sewers, broadcasting from somewhere in the basement.

Roosevelt was renominated on the first ballot. But then word came that FDR wanted Agriculture Secretary Henry Wallace as his vice president. A rebellion began to brew. Wallace was too liberal for many conservatives; he had never run for office— and he had once been a Republican.

FDR wouldn't budge: "Damn it to hell," he said. "They will go for Wallace or I won't run." To emphasize that he meant it, he wrote out a statement: if the Democrats could not

unite behind a liberal ticket, he would decline the honor of their nomination.

Eleanor arrived just before the vice presidential nominations began and took a seat beside Mrs. Wallace. When Wallace's name was introduced, delegates booed and jeered. Then, just before the vote, Eleanor rose to speak.

The convention fell silent. No first lady had ever spoken to a national convention before. She thanked Jim Farley for his lifetime of service to the Democratic Party and then called upon the delegates to rally to a cause greater than themselves. "This is no ordinary time, no time for weighing anything except what we can best do for the country as a whole. . . . This is only carried by a united people who love their country and who will live for it to the fullest of their ability, with the highest ideals, with a determination . . . and through doing what this country can, to bring the world to a safer and happier condition."

After Eleanor's speech, a united convention nominated Henry Wallace for vice president on the first ballot. The audience had been "just like lambs," she said. When Harry Hopkins escorted her back to the airport for the flight home she told him, "You young things don't know politics."

OPPOSITE Eleanor speaks at the Chicago convention. When she arrived, she reported that evening, "the atmosphere . . . was very much like the atmosphere one always finds on these occasions. Everybody was very busy, very troubled or very elated about one thing or another." But when she began to speak the great hall fell silent. The man in the dark suit behind the first lady is the convention chairman, Alben Barkley.

ABOVE Henry Wallace surrounded by reporters in Chicago: "I have always felt in him a certain shyness . . . that has kept him aloof from some Democrats," Eleanor wrote after she helped get him nominated for vice president, "but . . . I am sure they will soon find in him much to admire and love."

America's Answer to Hitlerism

As Willkie prepared to campaign across the country, Roosevelt sought to seem above politics. As a sign of bipartisanship, he had named two eminent Republicans to his cabinet—Henry L. Stimson, as secretary of war, and as secretary of the navy, Frank Knox, who had fought alongside Theodore Roosevelt as a Rough Rider.

Two issues demanded immediate attention—and either one could have lost him the election. First, he needed a military draft—it would be the first peacetime draft in U.S. history. Initially, he didn't dare publicly support a conscription bill that was working its way through Congress, for fear of Republican attack. Opponents besieged Capitol Hill—mothers' groups, college students, clergymen. "If you pass this bill," said Senator Burton K. Wheeler of Montana, "you slit the throat of the last democracy still living."

Then, Wendell Willkie defied his advisers and many in his own party and came out in favor of the draft as the best way to shore up the nation's defenses. A relieved Roosevelt now enthusiastically endorsed it, too; it was, he said, "America's answer to Hitlerism." More than sixteen million men between the ages of twenty-one and thirty-five would be registered on the draft rolls.

ABOVE Wendell Willkie kicks off his presidential campaign in his hometown of Elwood, Indiana. In front of an overwhelmingly isolationist crowd, he declared his support for the draft: "I cannot ask the American people to put their faith in me without recording my conviction that some form of selective service is the only democratic way to secure the trained and competent manpower we need for national defense." Without Willkie's backing, FDR later admitted, the conscription bill would not have passed.

RIGHT As Roosevelt looks on, Secretary of War Henry Stimson is blindfolded before drawing the first draft number from the fishbowl in front of him, September 16, 1940. "It was a brave decision on the part of the President," Stimson said, "not to delay the lottery until after election day."

OPPOSITE Army doctors examine new draftees at Fort Slocum, New York, 1940. Nearly half the men who reported to their local draft boards were rejected as unfit, most suffering from bad teeth, poor eyesight, heart problems, or venereal disease—or because they didn't measure up to fourth-grade educational standards.

The second compelling issue facing Roosevelt that autumn was finding a way to respond to Winston Churchill's desperate calls for help. German bombs were now falling on London. An all-out German assault across the Channel seemed imminent. Joseph Kennedy, Roosevelt's ambassador in London, believed Britain's surrender "inevitable." So did the president's top military commanders. They argued that America's military needs should take precedence over those of any foreign power.

FDR overruled them all. On September 2, 1940, without consulting Congress, he signed an executive order transferring fifty overage destroyers to Britain in exchange for leases on British bases in the Western Hemisphere. Arming Britain was "nothing more than a guess," FDR admitted to a member of his cabinet. If he guessed wrong and Britain fell he would have accomplished nothing—except to further enrage Hitler.

Wendell Willkie denounced the deal as "the most arbitrary and dictatorial action ever taken by a President of the United States." Isolationists were even angrier. There was talk again of impeachment. Students at Yale University formed the noninterventionist America First Committee,

dedicated to an "impregnable national defense"—but no help whatsoever for embattled Britain. Hundreds of thousands signed up, including the aviator Charles Lindbergh and the actress Lillian Gish; the poet Robert Frost; the composer Charles Ives and two soon-to-be-celebrated Ivy Leaguers, Gerald Ford and John F. Kennedy.

The Oyster Bay Roosevelts, like the rest of the country, were divided over the issue. Kermit Roosevelt, who had always remained friendly with Franklin and Eleanor, was already serving in the British army. But Theodore Roosevelt Jr. campaigned against U.S. involvement: he was "bitterly fearful of Franklin," who, he told his sister Alice, was "itching" to get into the war "partly as a means of bolstering himself and partly . . . because of megalomania." When Alice told a reporter that, rather than vote for a third term for Franklin, she'd cast her ballot for Hitler, the president told Eleanor he didn't want "to have anything to do with that damned woman again."

Less than a month after the president's destroyer deal was announced, Germany, Italy, and Japan signed the Tripartite Treaty, agreeing that if any one of them was attacked, the others would come to its aid.

OPPOSITE, TOP AND BOTTOM Londoners take shelter in an underground tunnel from the German bombs falling above; a small English boy and his stuffed animal, all that is left of his family after a direct hit.

ABOVE, LEFT Thousands of America Firsters and their supporters crowd into New York's Madison Square Garden to hear Charles Lindbergh attack both Roosevelt and Willkie as heedless interventionists, intent on getting America into a war against Germany he was sure it could not win.

ABOVE Alice Roosevelt Longworth, a charter member of the America First board of directors, sits on the Garden platform alongside the wives of isolationist senators Robert A. Taft and Burton K. Wheeler. "Franklin's trite pieties mean nothing," Alice wrote to her brother Ted. "He wants war . . . the only way he can retrieve his power which has been slipping so rapidly. . . . Only war can divert attention from his sweeping failures."

Safe on Third

Republicans tried to keep the third-term issue alive: reelecting Roosevelt would destroy America's "democratic way of life," Willkie said. But both sides realized the real issue was the war, and falling behind late in the race, the Republican candidate began to charge FDR with secretly planning to send America's sons into a European war.

Roosevelt had always been careful to say that the United States would never go to war—"*except in case of attack*." In Boston, where many Irish voters opposed any aid to Britain, he deliberately dropped even that qualifier. "And while I'm talking to you fathers and mothers," he told the crowd

in Boston Garden. "I give you one more assurance. I have said this before, but I shall say it again, and again, and again. Your boys are not going to be sent into any foreign war."

"That hypocritical son of bitch!" Willkie said when he heard Roosevelt's Boston pledge. "This is going to beat me."

On election night at Springwood, the returns were at first so close that even FDR's optimism faltered momentarily, and he asked to be left alone. But by the end of the evening, the tide had once again turned toward Roosevelt. In the end, he won 449 electoral votes to Willkie's 82.

Around midnight, a torchlight parade of townspeople wound its way onto the Roosevelt estate, following a tradition that had greeted Democratic victories since the days of the president's father. Roosevelt and his family went out to greet them. FDR was jubilant, roaring when he saw a small boy carrying a sign that read "SAFE ON THIRD." Eleanor was somber. "This is the first time a President has been [elected] for a third term," she wrote. "I looked at my children, at the President's mother, and then at the President himself, and wondered what each one was feeling down in [their] heart of hearts. I feel that any citizen should be willing to give all that he has to give to his country in work or sacrifice in times of crisis."

As the Roosevelts waved to their neighbors that evening, Nazi warplanes dropped fifteen hundred bombs on London.

OPPOSITE, BOTTOM The advantages of incumbency: Willkie gamely campaigns in downtown Jersey City, New Jersey, where Mayor Frank Hague has made sure no photograph of the Republican candidate fails also to advertise his Democratic opponent.

OPPOSITE, TOP Roosevelt winds up his campaign in Poughkeepsie. At the beginning of the race, he'd claimed the overseas crisis was too grave for traditional politicking. But he also considered it a "public duty" to correct what he called "falsifications of fact." "I will not pretend that I find this an unpleasant duty," he'd told a cheering crowd. "I am an old campaigner and I love a good fight."

ABOVE A triumphant FDR waves to his Hyde Park neighbors on election night, November 5, 1940. "We are facing difficult days in this country," he told them, "but I think you will find me the same Franklin Roosevelt you have known a great many years. My heart has always been here. It always will be." To the president's left are Franklin Roosevelt Jr. and his wife, Ethel du Pont Roosevelt; John Roosevelt and his wife, Anne Clark Roosevelt; Sara Delano Roosevelt and Eleanor.

The Arsenal of Democracy

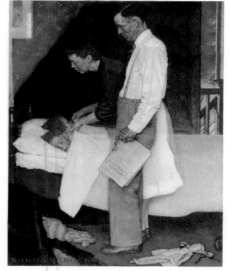

OURS...to fight for

FREEDOM FROM FEAR

Roosevelt redoubled his efforts at aiding Hitler's enemies. In a December fireside chat, he declared that the Nazis could never be appeased: "No man can tame a tiger into a kitten by stroking it." The only way to keep the United States out of the struggle against the Axis was to provide further aid to the Allies already engaged in fighting it. The United States must become the "arsenal of democracy," and, since Britain could no longer pay for arms, the president proposed continuing to provide ships, planes, tanks, and guns—so long as the British promised to return or replace them when the war was over. Roosevelt compared it to lending a neighbor a garden hose.

A few weeks later, in his 1941 State of the Union message, Roosevelt formally presented his "Lend-Lease" program to Congress and then tried to describe the kind of world he hoped would emerge from the war. It should be based, he said, "on four universal freedoms."

First is freedom of speech and expression—everywhere in the world.

The second is freedom of every person to worship God in his own way—everywhere in the world.

The third is freedom from want—which means economic understandings which will secure to every nation a healthy peacetime life for its inhabitants—everywhere in the world.

The fourth is freedom from fear—which, translated into world terms, means a world-wide reduction of armaments to such a point and in such a thorough fashion that no nation will be in a position to commit an act of physical aggression against any neighbor—anywhere in the world.

That is no vision of a distant millennium. It is a definite basis for a kind of world attainable in our own time and generation. That kind of world is the very antithesis of the so-called new order of tyranny, which the dictators seek to create with the crash of a bomb.

The battle over Lend-Lease was bitter and acrimonious, but the bill passed in March. Churchill called it the "most unsordid act in the history of any nation," but privately feared that the Americans were going to provide too little too late.

After Hitler sent his legions into the Soviet Union in June, Roosevelt persuaded Congress to extend Lend-Lease to Russia, as well. The Red Army would now be trying to repel the invaders with trucks made by the Ford Motor Company. And when Nazi submarines preyed on convoys carrying American supplies in the North Atlantic, FDR first ordered naval vessels to shoot on sight and then got Congress to arm American merchant ships. Soon, the United States would be engaged in a deadly but undeclared war at sea.

OPPOSITE, TOP Members of the "Mothers' Crusade" swarm Capitol Hill during the Senate debate on bill 1776, the law authorizing Lend-Lease. Their noisy prayers and incessant hymn singing so annoyed interventionist Senator Carter Glass of Virginia that he asked the FBI to see if they had any links to Nazi Germany—and while they were at it, he added, it might also be "pertinent to inquire whether they really are mothers. For the sake of America, I devoutly hope not."

OPPOSITE, BOTTOM "OURS . . . to fight for FREEDOM FROM FEAR," one of a quartet of Norman Rockwell paintings depicting Roosevelt's "Four Freedoms" that initially appeared in the *Saturday Evening Post*. After the United States entered the war, prints of them would be exchanged for $133 million in war bonds.

ABOVE, LEFT Nazi troops advance across Russia. In the summer of 1939, Hitler and Soviet leader Joseph Stalin had signed a ten-year nonaggression pact that allowed Germany to overrun Poland and Western Europe without interference from the East. Once that was accomplished, and less than two years after signing the agreement, Hitler turned on his temporary ally and launched Operation Barbarossa, sending three million troops into Russia along a thousand-mile front.

ABOVE An American tank intended for use in the war against Hitler being hoisted onto the deck of a cargo vessel bound for the Soviet Union, 1941

The Wrong War in the Wrong Ocean at the Wrong Time

Franklin Roosevelt faced a threat from the other side of the world, as well, where he feared Japan was about to make good on Theodore Roosevelt's old prophecy of an attack on American holdings in the Pacific that would lead to what TR had called "one of the most disastrous conflicts the world has ever seen."

The Japanese military had been on the move for a decade. They had seized Manchuria in 1931 and invaded China in 1937, killing hundreds of thousands of civilians and claiming Shanghai and other major ports along her coast. Now they seemed to be seeking to dominate the whole Far East, threatening vital American, Dutch, and British interests in the region.

Washington had formally objected to Japanese aggression over the years but did little else to stop it. Roosevelt did not want his country engaged in simultaneous conflicts on two fronts, and Germany seemed to present the greatest immediate threat. To go to war with Japan, he believed, would be "the wrong war in the wrong ocean at the wrong time." Instead, he instructed his State Department to "baby the Japs along."

He did have one nonmilitary weapon in his arsenal: the embargo. In order to continue to expand, Japan needed American strategic materials. One by one, Washington cut them off: steel and premium scrap iron, airplane parts, aviation fuel. When Japan responded in the summer of 1940 by signing the Tripartite Treaty with Hitler and Mussolini, the United States reciprocated by banning the export of all scrap iron as well as machine tools and hinted that oil might be next on the list. Eighty percent of Japan's fuel supply came from the United States; without it, the Japanese economy would collapse, and her military's dreams of further conquest would collapse with it.

In the summer of 1941, the Japanese occupied French Indochina, a major source of rubber, and seemed poised to attack British possessions and the oil-rich Dutch East Indies, as well. To slow their advance, Roosevelt froze Japanese assets in the United States and insisted that a government committee approve any further sales of oil. And, as a further deterrent, he dispatched a large part of the Pacific fleet to Hawaii, to the sprawling naval base at Pearl Harbor.

OPPOSITE Japanese troops on the move in China, 1941

ABOVE Chinese civilians killed by Japanese terror bombing in Chonqing

Let the Negro Masses Speak

The growth of defense industries put six million Americans to work in just twelve months, with thousands more signing on every day.

The focus on defense had begun to revive the economy, and Eleanor Roosevelt shared her husband's wish to ready the country for the war both feared was coming.

But she was also concerned that hundreds of thousands of Americans, through no fault of their own, were being left out.

Firms that had never hired black workers saw no reason to change their policy. "We have not had a Negro worker in twenty-five years," said the Standard Steel Corporation of Kansas City, "and do not plan to start now."

African Americans had voted overwhelmingly for Franklin Roosevelt in 1940, and were bitterly disappointed when the president backed away from what they had thought was a private pledge to end the old policy of segregating the armed forces and to allow black and white Americans to fight for their country, side by side.

Discrimination in defense jobs was the last straw. In the spring of 1941, A. Philip Randolph, president of the Brotherhood of Sleeping Car Porters, threatened to bring 100,000 black protesters to Washington on July 1 unless something was done about it. "Let the Negro masses speak," he said. "It will wake up Negro as well as as White America."

FDR feared bloodshed; Washington was a Jim Crow city. Randolph refused to back down. The president asked his wife to see what she could do.

The first lady had advocated an anti-lynching bill her husband had not felt able to support; had outraged white southerners by visiting black colleges and posing with their students; and, when a Birmingham, Alabama, policeman told her she could not sit among black citizens at a segregated meeting, she had moved her chair *between* the black and white sections to demonstrate the absurdity of the situation.

Now, she did as her husband suggested. "You know where I stand," she told Randolph. But, she went on, the march would be "a very grave mistake . . . I am afraid it will set back the progress which is being made . . . towards better opportunities and less segregation."

Randolph respectfully refused to back off. His deadline grew closer.

The first lady persuaded FDR that he had better meet with Randolph and her friend Walter White of the National Association for the Advancement of Colored People. Together, they helped negotiate the language of a new executive order. It created the Fair Employment Practices Commission to combat discrimination in defense plants. The FEPC had no enforcement powers. It could only investigate complaints and issue directives asking that discrimination be eliminated. But it represented the first federal action on civil rights since Reconstruction.

Randolph called off his march.

When Eleanor Roosevelt got word that her husband had finally signed Executive Order 8802, she wired him, "I hope from this first step we may go on to others."

ABOVE At the Bethlehem-Fairfield Shipyard in Baltimore, black and white welders work alongside one another on the USS *Frederick Douglass*, one of eighteen Liberty Ships named for distinguished African Americans. In 1942, African Americans held just 3 percent of the jobs in defense industries; by 1945 that percentage had nearly tripled.

"Mrs. Johnson"

ABOVE AND TOP Portrait of Lucy Mercer Rutherfurd, probably painted by her friend Elizabeth Shoumatoff; the page from the White House usher's diary for June 5, 1941, in which she first appears under the name "Mrs. Johnson." The president spent an hour and a half with her that day between visits to the bedside of Missy LeHand, who had suffered a stroke the night before.

On June 5, 1941, a new name appeared on FDR's appointment calendar: "Mrs. Johnson." Only Missy LeHand and a few other members of the president's innermost circle knew her true identity.

Back in 1918, Roosevelt had promised his wife he would never see his old love Lucy Mercer again and she had married Winthrop Rutherfurd, a wealthy widower far older than she. But she and the president had quietly kept in touch. He'd made sure she had a ticket to each of his inaugurations. White House operators had orders to put through calls from "Mrs. Johnson."

Now Lucy's husband, whom she had cared for faithfully for years, had been incapacitated by illness, and Franklin had invited her to come and see him at the White House. Eleanor was away. Lucy was discreetly led in a back way and ushered upstairs to the president's Oval Study.

The evening before Mrs. Rutherfurd's first visit, the president's personal secretary, Missy LeHand, who had always seen herself as the closest person to the man she called F.D., had collapsed at a staff party. She had suffered the first of two strokes that would rob her of the power of speech. She was put to bed in her room on the third floor of the White House. Roosevelt was wheeled in every day to visit. She did not improve, was sent to Warm Springs, brought back to the White House, and finally moved back in with her family in Somerville, Massachusetts.

As always, Roosevelt did his best to hide his feelings. But he quietly called in his lawyer and changed his will so that, in the event of his death, half of his estate would go to pay for her care. "I owed her that much," he told his son James. "She served me so well for so long and asked so little in return."

Meanwhile, Lucy Rutherfurd continued to come to the White House from time to time for tea or dinner, and sometimes she and the president took quiet rides together through Rock Creek Park—always when Eleanor was out of town.

ABOVE Missy LeHand in the White House Rose Garden. She loved and admired her boss, but she was also "the frankest of his associates," the president's speechwriter Samuel Rosenman remembered, "never hesitating to tell him unpleasant truths or to express an unfavorable opinion about his work."

Making a Get-Away

ABOVE FDR, braced against the ship's rail and holding the arm of his son Elliott, formally receives from Winston Churchill a letter of introduction from King George VI, August 9, 1941. "At last—we've gotten together," the president said. Churchill nodded, "We have." "There was warmth there on the deck from the start," one of the prime minister's aides recalled. (Elliott Roosevelt wears the uniform of a captain in the U.S. Army Air Corps; Franklin Jr., behind the prime minister, was a junior naval officer; all four Roosevelt sons were already in the service.)

All his life, FDR loved knowing secrets no one else knew, and so nothing pleased him more than to be able to sail north undetected to meet for the first time with the prime minister of Great Britain on August 3, 1941. The White House fed a cover story to the press that FDR was simply taking a few days off at sea, "away from the tension of duties which the critical international situation has made unusually wearing." Even Eleanor was fooled.

Roosevelt couldn't conceal his glee when writing to Daisy about it from aboard the USS *Augusta*, two days later:

> Even at my ripe old age I feel a thrill in making a get-away—especially from the American press. . . . Curiously enough the [presidential yacht] *Potomac* still flies my flag and tonight will be seen by thousands as she passes through the Cape Cod Canal . . . while in fact the President will be about 250 miles away.

It took four more days to reach the rendezvous point off Newfoundland in Argentia Bay. There, he told Daisy on August 9,

The huge new H.M.S. *Prince of Wales* came up the bay with two escorting corvettes and anchored alongside of us at 9:30. . . . Winston Churchill came on board at eleven. . . . We all met on the top deck and were duly photographed and then Churchill stayed on board and lunched with me alone. He is a tremendously vital person and in many ways is an English Mayor La Guardia. Don't say I said so! I like him—and lunching alone broke the ice both ways.

Their partnership would become one of the most important in history. During three days of talks, Roosevelt pledged more Lend-Lease aid, and promised that the U.S. Navy would help shield North Atlantic convoys from Nazi attack off the coast of Iceland, but he still could not commit American forces to the struggle against Hitler.

He and Churchill issued what became known as the Atlantic Charter. It called for "the final destruction of the Nazi tyranny," but also promised a postwar world in which every nation controlled its own destiny, an end to the kind of colonialism Winston Churchill had stood for all his life.

As the conference at sea ended, back in Washington Congress extended the tours of duty of draftees from twelve months to thirty—but by just a single vote. Had it not done so, it would have dangerously weakened the newly built army.

ABOVE Roosevelt, Churchill, their aides, and top commanders attend church services on the quarterdeck of HMS *Prince of Wales*. Churchill chose three hymns he was sure both Britons and Americans would know: "Eternal Father, Strong to Save," "O God, Our Help in Ages Past," and "Onward, Christian Soldiers." Churchill wept as they sang. "If nothing else had happened while we were here," Roosevelt told Elliott afterward, "that would have cemented us. 'Onward Christian Soldiers' we *are* and we *will* go on with God's help." "Nearly half those who sang were soon to die," Churchill later wrote; the Japanese would sink the *Prince of Wales* in early 1942. The slender civilian behind the prime minister is Harry Hopkins, whom FDR had secretly sent to London to arrange the meeting at sea.

He Was Always "My Boy . . ."

On Saturday morning, September 6, 1941, FDR made an unscheduled visit to Springwood. Sara Delano Roosevelt, now eighty-six, was failing. As always, she was eager to see him. "When my son comes and sits there beside me with the smile that is *not* reserved for the voters," she'd once told a friend, "I just look at his face and think it has everything—wisdom, goodness and sweetness."

He was rolled into her room and spent the day with her, telling her about his talks with Churchill, talking over old times, pausing only to read dispatches from the White House. Late that evening, she lapsed into a coma. She died of heart failure the following afternoon. A few minutes later, without wind or rain or lightning, the greatest of all the great oak trees on the Roosevelt estate groaned and toppled to the ground. Geologists would later blame an especially thin layer of earth that blanketed a base of solid rock, but those who had known Sara Delano Roosevelt were not so sure.

She was buried in the little graveyard behind St. James' Church where her husband had been laid to rest forty-one years earlier.

Eleanor Roosevelt wrote a friend that while she personally felt "no deep affection or sense of loss" at her mother-in-law's death, "it is hard on Franklin."

It *was* hard—and whenever he could in the coming years he, and sometimes his daughter, Anna, would stop by the grave of the mother who had taught him to believe he would succeed at whatever he set out to do, that no task was too great for him to take on.

Daisy Suckley understood the depth of his loss. "That big house without his mother seems awfully big and bare," she wrote. "She gave him that personal affection which his friends and secretaries cannot do in the same way. He was always 'my boy,' and he seems to me often rather pathetic, and hungry for just that kind of thing. . . . His wife is a wonderful person, but she lacks the ability to give him the things his mother gave him. She is away so much, and when she is here she has so many people around—the splendid people who are trying to do good and improve the world—the 'uplifters,' the President calls them—that he cannot relax and really rest."

The president's worshipful cousin had once dreamed of living with Franklin in the hilltop cottage she'd helped him plan. The war and the third term had shattered that dream. But FDR gave her a job as archivist in his new library so that she could be with him whenever he felt the need of quiet, admiring company. And she looked after Fala, the mischievous Scottie that was now the most celebrated dog on earth.

OPPOSITE A portrait of Sara Delano Roosevelt and her son, taken at Springwood toward the end of her life by the Philadelphia photographer Elias Goldensky. "I have always thought Franklin perfectly extraordinary," she once said, "and as I look back I don't think he has ever disappointed me."

ABOVE Daisy Suckley on her fiftieth birthday, photographed by FDR in his Oval Study at the White House. The lion skin on which she and Fala sit was given to FDR by the emperor of Ethiopia, Haile Selassie.

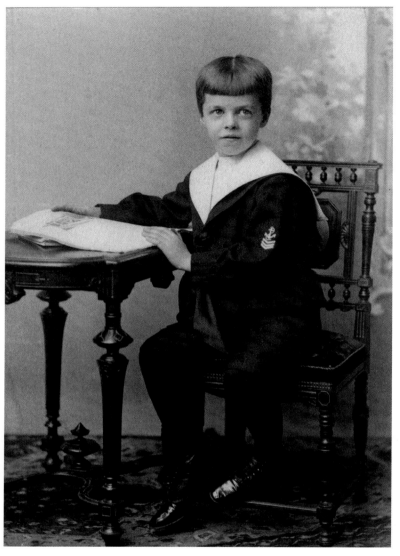

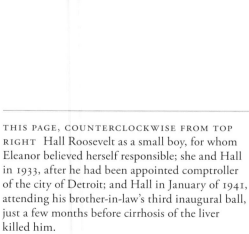

THIS PAGE, COUNTERCLOCKWISE FROM TOP
RIGHT Hall Roosevelt as a small boy, for whom
Eleanor believed herself responsible; she and Hall
in 1933, after he had been appointed comptroller
of the city of Detroit; and Hall in January of 1941,
attending his brother-in-law's third inaugural ball,
just a few months before cirrhosis of the liver
killed him.

My Idea of Hell

Eleanor Roosevelt suffered a loss of her own that same month. Hall Roosevelt, the younger brother for whom she'd felt responsible since the early deaths of their parents, died in a Washington hospital as she sat helpless at his bedside. He had been bright and promising when young, filled with all the Roosevelt energy, and had become an able engineer and city official. But the curse of alcoholism that had killed his father destroyed him, too.

"My idea of hell if I believed in it," Eleanor confided to her friend Joe Lash before the end came, "would be to sit . . . and watch someone breathing hard, struggling for words when a gleam of consciousness returns and thinking 'this was once the little boy I played with and scolded, he could have been so much and *this* is what he is.'"

On the morning of September 29—less than two weeks after her mother-in-law died, just two days after burying her brother—Eleanor left the White House grounds without an escort and walked eight blocks north to Dupont Circle to a brand-new office and a brand-new job. New York Mayor Fiorello La Guardia, director of the newly created Office of Civilian Defense, had asked her to become his unsalaried assistant in charge of civilian volunteers.

She saw her new job as a chance to keep the spirit of the New Deal alive—even under the threat of war. Effective defense, she insisted, demanded "better nutrition, better housing, better day-to-day medical care, better education, better recreation for every age."

But she quickly ran into trouble. Federal agencies resisted incursions onto their territory. Southern mayors resented her determination to recruit black as well as white volunteers. When she hired a dancer friend to help with physical training, Congress passed a resolution meant to ridicule her by banning the use of public funds for "fan-dancing."

"Mrs. Roosevelt," a Michigan woman wrote to her, "you would be doing a great service if you would simply go home and sew for the Red Cross. Every time you open your mouth the people of this country dislike and mistrust you more."

Within four months Eleanor Roosevelt would feel she had no choice but to resign. "People can . . . understand that an individual, even if she is a President's wife, may have independent views and must be allowed the expression of an opinion," she told a friend. "But actual participation in the work of the government, we are not yet able to accept."

TOP, LEFT Eleanor and Fiorello La Guardia at the Office of Civilian Defense on the day she was sworn in as his assistant, September 29, 1941

TOP, RIGHT Mayris Chaney meets the press on the day her friend the first lady appointed her to develop a recreational dance program for children in bomb shelters. A vaudeville performer who had entertained at the White House and invented a dance called the "Eleanor Glide," she was maligned on the House floor as a "strip-teaser."

ABOVE "Those Americans sure can attack . . . themselves!" The cartoonist Theodore Seuss Geisel, better known as "Dr. Seuss," criticized the first lady's critics in the liberal newspaper PM in early 1942.

Whatever Is Asked of Us

On Sunday morning, December 7, 1941, Japanese planes attacked Pearl Harbor. All afternoon news reports repeated the same meager information. The president did not plan to address Congress until the following day.

But that evening, on her weekly radio program, it fell to the first lady of the United States to try to reassure her frightened fellow citizens about what lay ahead.

TOP Black smoke pours from wrecked American warships, including the battleships USS *West Virginia* and USS *Tennessee*, at Pearl Harbor, December 7, 1941. Eighteen American ships were destroyed or heavily damaged that morning; 188 airplanes were destroyed on the ground; and 2,340 U.S. servicemen and 48 civilians were killed.

ABOVE White House reporters race for the telephones with official word of the Japanese attack.

OPPOSITE Eleanor Roosevelt in the studio from which she spoke to the American people on Sunday evening, December 7, 1941. She had been broadcasting every Sunday since October on a program sponsored by the Pan-American Coffee Bureau and carried by more NBC outlets across the country than the popular comedy program *Fibber McGee and Molly*.

Ladies and gentlemen, I'm speaking to you at a very serious moment in our history. The Cabinet is convening and the leaders in Congress are meeting with the President. The State Department and Army and Navy officials have been with the President all afternoon.

For months now the knowledge that something of this kind might happen has been hanging over our heads and yet it seemed impossible to believe, impossible to drop the everyday things of life and feel that there was only one thing which was important—preparation to meet an enemy no matter where he struck. That is all over now and there is no more uncertainty.

We know what we have to face and we know that we are ready to face it.

I should like to say just a word to the women in the country tonight. I have a boy at sea on a destroyer, for all I know he may be on his way to the Pacific. . . . Many of you all over this country have boys in the services who will now be called upon to go into action. . . . You cannot escape a clutch of fear at your heart and yet I hope . . . you [will] rise above these fears.

Whatever is asked of us I am sure we can accomplish it. We are the free and unconquerable people of the United States of America.

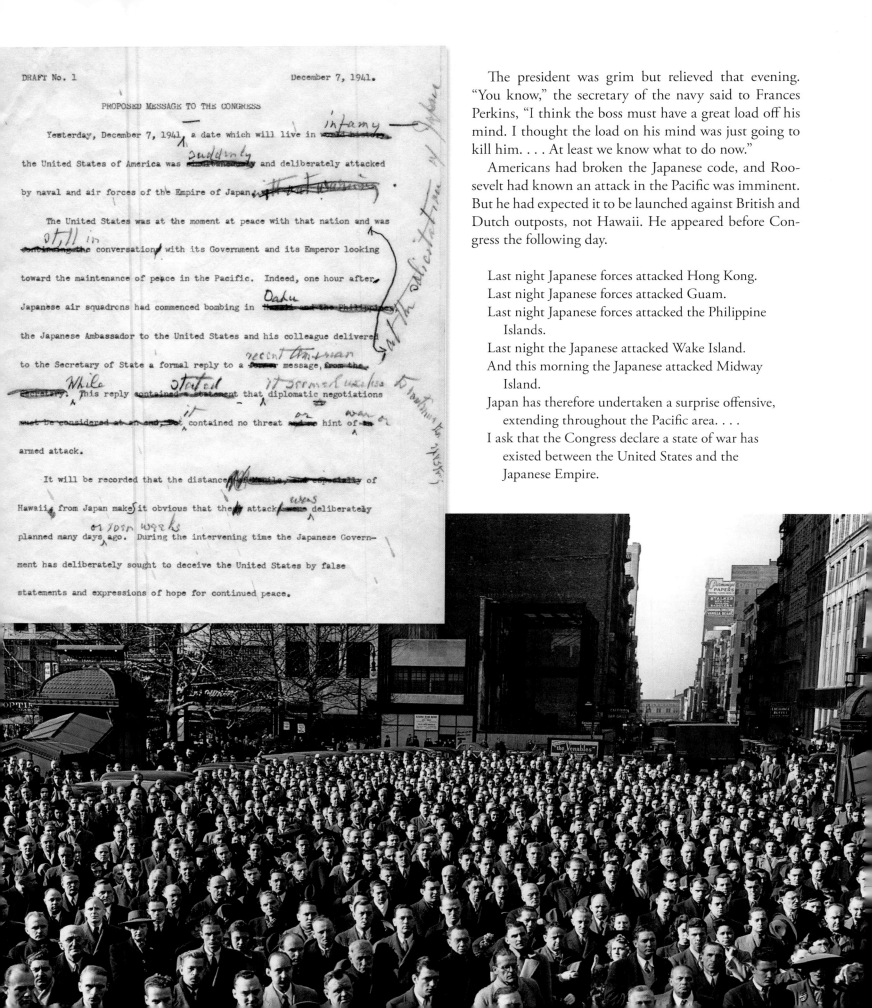

The president was grim but relieved that evening. "You know," the secretary of the navy said to Frances Perkins, "I think the boss must have a great load off his mind. I thought the load on his mind was just going to kill him. . . . At least we know what to do now."

Americans had broken the Japanese code, and Roosevelt had known an attack in the Pacific was imminent. But he had expected it to be launched against British and Dutch outposts, not Hawaii. He appeared before Congress the following day.

Last night Japanese forces attacked Hong Kong.
Last night Japanese forces attacked Guam.
Last night Japanese forces attacked the Philippine Islands.
Last night the Japanese attacked Wake Island.
And this morning the Japanese attacked Midway Island.
Japan has therefore undertaken a surprise offensive, extending throughout the Pacific area. . . .
I ask that the Congress declare a state of war has existed between the United States and the Japanese Empire.

On December 11, Hitler and Mussolini, siding with their Japanese ally, declared war on the United States. That same day, surrounded by senators and congressmen of both parties, FDR would sign the declaration of war.

Alice Longworth's initial reaction to the attack on Pearl Harbor had been characteristically acid. "Well, friends," she told some luncheon guests, "Franklin asked for it, now he's got it." But two weeks after Pearl Harbor, fifty-four-year-old Ted Roosevelt had asked to see the president and then told the press, "This is our country, our war and our president." He had long since resigned from America First and was already in uniform as commander of his old outfit, the 26th Infantry.

All four of FDR's sons had volunteered. So did all three of Theodore Roosevelt's surviving sons. Six of TR's grandsons, who were old enough to serve, signed on, as well. "It seems to me," Archie Roosevelt wrote FDR, "that regardless of the bitterness that many people feel toward the 'Hyde Park' Roosevelts or the 'Oyster Bay' Roosevelts, they have to admit that the whole clan has turned out to a man. . . . It is [something] in which I think we can take a certain amount of pride."

OPPOSITE, TOP AND BOTTOM The first page of the first draft of FDR's address to Congress, with emendations in his bold hand; and grim-faced New Yorkers, many with hats over their hearts, crowd into City Hall Park to hear the president's words, December 8, 1941.

ABOVE Four days after Pearl Harbor, the president, wearing a black mourning band in honor of his late mother, looks over the declarations of war against Germany and Japan just enacted by Congress and signed by him.

Nothing to Conceal

ABOVE On December 23, 1941, reporters crowd into the Oval Office for a joint press conference by the American president and the British prime minister—so many reporters that those in back were unable to see Winston Churchill. He accommodated them by climbing onto his chair and waving his cigar while they broke into applause. Did he think the war was now "turning in our favor?" he was asked. "I can't describe the feelings of relief with which I find . . . the United States and Great Britain standing side by side. It is incredible to anyone who has lived through the months of 1940. . . . Thank God." "How long will it take to lick these boys?" another reporter asked. Once Steve Early had explained to Churchill what "licked" meant in American jargon, he was happy to answer: "If we manage it well, it will take only half as long as if we manage it badly."

On December 22, 1941—just three weeks and a day since Pearl Harbor—the White House had a surprise guest: Winston Churchill, at considerable risk, had crossed the Atlantic to confer with Franklin Roosevelt. FDR had neglected to tell his wife Churchill was coming until that morning. "It had not occurred to him," she complained, that "this might require certain moving of furniture to adapt rooms for the purposes for which the Prime Minister wished to use them."

The White House had changed since December 7. Armed sentries now kept tourists off the grounds. There were machine gun emplacements on the roof and blackout curtains over the windows.

The prime minister would be the Roosevelts' guest for three weeks. At one of their first dinners, FDR raised his glass to "the common cause, which I can now truly say is a common cause." "We live here as a big family," Churchill wired to Clement Attlee, "and I have formed the very highest regard and admiration for the President." Night after night, the two men sat up until two

or three in the morning. Churchill needed little sleep but lots of alcohol: sherry before breakfast; Scotch and soda before lunch; champagne and brandy in the evening.

Eleanor Roosevelt disapproved of the drinking and the late hours and worried about the prime minister's unshakable devotion to the sprawling British empire, which both she and her husband believed should not be allowed to survive long after the war. But she liked him. He and her husband, she said, "looked like boys playing soldier. They seemed to be having a wonderful time."

Once, according to Harry Hopkins, the president came up with what he thought was a grand idea: the twenty-six countries now pledged to subscribe to the principles of the Atlantic Charter should be called the "United Nations." He had himself wheeled across the hall and entered his distinguished guest's bedroom without knocking so that he could tell him about it. Churchill had just climbed out of the bathtub, naked, pink, and gleaming. FDR apologized for bursting in. Nothing to apologize for, Churchill said. "The Prime Minister of Great Britain has nothing to conceal from the President of the United States."

ABOVE FDR and Churchill at the lighting of the White House Christmas tree. The Secret Service had urged the president to cancel the event, but he insisted on going ahead with it as a sign of continuity in wartime. "This is a strange Christmas Eve," Churchill told the crowd of twenty thousand. "Almost the whole world is locked in deadly struggle, and, with the most terrible weapons which science can devise, the nations advance upon each other." But for this one night, he continued, "the cares and dangers that beset us" should "be cast aside: Let the children have their night of fun and laughter. Let the gifts of Father Christmas delight their play. Let us grown-ups share to the full in their unstinted pleasures before we turn again to the stern task and the formidable years that lie before us, resolved that, by our sacrifice and daring, these same children shall not be robbed of their inheritance or denied their right to live in a free and decent world."

ABOVE Winston Churchill, flanked by British and American security men, strides toward the U.S. Capitol, where he was to address a joint session of Congress, December 26, 1941. In his speech, he questioned the sanity of the rulers of Japan: "What kind of people do they think we are?" he asked. "Is it possible they do not realize that we shall never cease to persevere against them until they have been taught a lesson which they and the world will never forget?" Senators and congressmen, Republicans as well as Democrats, rose and roared their approval.

OPPOSITE, TOP On the evening of February 23, 1942, FDR reenacts for the newsreel cameras a portion of the radio address he has just finished. In it, he explained that "the broad oceans which have been heralded in the past as our protection from attack have become endless battlefields."

OPPOSITE, BOTTOM A mother and grandmother in Singapore weep over children killed by Japanese bombs. The fall of the prize British colony—and the surrender of eighty thousand British and colonial troops there—on February 15, 1942, was nearly as devastating to the British as Pearl Harbor had been to Americans. It was "a heavy and far-reaching military defeat," Churchill told his people, but also an opportunity to demonstrate their "quality and their genius."

Roosevelt and Churchill received the war news together. It was all bad. In the Pacific theater, Japanese troops had landed in Thailand and Singapore, Burma and Borneo, Hong Kong and the Philippines—where they were driving American forces down the Bataan Peninsula. The American public was clamoring for revenge.

On the other side of the globe, the Germans occupied almost all of Europe and were threatening Egypt and the Suez Canal in North Africa, engaging the Russians along a thousand-mile front, and sinking Allied ships in the North Atlantic faster than they could be replaced.

Before Churchill returned to Britain, Roosevelt and he agreed that Germany, with its vast armies and mighty industrial machine, would have to be defeated first. But it would take time to mobilize, train, and equip a force powerful enough to destroy Hitler's armies. Until then, the Allies would have to remain on the defensive in the Pacific.

On February 23, FDR spoke to the country for the first time since Pearl Harbor. More than sixty-one million adults tuned in—80 percent of those who had access to a radio. He asked his listeners to have a world map at hand so that he could explain what was happening where, and what "the overall strategy has to be."

The United States was fighting "a new kind of war," he told them, fought on "every continent, every island, every sea, every air-lane in the world." The months ahead would not be easy. Sacrifices would be required of everyone. "But your government has unmistakable confidence in your ability to hear

the worst without flinching or losing heart." And once America's productive genius was fully mobilized, Roosevelt told his listeners, it would provide the Allies "the overwhelming superiority of military materiel necessary for ultimate triumph. . . . From Berlin, and Tokyo and Rome, we have been described as a Nation of weaklings, playboys, who would hire British soldiers, or Russian soldiers, or Chinese soldiers to do our fighting for us. [L]et them tell that to General MacArthur and his men. . . . Let them tell it to the boys in the Flying Fortresses. Let them tell that to the Marines!"

The speech was so effective, so reassuring, that an old friend urged Roosevelt to speak more often over the radio. FDR demurred: "The one thing I dread is that my talks should be so frequent as to lose their effectiveness."

Executive Order 9066

Within hours of Pearl Harbor, FDR issued identical proclamations authorizing the arrest and detention of any German, Italian, or Japanese noncitizens thought to be a threat to American security. All "enemy aliens" were required to register and were forbidden to own weapons, cameras, or shortwave radios or to move about after dark. Some eleven thousand Germans and more than three thousand Italians would be detained over the course of the war. Italians were officially struck from the enemy alien list on Columbus Day, 1943; "I don't care about the Italians," FDR told his attorney general, Francis Biddle. "They are a lot of opera singers."

But Japanese aliens—and American citizens of Japanese descent—living along the West Coast received far harsher treatment. On February 19, 1942, FDR signed Executive Order 9066. Its tone was carefully neutral: it authorized the War Department to designate "military areas" and then exclude anyone from them whom it felt to be a danger. But all the people of Japanese ancestry living along the West Coast were the real target. "A Jap's a Jap,"

said General John L. DeWitt, of the Western Defense Command. "It makes no difference whether he is an American citizen or not. I don't want any of them." His views mirrored those of many West Coast whites, whose resentment of hardworking Japanese immigrants and their offspring was decades old.

Over the course of the next few months, somewhere between 110,000 and 120,000 men, women, and children, two-thirds of them U.S. citizens whom the government renamed "non-aliens" to make their treatment seem less egregious, would be forced from their homes and businesses and interned in one or another of ten camps scattered across seven states. Armed guards and barbed wire ensured that no one got out.

Almost no one protested the government's plan, which also initially classified all Japanese Americans as unfit for military service. (Later, young internees would be allowed to form their own segregated outfit, the much-honored 442nd Regimental Combat Team.)

The FBI insisted that there was no justification for Roosevelt's action, and not a single documented wartime case of espionage would ever be registered against a Japanese American. But there is no evidence that the president ever regretted signing Executive Order 9066.

ABOVE, LEFT Two brothers wait atop their family's belongings for the bus that will take them from their home in Los Angeles to the hastily constructed assembly center at the Santa Anita Racetrack, where they would stay until housing was readied for them at Manzanar in the California desert.

ABOVE "Waiting for the Signal From Home." Millions of Americans across the political spectrum initially believed that no Japanese American living along the West Coast could be trusted, that somehow Pearl Harbor could never have happened without their help. This cartoon by Dr. Seuss appeared in the liberal New York newspaper *PM*, February 13, 1942, six days before FDR signed Executive Order 9066.

Roosevelt, C. in C.

The initial German invasion of the Soviet Union had stalled outside Moscow, but a summer offensive in 1942 sent 225 fresh divisions—more than four and a half million men—racing across Russia, and Joseph Stalin demanded that the Allies open a second front in western Europe to relieve the pressure on his beleaguered people.

American planners had a straightforward idea of how to beat the Germans: invade France in the spring of 1943 and drive right for Berlin.

But the British, haunted by memories of the butchery on the Western Front in the Great War, were wary of moving so fast: a defeat on the French coast, Churchill warned, was "the only way in which we could possibly lose this war." Instead, he favored attacking German and Italian forces in North Africa to keep Egypt and the oil fields of the Middle East from falling into enemy hands.

American commanders thought invading Africa would be a dangerous, wasteful diversion. Rather than accept the British plan, General Marshall proposed that the United States abandon the Germany-first strategy and go on the offensive in the Pacific.

Roosevelt overruled him. A premature attack in the Pacific was exactly what Germany wanted, he wrote; it would only mean the recapture of a "lot of islands," and would do nothing to help the Russians. The proposal was therefore "disapproved." He signed his response "Roosevelt, C. in C."—Commander in Chief.

ABOVE The president's handwritten note overruling his army chief of staff: "General Marshall. Copy to Admiral [Ernest J.] King [chief of naval operations] and General [Henry "Hap"] Arnold [commander, U.S. Army Air Force]. I have carefully read your estimate of Sunday. My first impression is that it is exactly what Germany hoped the United States would do following Pearl Harbor. Secondly, it does not in fact provide use of American troops in fighting except in a lot of islands whose occupation will not affect the world situation this year or next. Third: it does not help Russia or the Near East.

'Therefore it is disapproved as of the present.

'Roosevelt C. in C."

OPPOSITE A Russian woman watches helplessly as her home, set ablaze by advancing German troops, burns to the ground in the late spring of 1942.

ABOVE American troops surrender at Corregidor, May 6, 1942. That evening, their commander, General Jonathan Wainwright, wired President Roosevelt: "With broken heart and head bowed in sadness but not in shame I report to your excellency that today I must arrange terms for the surrender of the fortified islands of Manila Bay. . . . With profound regret and with continued pride in my gallant troops I go to meet the Japanese commander. Good-bye Mr. President." The Philippines had now fallen to Japan.

OPPOSITE, TOP The White House map room, modeled after a traveling version that Winston Churchill had brought with him to Washington. It was manned by army personnel twenty-four hours a day, and FDR had himself wheeled in frequently to get the latest war news.

OPPOSITE, BOTTOM FDR, Daisy Suckley, and fellow birders enjoy what Daisy called "the bird chorus at dawn," at Thompson's Pond, Dutchess County, May 10, 1942.

The invasion of occupied France would have to be delayed. Preparations began for American troops to land in North Africa. News from the Pacific continued to be bad.

But even the president's critics were astonished at his serenity.

Once he had made a decision, nothing seemed to faze him. Franklin had learned from his struggle against polio, his wife said, "that if there was nothing you could do about a situation, then you'd better try to put it out of your mind."

The president worked at his stamp collection, chatted with visitors, and presided over a carefree cocktail hour every afternoon.

He established his own secret map room in a former ladies' cloakroom in the White House basement so that he could personally follow the movements of American ships and armies. A special pin marked the whereabouts of the destroyer aboard which his son Franklin was serving. When Roosevelt was rolled into the map room every morning that was always the first pin he looked for.

Wartime security allowed the president to spend as much time as possible out of public sight and away from the White House—in the cottage he'd

built for himself at Warm Springs; at a new hideaway in the Catoctin Mountains of Maryland that he called "Shangri-La," which would later come to be called Camp David; and at home at Springwood, where the grounds were now patrolled day and night.

He was there on May 6 when he learned that Corregidor, the last American outpost in the Philippines, had surrendered.

Just four days later, before dawn, he, Daisy Suckley, and a handful of aides and Secret Servicemen drove to a nearby pond to take part in the annual census of Dutchess County birds. From the backseat of his car, a seemingly unconcerned FDR claimed to have identified 108 species—22 of them by their songs alone. Daisy was delighted: "He seemed really to enjoy every minute. It is the kind of thing he has privately given up any idea of ever doing again, so it did him lots of good. In that far-off silent place, with myriads of birds waking up, it was quite impossible to think much of the horrors of war."

TOP, LEFT The first lady smashes a champagne bottle over the bow of the brand-new liner SS *America* at Newport News, Virginia, in 1939. Acquired by the navy and renamed the USS *West Point* in 1941, she became a transport ship and carried 350,000 U.S. troops to and from battle over the course of the war, more than any other vessel.

TOP, RIGHT The Boy Scouts of Stevens Point, Wisconsin, answer the president's call for rubber with eighty tons of old tires.

ABOVE The 1,500-ton submarine USS *Peto* is launched sideways into Lake Michigan by the Manitowoc Shipbuilding Company at Manitowoc, Wisconsin, 1941. She would see action in the Pacific and survive the war.

Here's Our Answer President Roosevelt

Congress granted Roosevelt sweeping wartime powers to reorganize American industry, and he made the most of them. The result was improvised, inconsistent, and often inefficient—six new federal agencies with overlapping responsibilities were established in a single year. But it would ultimately make possible the defeat of Germany, Italy, and Japan.

"If you are going to try to . . . prepare for war in a capitalist country," Secretary of War Stimson said, "you have to let business make money out of the process."

FDR now found himself working hand in glove with many of the "economic royalists" whose hatred he'd welcomed just five years earlier.

The biggest companies got the biggest contracts—and earned the biggest profits. Antitrust laws were overlooked. Taxes on ordinary Americans rose.

Again and again, the president urged industry to greater efforts. When advisers handed him estimates of what they thought could realistically be achieved, he crossed them out and wrote in larger numbers of his own. "The production people can do it if they really try," he said. They did try—and they did do it.

Idle factories were soon back in business. Nearly all manufacturing was converted to the war effort. In 1941, more than three million cars had been manufactured in the United States. Only 139 more were made during the entire war. Instead, Chrysler made fuselages; General Motors made airplane engines, guns, trucks, and tanks. And at its vast Willow Run plant in Ypsilanti, Michigan—sixty-seven acres of assembly lines under a single roof that one observer called "the Grand Canyon of the mechanized world"—the Ford

Motor Company performed something like a miracle, twenty-four hours a day. The average Ford car had some 15,000 parts. The B-24 Liberator long-range bomber had 1,550,000 parts. By 1944, one was coming off the line at Willow Run every sixty-three minutes.

War mobilization would give the Allies the "crushing superiority" in arms Roosevelt insisted they needed for victory. It also brought the Great Depression to an end, creating so many new jobs so fast that for the first time in a generation there was soon a labor shortage in the United States.

TOP, LEFT B-24 Liberator bombers lined up at the Ford Willow Run plant, 1943. The following year, American workers would produce 96,318 warplanes, exceeding the combined output of Britain, Germany, and Japan.

TOP, RIGHT New jeeps parked and ready for shipment overseas, outside the Willys-Overland plant in Toledo, Ohio. Before the war ended, some 640,000 of them would roll off the assembly lines.

LEFT Women welders at work in a U.S. shipyard. Initially, shipbuilders were often reluctant to hire them, but they quickly proved their worth. "Let me tell you," said one personnel director, "it takes stuff to handle a welding arc all day long—stuff and skill."

ABOVE Artillery shells stored at the Picatinny Arsenal in Dover, New Jersey, 1940. Four years later, the United States would be producing 60 percent of all Allied munitions and 40 percent of the world's total arms.

Dear God, Please Make Eleanor a Little Tired

ABOVE, LEFT AND RIGHT Eleanor Roosevelt during her three-week whirlwind tour of Great Britain in the fall of 1942: she salutes during a lightning visit to her son Elliott's photo-reconnaissance unit at Steeple Morden, not far from Cambridge, and meets with flag-waving workers at a Women's Voluntary Services nursery in London. During the nursery visit, a British reporter asked if she ever relaxed, slept late, or missed an appointment. "Not since I can remember," she said. "Why do you ask?" "Because," the newspaperman said, "I wish you would [rest] now—because *I'm* tired out."

A wartime Washington story had it that the president prayed every night, "Dear God, please make Eleanor a little tired." The story was apocryphal, but the sentiment was understandable. Eleanor Roosevelt shared her husband's sense of urgency about American defense, and, like any other mother, she had wept when her boys went off to war. But she was also unhappy with what seemed to her to be FDR's abandonment of reform.

The president was "Dr. Win-the-War" now, he explained, no longer "Dr. New Deal." He made only token objections when Congress voted to end the Civilian Conservation Corps, the Works Progress Administration, and the National Youth Administration. Further domestic progress would have to wait until the fighting ended.

Eleanor could not easily accept that decision. For her, the challenge was to defeat fascism abroad while extending the benefits of democracy at home to every citizen regardless of color, creed, or sex.

If her husband was no longer interested in listening to other New Dealers, she would speak for them. "No one who ever saw Eleanor Roosevelt . . . facing her husband," an aide remembered, "and, holding his eye firmly, say to him, 'Franklin, I think you should . . .' or, 'Franklin, surely you will not . . .' will ever forget the experience."

She was an early and enthusiastic champion of women in war industries. "I'm pretty old, 57 you know, to tell girls what to do with their lives," she

said, "but if were a debutante of a certain age I would go into a factory—and any factory where I could learn a skill and be useful." Eventually, women would comprise 60 percent of the workforce in defense industries.

In the spring of 1943, word reached the White House that conditions within the Japanese American relocation camps were breeding dangerous resentment, that internees who had once been willing to accept the government's policy "philosophically" were growing increasingly angry at their government for keeping them behind barbed wire. FDR sent Eleanor to the Gila River Relocation Center near River, Arizona, to assess conditions for herself. She had loyally supported her husband's decision to sign Executive Order 9066—"I regret the need to evacuate," she told a friend, "but I recognize it has to be done"—but had subsequently learned that there had been no truth to the early stories of spying and sabotage by Japanese Americans.

She came away from her visit convinced that all internees should be allowed to return to their homes and resume their lives, and was only dissuaded from bringing an interned family home to live in the White House when the president told her the Secret Service would not allow it. Internment had been a "mistake," she told him, and mistakes needed to be "corrected."

The president never conceded that he'd made a mistake, and he ordered that any internees whom the War Department deemed likely to be trouble-makers be segregated in a single camp near Tulelake, California, but he also

JUST DON'T BE SURPRISED, THAT'S ALL

MY DAY HAS BEEN RATHER A BUSY ONE...

TOP, LEFT AND RIGHT Eleanor meets internees at the Gila River Relocation Center and inspects their camp with Dillon S. Myer, director of the War Relocation Authority, April 1943. Both agreed that all ten internment camps should be closed as soon as possible. "This is just one more reason to hate war," she told a friend. "Innocent people suffer for a few guilty ones."

ABOVE The first lady's propensity for turning up in unexpected places delighted the press. Herblock's cartoon "Just Don't Be Surprised, That's All" was published by the Newspaper Enterprise Association during Eleanor's visit to England, the first overseas trip ever taken by a first lady on her own.

agreed that individuals who had jobs and homes to go to could begin to leave the camps, along with young men willing to join the army. (Still, he did not agree to close the camps until after the 1944 election.)

Eleanor was also painfully aware of the absurdity of continuing to ask young African Americans to fight for democracy while serving in armed forces that were still stubbornly segregated. She did all she could behind the scenes to improve things.

She often cautioned black citizens to be patient—and some young African Americans criticized her bitterly for it—but her unshakable devotion to their cause infuriated some whites. When black women in the South began giving up their jobs as domestics for better pay in defense industries, the rumor spread that they belonged to secret "Eleanor Clubs" devoted to getting black women out of white kitchens. When the FBI found the rumors baseless, she was relieved: "Instead of forming clubs of that kind," she wrote, "they should enter a union and make their household work a profession."

During the war, hundreds of thousands of black Americans moved north, where they found defense jobs—and encountered trouble from a society not yet willing to accommodate them. In 1943 alone there were race riots in forty-seven cities. Some blamed the first lady for all of it. "It is blood on your hands, Mrs. Roosevelt," wrote the editor of the *Daily News* in Jackson, Mississippi. "You have been personally proclaiming and practicing social equality at the White House and wherever you go. What followed is now history."

"Unless we make the country worth fighting for by Negroes," she answered her critics, "we [will] have nothing to offer the world at the end of the war."

ABOVE Over the protests of the Secret Service, flight instructor Charles A. Anderson, the first African American ever to earn an air transport license, prepares to take the first lady for an hour's flight above the Tuskegee Army Air Field at Tuskegee, Alabama. Eleanor's advocacy—and this photograph—helped persuade her husband to approve combat missions for the all-black 99th Fighter Squadron, which came to be called the Tuskegee Airmen. They would distinguish themselves escorting bombers over North Africa and Europe.

LEFT, TOP AND BOTTOM The first lady pins a medal on a black serviceman in Seattle, 1943, and shakes the hand of an African American delegate to a Democratic Women's Council meeting in Pittsburgh the following year. When a white woman wrote to ask if she had "colored blood in your family as you seem to derive so much pleasure from associating with colored folks," Eleanor answered, "I haven't as yet discovered . . . any colored blood, but, of course, if any of us go back far enough, I suppose we can find that we all stem from the same beginnings."

ABOVE A black man, already bleeding from a beating, tries to outrun his tormentors during a three-day Detroit race riot that left thirty-four dead and ended only after FDR sent in federal troops in June 1943. Afterward, there were calls for the president to address the nation about race. He demurred, convinced, Eleanor explained to a disappointed friend, that "he must not irritate the southern leaders as he feels he needs their votes for essential war bills."

We Are Dealing with an Insane Man

leanor Roosevelt had also continued to argue on behalf of admitting Jewish refugees to the United States for as long as the Nazis were willing to grant them exit visas. Restrictive immigration laws frustrated her. So did the actions of obstructionists within the State Department—some genuinely concerned that German or Soviet spies would slip into the country along with genuine refugees, some blatantly anti-Semitic—who erected what Albert Einstein called "a wall of bureaucratic measures" meant to keep refugees out.

"I do not know what we can do to save the Jews of Europe and to find them homes," Eleanor wrote in 1943, "but I do know that we will be the sufferers if we let great wrongs occur without extending ourselves to correct them."

From FDR's point of view, he and the Allies were already extending themselves. No other world leader reacted more decisively to Nazi crimes against Jews than Franklin Roosevelt did. In 1938, he had called for an international conference to deal with the refugee problem, only to find that no Western nation was willing to admit significant numbers of Jewish refugees. Later that year, he found himself the sole leader of a democratic nation willing to call home his ambassador and denounce Nazi brutality following *Kristallnacht* and was made the target afterward of bigots at home and in Berlin for doing the bidding of international Jewry.

In 1942, when rumors began to filter out of occupied Europe that the Nazis had moved from mistreatment of the Jews to mass murder, they were met at first with disbelief; the State Department thought they were of a "fantastic nature," reminiscent of the false propaganda employed by both sides in the First World War. But when Rabbi Stephen S. Wise and the heads of four major Jewish organizations presented Roosevelt with irrefutable proof, the president agreed to warn the Nazis that they would be held to "strict accountability." Just nine days later, he persuaded Churchill and Stalin to join him in promising to prosecute as "war criminals" those responsible for what they called this "bestial policy of cold-blooded extermination."

But he also asked the rabbis while they were still in the Oval Office for suggestions as to what more he could do to save European Jewry. They had no answer. Hitler remained the master of Europe. The Jews were his prisoners—and his intended victims. "We are dealing with an insane man," FDR told his visitors. "Hitler and the men around him represent . . . a national psychopathic case. We cannot act toward them by normal means." In the end, he believed there was nothing he could do other than work night and day to obliterate that madman and his monstrous regime.

Then, in 1944, persuaded by his friend and secretary of the treasury, Henry Morgenthau Jr., he created the War Refugee Board, which authorized funds to help Jews flee from the edges of the crumbling Nazi empire. As many as 200,000 men, women, and children may have been saved—a minute fraction compared to those who were murdered, but more than any other Allied agency managed to rescue.

ABOVE Breckinridge Long, the assistant secretary of state in charge of immigration. In 1940, he wrote a memorandum urging consular officials to block efforts to assist endangered Jews hoping to find sanctuary in America: "We can delay and effectively stop . . . the number of immigrants into the United States," he wrote, "by simply advising our consuls to put every obstacle in the way . . . and to resort to various administrative devices which would postpone . . . the granting of the visas."

OPPOSITE A Ukrainian Jew, about to be shot by an SS executioner, kneels at the edge of a mass grave near the town of Vinnitsa, September 22, 1941. This snapshot, made by another SS man, was pasted in his personal album and labeled "The Last Jew of Vinnitsa." Twenty-eight thousand other Jewish men, women, and children had already been slaughtered in and around the town. Within a few months, secret plans would be under way for what Hermann Göring was the first to call the "final solution of the Jewish question"—the systematic, mechanized extermination of the Jews of Europe.

Unconditional Surrender

On Saturday, November 8, 1942, FDR, Daisy Suckley, Harry Hopkins, and a handful of others were spending the weekend at "Shangri-La," hidden in the Catoctin National Forest, seventy-five miles from Washington.

"For weeks," Daisy noted in her journal, "the P[resident] has had something exciting up his sleeve. Only a handful knew about it. . . . He spoke of an egg about to be hatched. . . . After dinner, as we were getting settled in chairs, [the president] . . . said at nine that something will break on the radio . . . and at nine we got the news of the landing of our troops on North Africa. . . . It was thrilling and for the President it was a tremendous climax."

The simultaneous landings in Morocco, Algiers, and Tunisia went smoothly and came as a complete surprise to the enemy. Casualties were low. "Thank God!" Roosevelt said. "Thank God!"

It took just four days to force the Vichy French to agree to an armistice, but their German and Italian allies proved far more formidable foes and the raw U.S. troops soon found the fighting that followed much tougher than they'd expected. Elliott Roosevelt, who had pulled strings to get into combat despite his bad eyesight, was among those fighting there, piloting unarmed reconnaissance planes again and again over enemy territory. It would take seven bloody months to drive the enemy from North Africa.

In January of 1943, Roosevelt and Churchill made their way to the war zone, to Casablanca in Morocco, where FDR declared the Allies united in their goal—nothing less than "unconditional surrender."

In the Pacific, American naval forces had already badly damaged the Japanese fleet at Midway. The Marines had captured most of Guadalcanal—though at a fearful cost—and had raided Makin Island, too, where the president's eldest son, Major James Roosevelt, was awarded the Navy Cross for "extraordinary heroism."

Within a few weeks, the Nazi invasion of the Soviet Union would finally be halted at Stalingrad.

Allied troops would soon invade Sicily—where Franklin Jr.'s destroyer would be badly damaged. He would win the Silver Star for carrying one of his wounded sailors to safety under fire.

Then the Allies would have to begin the long, bloody struggle to take Italy. But the cross-Channel invasion of France that the Russians were demanding—and that everyone including the enemy knew had to come—had been postponed yet again and was still more than a year away.

OPPOSITE GIs about to land in North Africa as part of Operation Torch, fulfilling Roosevelt's pledge that American troops would at last be fighting the Germans somewhere in 1942

ABOVE From a lofty tower in Marrakesh, Roosevelt delights in the sunset over the roofs and minarets of the city and the snow-covered slopes of the Atlas Mountains beyond them. Churchill, just visible in the shadow, thought this "the most lovely spot in the whole world" and encouraged the president to allow himself to be carried up sixty steps to see it for himself.

The Bottom Has Dropped Out

Kermit and I are much alike," Theodore Roosevelt once said of his second son. Kermit shared his father's love of books and adventure. He helped build bridges and railroads in Brazil, accompanied his father to Africa and down the Rio Roosevelt, shot tigers in Nepal and bears in Alaska, and wrote vivid books about it all. But he lacked his father's ambition, could not find a way to outpace the depression that he also inherited, and never quite got over his father's death: "You well know," he told his mother afterward, "how the bottom has dropped out for me."

He married an heiress with whom he had four children, but he disliked the social whirl she loved. He launched a steamship line but was never much interested in business, and lost most of his wife's fortune in the Depression.

He began to drink far too much and took up with a mistress, just as his uncle Elliott had. When the war began he rejoined his old British regiment as a major in the hope that having a real mission might steady him. He fought bravely against the Germans in Norway, and served in North Africa until ill health forced him home. When he was picked up by the police too drunk to stand, his brother Archie had him committed to a sanitarium for a time.

In the summer of 1942, his wife appealed to FDR to find something for him to do. The president sent him to an air base in Alaska where he was to help establish a Territorial Guard of Aleuts and Eskimos to serve as guerrilla fighters in case of Japanese invasion—just the kind of assignment his father would have relished.

It was too late. On May 31, 1943, U.S. forces destroyed the enemy garrison on the island of Attu in the Aleutians. The Japanese threat to Alaska had been lifted. Four days later, Kermit put his service revolver under his chin and pulled the trigger. A telegram explained that he had killed himself "due to despondence resulting from exclusion from combat duties."

It was thought best to tell his mother, Edith—eighty-one years old and still living at Sagamore Hill—that he had died of a heart attack.

ABOVE, LEFT AND RIGHT Major Kermit Roosevelt in Alaska, still hoping for action against a Japanese invasion force that would never come, and the simple marker on his grave at Fort Richardson

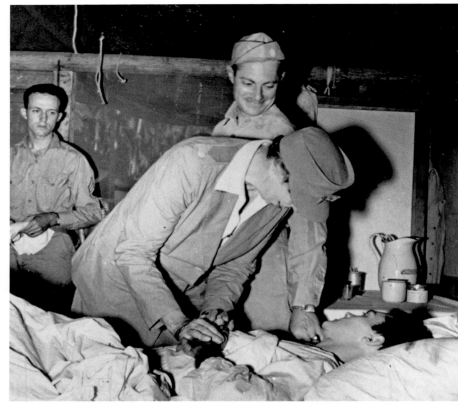

An American Mother

In the summer of 1943, Eleanor Roosevelt undertook a five-week 25,000-mile trip to the South Pacific on behalf of the Red Cross. She had no illusions about how it would be received by her husband's enemies at home. "This trip will be attacked as a political gesture," she told a friend, "and I am so uncertain whether or not I am doing the right thing that I will start with a heavy heart. . . . I'll go because other people think I should . . . and where I do see our soldiers I'll try to make them feel that Franklin really wants to know about them."

She did just that in Hawaii, Australia, and New Zealand and on seventeen other Pacific islands, including Bora Bora, Samoa, Fiji, New Caledonia, Christmas Island—and Guadalcanal, where she got to see her young friend Joe Lash, now a sergeant in the army.

Admiral William F. "Bull" Halsey, commander in the South Pacific, had been against her coming. He had a war to fight, he said, and no time to waste welcoming a visiting "do-gooder." But when the first lady turned up and went to work, Halsey quickly changed his mind.

Here is what Eleanor Roosevelt did in twelve hours: she inspected two Navy hospitals, took a boat to an officer's rest home and had lunch there, returned and inspected an Army hospital, reviewed the 2nd Marine Raider

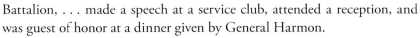
Battalion, . . . made a speech at a service club, attended a reception, and was guest of honor at a dinner given by General Harmon.

When I say that she inspected those hospitals, I don't mean that she shook hands with the chief medical officer, glanced into a sunroom and left. I mean that she went into every ward, stopped at every bed, and spoke to every patient: What was his name? How did he feel? Was there anything he needed? Could she take a message home for him? I marveled at her hardihood, both physical and mental. . . . And she saw patients who were grievously and gruesomely wounded. But I marveled most at their expressions as she leaned over them. It was a sight I will never forget.

"Over here," one soldier said, "she was something . . . none of us had seen in over a year, an American mother." The family of every wounded soldier and sailor she visited got a personal letter. But, just as her experience with the wounded of World War I had affected her, it took weeks for her to get over the impact of the horrors she had seen. To the end of her life, she would remember the smell of the burn wards.

When she got back, just as she had predicted, Republicans attacked her for junketeering at the public's expense. "The outcry in Congress is so great," she confided to a friend, "that FDR feels I should not use Government transportation or even go on any [long] trips for awhile. . . . Later, I'm sure he'll say go ahead again, but just now it seems he wants a little peace."

CLOCKWISE FROM OPPOSITE BOTTOM Eleanor Roosevelt in the Pacific: speaking to troops; with Admiral William "Bull" Halsey, who began as her critic and became an admirer; visiting a wounded soldier; receiving three cheers aboard ship; and examining the wreckage of a downed Japanese plane.

TOP The first lady's trip drew enough worldwide attention that a Nazi cartoonist was assigned to produce a series of vicious caricatures of her. The German caption beneath this one reads, "I was the first white woman that the Americans stationed on the Pacific Island had seen for ten months."

The Final Authority

At the end of November 1943, the president set out on a demanding eight-thousand-mile journey by sea and air, first to Cairo, where he conferred again with Churchill, and then on to Tehran, Persia (now Iran), to meet for the first time with Soviet Premier Joseph Stalin.

Stalin was surprised to see the extent of the president's handicap. "Tell the president that I now understand what it has meant for him to make the effort to come on such a long journey," he told his interpreter. "Tell him the next time I will go to him."

The Soviet dictator was taciturn, guarded, and perpetually suspicious, but FDR was convinced the Roosevelt charm that had worked so well for him throughout his career would work with Stalin, as well.

The bargaining was often tense.

Stalin, whose Red Army was still bearing the brunt of the fighting, was determined to hold on to the eastern European countries his men were capturing as they pushed the Germans back toward Berlin. And he insisted upon the fastest possible opening of a second front in western Europe.

Churchill resisted, still hoping an assault on France could be delayed or somehow avoided altogether.

Roosevelt, an aide remembered, "sat in the middle, by common consent the moderator, arbitrator and final authority."

In the end, the Big Three set the stage for victory. The Americans and British would invade occupied France in the spring of 1944. The Soviets would mount a simultaneous offensive from the east. The hope was that the Nazis would be crushed between them. Once the Germans had been defeated, the Soviet Union would enter the war against Japan.

At the final dinner, each of the leaders toasted the other two. Then, Stalin asked to make another toast—to the special contribution made by Roosevelt and the United States. "The most important things in this war are the machines," he said. "The United States is a country of machines. Without the use of those machines, through Lend-Lease, we would lose this war."

But even with all those machines, victory in Europe—and in the Pacific—still seemed a long way off.

OPPOSITE FDR and General Dwight D. Eisenhower review troops at Castelvetrano, Sicily, December 8, 1943. The preceding day, the president had named Eisenhower to command Overlord, the long-delayed Allied assault on western Europe. "Eisenhower is the best politician among the military men," the president explained to his son James. "He is a natural leader who can convince other men to follow him, and this is what we need in his position more than any other quality."

TOP Together at last, the Big Three—Stalin, Roosevelt, and Churchill—in Tehran

ABOVE Roosevelt returns from the Tehran conference, greeted by (left to right) Senate Majority Leader Alben Barkley, House Majority Leader John McCormack of Massachusetts, Vice President Henry Wallace, and House Speaker Sam Rayburn of Texas.

There Must Be Something Definitely Wrong

Roosevelt returned from Tehran exhausted and suffering from what Admiral Ross McIntire, his physician and the surgeon general, diagnosed as the flu. Weeks went by. He did not get better. Grace Tully, his longtime secretary, who had taken over for Missy LeHand, noticed that his hands now shook so badly that he had trouble lighting his cigarettes and he sometimes seemed to doze for a moment during dictation.

She and Daisy Suckley were worried. So was the president's daughter, Anna. With her second husband overseas, she had recently moved back into the White House with her children, and—with her mother often away—was now acting as her father's hostess.

All three women feared that Admiral McIntire was not up to the job of caring for the president. His expertise was sinuses.

Something else was wrong, and Anna insisted on answers. On March 27, 1944, her father agreed to be wheeled into Bethesda Naval Hospital for an off-the-record examination by the chief of cardiology, Lieutenant Commander Howard G. Bruenn.

The doctor was horrified by what he found: the president was suffering from congestive heart failure. His heart was "markedly enlarged"; he was short of breath; and he was suffering from severe hypertension, for which there was then no effective treatment. Four days later, three senior physicians confirmed the diagnosis.

To reduce and slow the heart and to ease the strain on it, FDR was prescribed digitalis and put on a diet. He was told to cut his smoking in half and urged not to work more than four hours a day.

Everyone was sworn to the strictest secrecy.

Admiral McIntire assured the press that FDR just had a touch of persistent bronchitis; "for a man of 62-plus," he said, he was doing fine.

"I am more worried than I let anyone know," Daisy Suckley confided to her diary. "There must be something definitely wrong or they wouldn't have these consultations."

Nineteen forty-four was another presidential election year. The cross-Channel invasion of Europe was still weeks away. American forces had only just begun to fight their way island by island across the Pacific toward Japan. And, although just a handful of people knew it, the commander in chief—the most powerful man on earth—was seriously, perhaps fatally, ill.

LEFT Dr. Howard Bruenn's notes of his first meeting with FDR, during which he diagnosed congestive heart failure, March 27, 1944, and the determinedly optimistic White House statement on the president's health as it appeared in the *New York Times* three days later

OPPOSITE Bundled against the cold, the president and Mrs. Roosevelt lay a wreath at the Lincoln Memorial on Lincoln's Birthday, February 12, 1944. Daisy Suckley feared that his drive in an open car on a wintry day would be bad for FDR. He had a constant headache, she wrote. "I feel it must come from being constantly tired—never getting *really* rested, specially since having the flu."

CHAPTER 7

A Strong and Active Faith

1944–1962

A Very Quiet Time

In April of 1944, in the midst of the Second World War, the president of the United States seemed to have vanished. Wartime security had obscured Franklin Roosevelt's movements ever since the Japanese attack on Pearl Harbor, but this was different. He was said to be vacationing "somewhere in the South," getting over a bout of bronchitis.

Actually, he was resting on the sprawling South Carolina estate of the financier Bernard M. Baruch. Coast Guard men and Marines guarded the perimeter. He had been secretly diagnosed with congestive heart failure, and his doctors feared for his life.

Reporters from the three wire services, housed eight miles away, were told nothing about the president's actual condition, and were rarely able even to lay eyes on him. They were told to "stay out of the old man's way," Merriman Smith of the United Press recalled. "He wanted seclusion and lots of it."

FDR's uncharacteristic silence was interrupted by embarrassing headlines about him and his family.

Elliott's second wife won a divorce on the grounds of "unkind, harsh and tyrannical" treatment. When his sons Marine Lieutenant Colonel James Roosevelt and Navy Lieutenant Commander Franklin Roosevelt Jr. both received promotions, Republican newspapers charged favoritism. Despite the courage all of the Roosevelt boys had shown in combat, GOP congressmen routinely attacked their war records, claiming that they were somehow being protected against harm. Elliott Roosevelt, who won the Distinguished Flying Cross, had written to his father that "I sometimes really hope that one of us gets killed so that . . . they'll stop picking on the rest of the family."

Democratic Senator Harry S. Truman of Missouri insisted that the White House respond formally to a letter from a constituent claiming that Mrs. Roosevelt was using four cars and burning up two thousand gallons of precious rationed gasoline a month, gallivanting around the country. Montana Senator Burton K. Wheeler, an isolationist Democrat who had long since broken with the president, predicted that FDR's health would prevent him from running again, adding, "I wouldn't vote for my own brother for a fourth term."

TOP In a frame from a home movie made by one of the president's guards, two aides lean over FDR, who has been carried out to the beach for a little time in the sun.

ABOVE Portraits of the president's sons in uniform that Roosevelt kept on his White House desk throughout the war: (left to right, top to bottom) Elliott, James, Franklin Jr., and John

Franklin and Eleanor Roosevelt had already occupied the White House for more than eleven years. Millions of Americans could remember no other first family, and had a hard time imagining another, especially so long as the country—and the world—were still at war.

FDR wanted to see the struggle through to victory—and then to do what Woodrow Wilson had been unable to do after the First World War: bring the United States into a new international organization strong enough to ensure that the world would not go to war again. Then, he told his devoted cousin Daisy Suckley, he thought he might break yet another presidential precedent and retire from office before his fourth term ended.

Meanwhile, he would maintain the strictest secrecy about his own condition—even from his wife. "I wouldn't discuss [the President's health] with him," she recalled, "because I hated the idea and he knew I hated it. Either he felt he ought to serve a fourth term and wanted it or he didn't. That was up to the man himself to decide and no one else."

When FDR finally returned to the White House, Daisy Suckley and Anna were relieved to see that a month in South Carolina had cleared up the president's supposed "bronchitis."

"Everyone wanted to greet the President and see how he looked and felt," Daisy wrote on May 10. "Anna and I held long talks about his 'routine,' and how difficult it is going to be to keep him to it. Anna . . . had the brilliant thought of suggesting a nice cool lunch on the porch. . . . The lawn looking 'green as green.' The President looked across at the Jefferson Memorial and decided to give instructions for trimming the trees back, [for the] vista."

FDR did his best to follow his doctor's regimen and was pleased to be los-

ing weight because it would allow him more easily to stand in his braces. But he remained listless and easily tired.

Despite his frailty and the relentless demands of the continuing struggle overseas, Roosevelt had ambitious postwar plans for his country. In his latest State of the Union message, he had called for a new "Economic Bill of Rights" that would guarantee to every American a living wage, a decent home, a good education, and adequate medical care. "Unless there is security here at home," he said, "there cannot be a lasting peace in the world."

The GI Bill of Rights—signed by the president after it was passed by Congress without a single dissenting vote—would provide almost eight million returning veterans with vocational or college educations, help more than two million more to buy new homes, and offer other kinds of loans to launch hundreds of thousands of new businesses. No other single piece of legislation would do more to expand the American middle class.

Eleanor applauded her husband's renewed call for reform and was determined to make sure he did not abandon it. But she thought he was exaggerating his medical condition for attention and complained that by dining alone with Anna and Daisy he was cut off from the dissenters she had always invited to speak their minds to him over the dinner table.

FDR craved company—but not that kind. He asked Anna if she would quietly arrange to have Lucy Rutherfurd come to dinner again. One evening, Franklin Jr., home on leave, returned to the White House unannounced and was startled to find his father in the Oval Study, a strange woman massaging his legs. He had no idea who she was. His father simply said, "This is an old friend." They shook hands, and the younger Roosevelt went on his way. Years later, he realized it had been Mrs. Rutherfurd.

OPPOSITE, TOP The Roosevelts in 1944. There were times, their daughter, Anna, remembered, when it was clear that FDR's blood was not pumping the way it should. "I saw this with my own eyes, but I don't think Mother saw it. . . . [She wasn't] interested in physiology."

OPPOSITE, LEFT FDR on his return from Hobcaw, May 7, 1944. "Brown as a berry, radiant and happy," William Hassett noted in his diary. "But he is thin and although his color is good I fear that he has not entirely shaken the effects of the flu, followed by bronchitis, which have bedeviled him for many weeks now."

ABOVE Roosevelt signs the GI Bill of Rights, June 22, 1944. "Lack of money," he said, "should not prevent any veteran of this war from equipping himself for the most useful employment for which his aptitude and willingness qualify him." Among the legislators crowded into the Oval Office for the ceremony is Republican Congresswoman Edith N. Rogers of Massachusetts, who helped draft and then cosponsored the bill.

Pride of Our Nation

On the morning of May 19, 1944, the president and Daisy Suckley drove up to Top Cottage to see the dogwood in bloom. By then, the world had been waiting nearly thirty months for the Allies to launch their invasion of Nazi-occupied western Europe. "We put a couple of chairs in the sun, north of the porch," she wrote, "and just talked quietly about the view, the dogwood, a little about the coming invasion of Europe. Next week is the time, the exact date depending on wind and weather and tide. . . . How that event hangs over us—has been hanging over us for months—and here it is, almost at hand."

In the end, the invasion began with five coordinated landings along the coast of Normandy on June 6, 1944—D-Day. As the attacks started, FDR broadcast a prayer he'd written with help from Anna and her husband, John Boettiger.

> Almighty God: Our sons, pride of our nation, this day have set upon a mighty endeavor, a struggle to preserve our Republic, our religion and our civilization, and to set free a suffering humanity. Lead them straight and true; give strength to their arms, stoutness to their hearts, steadfastness in their faith. They will need Thy blessings. Their road will be long and hard for the enemy is strong. He may hurl back our forces. Success may not come with rushing speed, but we shall return again and again; and we know that by Thy grace, and by the righteousness of our cause, our sons will triumph.

The American commander who had been assigned to take Utah Beach on D-Day was the oldest man in the invasion force: fifty-seven-year-old Brigadier General Theodore Roosevelt Jr., the oldest son of the twenty-sixth president of the United States and the fifth cousin of the thirty-second. Drifting smoke that had obscured the target and strong currents that drove their landing craft off course had brought his men onto Utah Beach more than two thousand yards from the spot chosen by the D-Day planners. Roosevelt limped badly from arthritis and his World War I wounds, but he refused to seek cover. He had explained to his wife, "It steadies the young men to know that I am with them, plodding along with my cane." He rallied his men who took the beachhead in less than an hour, then accompanied them as they fought their way inland, despite sporadic chest pains that he kept to himself. A little over a month later, he died of a massive heart attack.

"Ted's death did something to me from which I shall not recover," Edith Roosevelt told her daughter Ethel. She had now outlived her husband and three out of four of her boys.

Theodore Roosevelt Jr. was posthumously awarded the Medal of Honor for gallantry and courage at Utah Beach, the same medal his father had once sought for himself after the battle of San Juan Hill.

OPPOSITE, TOP FDR and Fala, photographed by Daisy Suckley at Top Cottage, where he alerted her to the imminent cross-Channel invasion

OPPOSITE, BOTTOM Brigadier General Theodore Roosevelt Jr. and his battered jeep, "Rough Rider," photographed in Sicily, where he fought before taking part in the D-Day landings. "We've had a grand life," he wrote to his wife on the eve of the invasion, "and I hope there'll be more. Should it chance that there's not, at least we can say that in our lives together we've packed enough for ten ordinary lives."

ABOVE AND LEFT D-Day, June 6, 1944, the ramp falls and a rifle company of the 18th Infantry Division steps off into the surf at Omaha Beach in the face of deadly fire from the cliffs above; a stunned GI shivers on the shale after making it to cover.

The Berkshire Evening Eagle, Pittsfield, Mass. Friday, July 21, 1944.   Page Three

President Urges Government Be Left in Experienced Hands

Roosevelt Accepts Democratic Nomination

Says Great Task Ahead Is To Prevent Any Future Wars From Disrupting Our Lives

WITH PRESIDENT ROOSEVELT AT A PACIFIC COAST NAVAL BASE (UP)—President Roosevelt, climaxing a cross-country trip made in tight war-time secrecy, last night accepted the Democratic presidential nomination for the fourth term, speaking from an undisclosed Pacific Coast naval base and warning the country not to "turn over this 1944 job—this world-wide job—to inexperienced and immature hands."

Text of Speech

The text of the President's speech follows:

Members of the convention, my friends:

I have already indicated to you why I accept the nomination which you have offered me—in spite of my desire to retire to the quiet of a private life.

You in this convention are aware of what I have sought to gain for the nation, and you have asked me to continue.

It seems wholly likely that within the next four years our armed forces, and those of our allies, will have gained a complete victory over Germany and Japan, and that the world once more will be at peace—under a system, we hope, which will prevent a new world war. In any event, new hands will then have full opportunity to realize the ideals which we seek.

I shall not campaign in the usual sense, for the office. In these days of tragic sorrow, I do not consider it fitting. Besides, in these days of global warfare, I shall not be able to find the time. I shall, however, feel free to report to the people the facts about matters of concern to them and especially to correct any misrepresentations.

In the last three elections the people of the United States have transcended party affiliations. Not only Democrats but also forward-looking Republicans and millions of independent voters have sought consistently—and with fair success—to advance the lot of the average American citizen who has been so forgotten during the period after the last war. I am confident that they will continue to look to that same kind of liberalism to build our economy for the future.

Obligation To Serve

I am sure that you will understand me when I say that my decision, expressed to you formally tonight, is based solely on a sense of obligation to serve if called upon to do so by the people of the United States.

...ation, improvement is necessary in other fields—in the physical things which are part of our daily lives, and also in the concepts of social justice at home and abroad.

I am now at this naval base in the performance of my duties under the constitution. The war waits for no elections. Decisions must be made...

Gabreski Bags His 31st Plane

AN AMERICAN FIGHTER BASE, England (U)—Lt. Col. Francis S. Gabreski of Oil City, Pa., America's leading air ace, destroyed a twin-engined German...

Polish Concert At Vatican Honors Sikorski

ROME—The Polish victory at Ancona and the first anniversary of former Premier Gen. Wladislaw Sikorski's death provided...

PRESIDENT ROOSEVELT FROM A PACIFIC COAST NAVAL BASE, accepts nomination for a fourth term. In the car with him are his son and daughter-in-law, Col. and Mrs. James Roosevelt. (INP Soundphoto.)

FUEHRER ADOLF HITLER, left, talks with Reichsminister Herman Goering, second from right, and Adjt. Col. Schmundt, right, in this German photo captioned as made at Hitler's headquarters on the Western Front in 1940. It was announced in Berlin July 30 that Hitler suffered "slight burns and bruises" in a bomb attempt on his life. The British radio said that Hitler also sustained a brain concussion. A Lt. Gen. Schmundt was reported "seriously injured," presumably the adjutant colonel shown in this photo.

Democratic Platform
Abstract of Party's Promises

CHICAGO STADIUM (AP)—The Democratic national convention adopted a platform last night calling for American participation in an international peace-preserving organization and pledging continuation and improvement of the present administration's domestic program.

The platform promised the "earliest possible release" of war...

...was ready to stand or fall on President Roosevelt's record.

The platform pledged party support to the Atlantic Charter and the four freedoms—freedom of speech, freedom of worship, freedom from fear and freedom from want.

On domestic policy, the statement of party principles and philosophy embodied in a large...

The Contrariest Goddamn Mule

Two days after D-Day, Admiral McIntire, the president's official physician, issued one of his cheery periodic bulletins: the president's health, he assured the press, was "excellent in all respects."

As the Democratic convention approached, fewer and fewer Democratic insiders believed him. But the Allies had not yet begun to fight their way through the hedgerows that boxed them in behind the Normandy beaches, and in the Pacific, American forces were still months away from beginning the campaign to retake the Philippines.

No one was willing publicly to admit that Roosevelt was too ill to survive a fourth term. But now the choice of a vice presidential candidate assumed an importance it had never had before.

Conservatives insisted on replacing the liberal Henry Wallace. Even some of Wallace's supporters found him dreamy, impractical, aloof.

Eleanor Roosevelt wrote a column praising him. The president told her not to publish it until the convention was over.

He took no public position on who should be his running mate, but this time made no objection to the choice of the party's more moderate leaders: Missouri Senator Harry S. Truman, who initially said he had no interest in the job.

On July 20, the day the delegates were to nominate their vice presidential candidate in Chicago, the president was in San Diego, on his way to Hawaii for a conference about strategy in the Pacific.

He telephoned Robert Hannegan, chairman of the Democratic

National Committee. "Have you got that guy lined up yet on that Vice President?" he asked.

"No," Hannegan answered. "He's the contrariest goddam mule from Missouri I ever saw."

"Well," FDR said, "you tell him if he wants to break up the Democratic party in the middle of the war and maybe lose that war, it's up to him."

Truman gave in.

Roosevelt accepted his party's nomination from his railroad car on a siding in San Diego. An Associated Press photographer caught him looking especially gaunt and slack-jawed. The picture startled newspaper readers across the country, and the president's press secretary kicked the photographer off the train. But Walter Trohan, a reporter for the *Chicago Tribune,* noticed something else in the uncropped picture: a uniformed stranger who turned out to be FDR's cardiologist, Lieutenant Commander Howard Bruenn, assigned to be at the president's side wherever he went. Rumors that Roosevelt was even sicker than he looked began to spread.

On Sunday evening, July 30, 1944, in Somerville, Massachusetts, Missy LeHand was taken to the movies. She had suffered two serious strokes three years earlier, but seemed to be improving. Then she saw the newsreel of FDR accepting his party's nomination aboard his railroad car in San Diego. She hadn't seen him for nearly a year. He looked like a different man—haggard and ill.

Back home from the theater, Missy leafed through pictures of them both when they were young. That night, she suffered a third stroke. She died the following day.

OPPOSITE, BOTTOM Democratic convention delegates cheer their presidential candidate for the fourth time. FDR himself was less enthusiastic. "His mind was on the war," James remembered. "His attitude toward the coming political campaign was one of, 'let's get on with it.'"

OPPOSITE, TOP AND ABOVE, LEFT The cropped photograph of a frail-looking president accepting his party's nomination from San Diego, as it appeared in most newspapers, and the uncropped original that revealed to one sharp-eyed reporter that a navy cardiologist, Dr. Howard Bruenn (lower left), was in attendance.

BELOW Roosevelt and Truman lunch on the South Lawn of the White House, August 18, 1944, so that photographers can take pictures of them together. Truman noticed that the president's hand trembled so badly he poured more cream into his saucer than into his tea.

To David from a girl he never knew

Eleanor Roosevelt

A Girl He Never Knew

Throughout her public life, Eleanor Roosevelt had always had a small circle of friends in whom she could confide her private thoughts and feelings: Nancy Cook and Marion Dickerman, Earl Miller, Lorena Hickok, Joseph Lash and his wife, Trude.

Now, a new friend was often at her side, her New York physician, an expert on polio, eighteen years younger than she, named David Gurewitsch.

He became her confidant and constant companion as well as her doctor. Her friend Esther Lape, who had known her since her first forays into reform, believed he was "dearer to [her] than anyone else in the world." "I love you," Eleanor once wrote him, "as I love and have never loved anyone else."

When Dr. Gurewitsch became engaged to a young woman named Edna Perkel, it took both women a little time to adjust. Mrs. Roosevelt and the Gurewitsches eventually bought a house together at 55 East Seventy-fourth Street, just nine blocks from the twin brownstones Sara Delano Roosevelt had built for herself, Eleanor, and Franklin more than half a century before.

"Mrs. Roosevelt never had dinner alone if she could help it," Edna Gurewitsch remembered, "because she was, as David said, 'A chronically lonely person.'" One evening, early in their time together, she continued, "Mrs. Roosevelt came upstairs, she marched into the kitchen and said, 'May I help you, dear?' And my heart sank because Mrs. Roosevelt had no clue about what happens in a kitchen. So I thought she could do the least harm if I asked her to wash the lettuce. And so she stood beside me at the sink washing lettuce. And I said after a few moments, 'Would you excuse me, Mrs. Roosevelt?' I went in to my husband and I said to David, 'Find an excuse to get her out of the kitchen because we're standing in water up to our ankles.' And she never helped me in the kitchen again."

OPPOSITE AND TOP A photograph of Eleanor at fourteen, given by her to David Gurewitsch with the inscription, "To David from a girl he never knew. Eleanor Roosevelt"; and a photograph of David Gurewitsch, which she carried with her wherever she went. "Above all others," she once told him, "you are the one to whom my heart is tied."

RIGHT The East Side townhouse Eleanor Roosevelt shared with David and Edna Gurewitsch from 1959 until her death

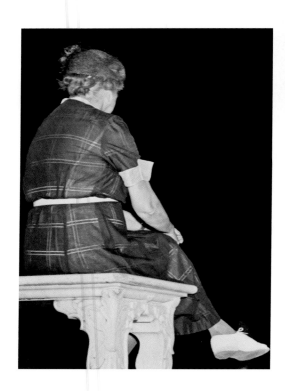

We Will Have to Talk

The constant travel that had won Eleanor Roosevelt both admiration and criticism during her time in the White House only accelerated after she left it. She was often away from home two weeks out of every month, delivered some 150 speeches each year, and undertaking journey after fact-finding journey overseas, serving as an unofficial ambassador for her country. Israel, Pakistan, India, Indonesia, Japan, Morocco, the Soviet Union—she seemed to be everywhere, taking note of everything, asking what she could do to help. She was an American phenomenon, said one admiring Indian diplomat, "comparable to Niagara Falls."

She had few illusions about the Soviet government or about American communists: in 1947, she'd helped found the liberal Americans for Democratic Action, which specifically barred them from membership, and she opposed her old friend Henry Wallace's third-party bid for the presidency the following year in part because she believed communists had too great an influence on his campaign.

But she was a reluctant Cold Warrior and continued to share her husband's hope that a way could be found to build a lasting peace. She championed economic rather than military aid to the Third World, pleaded for greater understanding of the needs and wishes of people newly freed from colonialism, and urged Washington to do less reacting to Soviet actions and undertake more initiatives of its own.

And through it all, she sought to remind the American people that one could oppose communism without demonizing communists or undermining the civil liberties that were the hallmark of American democracy. If Americans grew to fear one another, she said at her seventieth birthday party, they

would never succeed: "I would like to see us take hold of ourselves, look at ourselves and cease being afraid."

When criticized for continuing to urge dialogue with Moscow when relations with Washington were especially tense, she was unrepentant: "We have to face the fact that either all of us are going to die together or we are going to learn to live together and if we are to live together we will have to talk."

ABOVE Mrs. Roosevelt interviews Soviet premier Nikita Khrushchev on the porch of his summer house in Yalta. Afterward, Khrushchev asked his visitor if he could tell the press they'd had "a friendly conversation." She answered, "You can say that we had a friendly conversation but that we differed." The premier smiled. "At least we didn't shoot each other," he said.

LEFT The canvas suitcase, marked with the initials "E.R.," that accompanied Eleanor Roosevelt wherever she went.

A Liberal Conscience

Eleanor Roosevelt had been her husband's liberal conscience, always urging him to do what she saw as the right thing. During her last years, she served her party—and her country—in the same role.

Over the next decade she continued her work on behalf of civil rights—championing integration of the armed forces, applauding the integration of the schools, publicizing instances of discrimination, supporting the Freedom Riders, and ignoring the death threats that never stopped coming her way.

In 1949, Mrs. Roosevelt had found herself in conflict with Cardinal Francis Spellman of New York. She backed a bill—on constitutional grounds—that barred parochial schools from receiving direct aid from the federal government. The cardinal denounced her as anti-Catholic, and went on to accuse her of actions "unworthy of an American mother." Her friends were furious on her behalf. She remained cool in her response. "The final judgment, my dear cardinal, of the worthiness of all human beings is in the hands of God." In the end, the cardinal had to call upon her at Val-Kill to make his peace.

She was not intimidated by Senator Joseph McCarthy's anti-communist crusade, either. "The day I'm afraid to sit down with people I do not know," she said, "because five years from now someone will say five of those people were Communists and therefore [I am] a Communist—that will be a bad day."

She had bad days of her own, most often connected with her troubled children, whose continuing problems she was unable to solve. Sometimes, she confided to David Gurewitsch, they brought her close to suicide.

As always, her work was her salvation.

ABOVE At a Val-Kill picnic, Mrs. Roosevelt speaks with one of the boys from the Wiltwyck School, an interracial home for troubled youth located across the Hudson in Esopus, New York, for which she helped raise funds for many years.

RIGHT The pistol permit Mrs. Roosevelt carried in her wallet and presumably had renewed annually after 1933, when the Secret Service insisted that she carry a revolver whenever she was not under their protection.

TOP, RIGHT A "Saralee Doll," created in the early 1950s so that black children could have a doll to play with that looked like themselves, and enthusiastically promoted by Mrs. Roosevelt as "a lesson in equality for little children, . . . [and a contribution] to race pride without condescension."

OPPOSITE Mrs. Roosevelt works on her correspondence with her last secretary, Maureen Corr. Every letter was answered no matter how late it got: "Usefulness, whatever form it may take," she once wrote, "is the price we should pay for . . . the privilege of being alive."

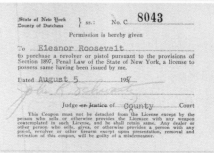

I Know Nothing of Politics

When Eleanor Roosevelt was asked a political question she didn't want to answer, she liked to say, "I know nothing of politics." In fact, she could be as politically shrewd—and as unforgiving—as her old friend and political mentor Louis Howe had been.

In 1954, when her son Franklin was denied the Democratic nomination for governor of New York by the boss of Tammany Hall, Carmine De Sapio, she vowed to get even. In order to get ahead more than forty years earlier, her husband had made peace with the Tammany boss of his era. This time, his widow had other ideas. It took her six years, but she helped establish a reform organization to combat boss rule, campaigned from the roofs of sound trucks in the summer heat, and eventually ended the career of the man who'd double-crossed her son. "I told Carmine I would get him for what he did to Franklin," she told a reporter on election night, "and get him I did."

In 1956, she helped the worldly, well-traveled governor of Illinois, Adlai Stevenson, win the Democratic presidential nomination for the second time.

It was imperative that the Democrats return to power, she said, "but they must come back with the right leaders." For her, even though Dwight Eisenhower had already beaten Stevenson once back in 1952, he was that leader, and during the campaign that followed she offered him practical advice on how to reach the voters: get to know more ordinary people, she told him, speak as if you're talking to one person; every speech need not be the Gettysburg Address.

Eisenhower crushed Stevenson again, but four years later, Eleanor was still for him—and against the front-runner, Senator John F. Kennedy of Massachusetts. She thought Kennedy too inexperienced, too willing to cut corners, too close to his father, Joseph, her husband's pre-war ambassador to the Court of St. James's, whose defeatism she had not forgotten—and she said all of this and more on television. When Kennedy complained that she was being unfair, she wired him right back. "My dear boy," she wrote. "I only say these things for your own good. I have found in [a] lifetime of adversity that when blows are rained on one, it is advisable to turn the other profile."

Stevenson proved a disappointingly tentative candidate in 1960 but Mrs. Roosevelt went to the convention in Los Angeles on his behalf anyway, hoping somehow to stop the Kennedy bandwagon. When the delegates spotted her entering the hall they stood and cheered for seven minutes. She pretended

OPPOSITE At a Memorial Day service at Springwood, Adlai Stevenson gets a little last-minute help with his prose.

ABOVE Mrs. Roosevelt in 1960. "We cannot exist as a little island of well-being in a world where two-thirds of the people go to bed hungry every night," she said just before the Democratic convention that year. "I want unity but above everything else I want a party that will fight for the things that we know to be right at home and abroad."

ABOVE Mrs. Roosevelt was warmly received in 1960 by the Democratic delegates in Miami as "the First Lady of the World," but her hopes that Adlai Stevenson would be nominated for a third time were dashed. The smiling man to her left is the convention chairman, Governor LeRoy Collins of Florida.

RIGHT Eager for Mrs. Roosevelt's approval, the Democratic presidential nominee, John F. Kennedy, lunches at Val-Kill, August 10, 1960. She endorsed him, and afterward wrote a reassuring letter to several fellow Stevenson supporters: "I gather that [Kennedy's] understanding of the difficulties of the campaign that face him have matured him in a short time. . . . I liked him better than I ever had before because he seemed so little cocksure, and I think he has a mind that is open to new ideas."

not to notice for as long as she could, because, she said, it would have been impolite to the speaker to acknowledge the applause. She later wrote him a letter of apology.

In the end, despite her efforts, Kennedy was nominated on the first ballot.

A few weeks later, the nominee arranged to call upon Mrs. Roosevelt at Val-Kill, hoping for her political blessing. The day before he was to appear, one of her granddaughters fell from a horse and was killed. Kennedy offered to cancel the meeting. She said to come ahead; she understood how difficult it was to alter a campaign schedule.

Kennedy left their lunch "absolutely smitten by this woman," a friend remembered, and she agreed to support his candidacy.

On election night, she watched the returns at her New York home. Guests came and went. When they cheered at good news from one Democratic stronghold or another she remained unmoved: "Why are they applauding?" she asked Edna Gurewitsch. "What do they expect?"

She was glad Kennedy won. But she did not hesitate to urge him on to greater efforts on behalf of peace, progress for women, and equal rights for all Americans—just as she had urged her husband on. And when she thought him wrong, she did not hesitate to criticize him, either. That, too, was what she had always done.

ABOVE Campaigning in Manhattan with Kennedy and his running mate, Lyndon B. Johnson, the evening before election day

A Good Deal of My Uncle Theodore

On Mrs. Roosevelt's seventy-seventh birthday in 1961 someone asked her if she should slow down. "I suppose I should," she said. But "I think I have a good deal of my Uncle Theodore in me, because I could not, at any age, be content to take my place in a corner by the fireside and simply look on."

But in fact she was beginning to slow down. In July of 1962, she was hospitalized for a time with intermittent fever and infections. David Gurewitsch diagnosed aplastic anemia, a rare condition in which the body fails to produce enough new blood cells.

Later that summer, she, David, Edna, and Maureen Corr, made a trip to Campobello, the island where she had had the first home she considered truly her own, and where Franklin had taught his children to sail. But it was also the place where during the Great War she had fretted over his closeness to Lucy Mercer, and where she had watched helplessly as infantile paralysis ravaged his body.

She was too frail to walk very far, but her friends helped her make it to her favorite picnic spot. She loved the island in the daytime, she said, but after dark the memories flooded back. "The night," she said, "has a thousand eyes."

She was hospitalized again when they got back to the city and grew steadily worse despite everything the doctors tried to do. When Dr. Gurewitsch told her she could still be saved, she shook her head. "David," she said, "I want to die." Life for her without being able to be useful was not worth living.

She insisted on being taken home to her apartment—and worried after she got there that she'd failed to be sufficiently grateful to the men who'd carried her stretcher.

Eleanor Roosevelt died in her own bedroom on November 7, 1962. She was seventy-eight years old.

OPPOSITE Mrs. Roosevelt in her bedroom on East Seventy-fourth Street, 1962. Pictures of friends and family members cover the wall and dresser; correspondence and articles marked for reading lie heaped on nearly every surface.

ABOVE Cutting marigolds to fill the vases in her guest rooms at Val-Kill

TOP With Edna and David Gurewitsch, picnicking on Campobello Island, August 1962. She had to be helped to stand, David remembered, but never complained and, "though her strength was rapidly dwindling, . . . was full of plans for the autumn and winter."

The Great Organizer

ABOVE Eleanor Roosevelt is laid to rest next to her husband in the Springwood rose garden, November 10, 1962. A week later, her friend Adlai Stevenson spoke at a memorial service in Manhattan: "We pray that she has found peace, and a glimpse of sunset. But today we weep for ourselves. We are lonelier, someone has gone from one's own life who was like the certainty of refuge, and someone has gone from the world who was like the certainty of honor."

OPPOSITE Three presidents and a president-to-be were among the mourners: (left to right) Jacqueline and John F. Kennedy, Vice President Lyndon Johnson, Harry and Bess Truman, Dwight Eisenhower, and, over his shoulder, Margaret Truman Daniel.

The funeral was to be held in Hyde Park. David Gurewitsch would accompany her casket up the Hudson River. Edna Gurewitsch watched from the window as the hearse moved west on Sixty-fourth Street. When it reached the corner and stopped for a red light, she recalled, "I was amazed because I couldn't believe the traffic lights were still working."

President and Mrs. Kennedy, Vice President Lyndon Johnson, and former Presidents Harry Truman and Dwight Eisenhower all watched alongside her children, her friends, and her neighbors as she was buried next to her husband in the heart of her mother-in-law's rose garden, just as Franklin had wished her to be.

It had rained all morning, Edna Gurewitsch remembered, but as everyone gathered for the final rites, "suddenly it stopped raining. There was a burst of sunshine. All of us looked at each other and smiled because we knew why that happened. And just at the close of the service, it began to rain again. And we all said the same thing, 'the Great Organizer.' Mrs. Roosevelt was 'the Great Organizer.'"

Not long before she died, Eleanor Roosevelt was asked if she believed in an afterlife. "I don't know whether I believe in a future life," she said. "I believe that all that you go through here must have some value. . . . I think I am pretty much of a fatalist. You have to accept whatever comes and the only important thing is that you meet it with courage and with the best that you have to give."

Epilogue

One hot August afternoon back in 1939, the White House press corps crowded into FDR's tiny office at Springwood. The war was then still weeks away, and there wasn't much news. The sheikh of Bahrain was coming for a visit. The president was glad that the Supreme Court had seemed more reasonable lately. The opposition in Congress was being shortsighted about national defense.

Eleanor Roosevelt happened to be there too, and she and Franklin began to reminisce about visits with Theodore Roosevelt at Sagamore Hill that each had made when they were children.

When they went swimming, Eleanor remembered, Uncle Ted always insisted that all the children *run* down the dune to Oyster Bay.

"It was awfully steep," FDR said, "the sand went down with you and you were darned lucky if you didn't end [up] halfway down, going head over heels."

And climbing back up, Eleanor recalled, you slipped down one step for every two you took. But you kept at it, and eventually the fear was worn away.

OPPOSITE The dune called Cooper's Bluff at Oyster Bay, as the Roosevelts remembered it

Acknowledgments

This book is dedicated to two great historians of the Roosevelt era, Arthur M. Schlesinger, Jr., and William E. Leuchtenburg.

In 1982, when I first set out to write about the young FDR, I wasn't at all sure I was up to the job. I'd been an editor, not a writer; had been trained as a painter, not a biographer. Arthur would have none of it. He welcomed me into the Roosevelt world, took me to lunch again and again to see what I'd uncovered lately, and then asked me shrewd questions that sent me back in search of answers. The memory of his generosity with his time and his boundless enthusiasm for the subject we shared still astonishes me.

Bill Leuchtenburg, whom I first got to know thirty-one years ago when Ken Burns asked me to try my hand at writing a film about Huey Long, has been an adviser on every project we've worked on together since. He is omniscient about the Roosevelts and their America—and pretty nearly omniscient about everything that happened here before and after them, as well. But more than an adviser, he's been a friend to all of us, filled with an infectious belief that history matters and full of good ideas on how to make our work better.

I'll always be grateful to both of them.

On this project, I want first of all to thank Ken, who saw right away that something fresh could be done by interweaving the stories of the three greatest members of the Roosevelt clan. He remains creatively the least easily intimidated person I know, and I count myself fortunate that his willingness to take on challenging topics has allowed me to become engaged with so many of them, too.

I'm also profoundly grateful to my two teammates on this project: Maggie Hinders, who came up with the book's novel and inviting design, laid out the pages, and endured without complaint more changes of mind than I can count; and Susanna Steisel, whose tireless enthusiasm provided us with more than twenty thousand images of the three Roosevelts and their worlds upon which to draw, and then, when she wasn't satisfied with what we had on hand, took it upon herself to track down still more.

It's been a joy to work with my old friends Paul Barnes and Pam Tubridy-Baucom, coproducers of our film series. Their affection for all three Roosevelts now rivals my own. Both were tireless in their efforts to do justice to our subjects, and I owe a special debt to Paul, a master chef as well as a

ABOVE The morning fog lifts on Campobello Island

masterful film editor, who generously offered me sustenance and shelter during any number of New Hampshire's winter storms.

We are grateful as well to Evan Barlow, Brian Lee, and Dan White—all of Florentine Films—for their help in improving vintage images without altering them and for helping us to isolate never-before-published stills from newsreel footage.

As someone who has worked at the Franklin D. Roosevelt Library off and on for a very long time, it gives me special pleasure again to thank its extraordinary staff for all the help they gave us—Lynn Bassanese, Robert Clark, Michelle Frauenberger, Matthew Hanson, and Herman Eberhardt. We also want to give special thanks to Michelle Balos, Tara McGill, and Bill Urbin at the Roosevelt-Vanderbilt National Historic Site.

Susanna and I want to acknowledge a number of other individuals who went above and beyond the call of duty in answering our requests for illustrations and information: Allida Black, Heather Cole, and David Remington at the Theodore Roosevelt Collection at Harvard University; Andrew Conti and Ann Hartman at Corbis; Robin Glass at the Little White House State Historic Site; Steve Laise at the Theodore Roosevelt Birthplace; F. Kennon Moody in Hyde Park; Lisa Smith at AP Images; Gesine Stross at Getty Images; Amy Verone at the Sagamore Hill National Historic Site; and Linda and Duane Watson at Wilderstein.

We'd also like to express our gratitude to our invaluable interns: Carrie Hall, Megan Ruffe, Ali Scattergood, and Sam Vail.

I'd like to thank everyone at Knopf who first gave us permission to create a different kind of book and then brought to it the care and attention to detail for which they are so deservedly famous—Kevin Bourke, Kathy Hourigan, Andy Hughes, Sonny Mehta, and Andrew Miller.

Finally, I'd like to thank Carl Brandt, my agent and dear friend of more than thirty years , who did not live to see this book. I hope very much that he would have liked it.

—Geoffrey C. Ward

A Word About Sources

This book represents more than three decades of thinking and writing about the Roosevelts. It draws upon hundreds of books and thousands of documents read or consulted over that time, far too many and too various to cite here. But it could never have been written without the work of a host of other writers, including Jonathan Alter, Bernard Asbell, James McGregor Burns, Blanche Weisen Cook, Robert Dallek, Kathleen Dalton, Kenneth S. Davis, Frank Freidel, John Gunther, Edna Gurewitsch, Doris Kearns Goodwin, Joseph Lash, William E. Leuchtenburg, David McCullough, Jon Meacham, Edmund and Sylvia Morris, Patricia O'Toole, Carleton Putnam, Arthur M. Schlesinger, Jr., Robert E. Sherwood, and Edward Wagenknecht.

—G.C.W.

LEFT A portrait of Theodore Roosevelt, Sr., overlooks his son's study at Sagamore Hill

Index

ABOVE A vase of Safrano roses, the
favorite flower of Theodore Roosevelt, Sr.'s,
photographed at the Theodore Roosevelt
birthplace on Manhattan's East Twentieth
Street

ABOVE Stuffed birds shot by the young
Franklin Roosevelt and proudly displayed by
his mother in the foyer of Springwood, her
Hyde Park home

ABOVE The view of the Hudson from Eleanor Roosevelt's bedroom at Oak Terrace, her grandmother's home at Tivoli, New York

ABOVE Hunting trophies line the walls of Theodore Roosevelt's library at Sagamore Hill

ABOVE TR's desk at Sagamore Hill

ABOVE The desk at which FDR worked at his stamp collection in the Springwood parlor; the photograph is of his half brother, Rosy

ABOVE Val Kill, Eleanor Roosevelt's cottage
at Hyde Park

Illustration Credits

When there is more than one credit for a page the images will be listed clockwise from top left.

ABBREVIATIONS
AP   The Associated Press
FDRL   Franklin D. Roosevelt Presidential
    Library, Hyde Park, NY
Getty   Getty Images
HU   Theodore Roosevelt Collection, Houghton
    Library, Harvard University
LOC   Library of Congress Prints and
    Photographs Division
LWH   Roosevelt's Little White House State
    Historic Site and the Georgia Department of
    Natural Resources
NARA   National Archives and Records
    Administration
R-VNHS   Roosevelt-Vanderbilt National
    Historic Site, National Park Service
SAHI   Sagamore Hill National Historic
    Site
THRB   Theodore Roosevelt Birthplace
    National Historic Site

ENDPAPERS
Theodore Roosevelt Collection, Houghton
    Library, Harvard University

FRONTMATTER
viii–ix: NARA Motion Pictures 200 UN 1894
    X 3
xiii: HU olvwork408254
xiv: FDRL 54–18 (76)
xv: Culver Pictures PEO127 CP005 161
xvi–xvii: Brown Brothers, Sterling, PA
xviii–xix: LWH
xx–xxi: Corbis BE002835

CHAPTER I
xxii–1: HU olvwork448672
2: FDRL Exterior(1) 48–22:3790 (373); SAHI
    7756 TR & Politicians-Oversized
3: The Bridgeman Art Library NYH 154219
4: THRB 1091
5: HU TRC-PH-2 (570.R67m); THRB 1090
6: HU olvwork414377
7: THRB
8: Getty 90953712; THRB 753
9: THRB 751
10: LOC LC-USZ61–942; HU olvwork408285;
    Theodore Roosevelt Association, courtesy

Harvard University; American Antiquarian
Society
11: HU olvwork592795
12: THRB 1065
13: American Museum of Natural History
    Library 334521; HU bMS Am 1541(288,no.2)
14: HU olvwork408290
15: HU TRC-PH-2 (570.R67Sr)
16: THRB 810; HU MS Am 1454.36; HU
    olvwork361403
17: HU olvwork417631
18: HU olvwork417691
19: FDRL MO 2000.18
20: HU olvwork589985; THRB Civilian People
    & Groups, Folder 1
21: HU MS Am 1541.9 (130)
22: FDRL 48–22: 3646 (3)
23: FDRL James II Ind/Informal/Over. 48–22
    3647(13)
24: FDRL MO 2008.30
25: FDRL 47–96:119 &121
26: THRB 1105
27: NY State Archives A3045–78_1922
28: HU MS Am 1834 (958)
29: HU MS Am 1541.9 (133); LOC Manuscripts;
    HU MS Am 1541.9 (142)
30: HU olvwork377809

31: LOC LC-DIG-ds-04077
32: HU olvwork377852
33: HU olvwork422646
34: HU olvwork419533; HU olvwork420669
35: LOC LC-USZ62–91139
36: *In Thackery's London*; THRB 823
37: HU olvwork592797
38: THRB; HU olvwork375797
39: HU olvwork586918
40: THRB 3013; SAHI 1746 Album-Roma
41: HU olvwork376064; HU olvwork375846
42: Dartmouth College Library
43: Corbis IH179693
44: FDRL 91–171(1)
45: FDRL PX 91–174(68)
46: Culver Pictures peo127-cp005–162; Getty
    51966728
47: FDRL 65–25; FDRL 56–164
48: FDRL 63–520; FDRL 1898,48–22:4289(3)
49: FDRL 1900,47–96:2512; FDRL MO
    1970.29a
50: HU olvwork443833

ABOVE The chair in which FDR suffered his
fatal hemorrhage in the Little White House at
Warm Springs

51: THRB 3514; Culver Pictures NYC017 CP001 215

52: FDRL 47–96:210B; FDRL 47–96:145

53: FDRL 43–183–142

54: FDRL 1888,48–22:4182; FDRL 1897,48–22:4240(1); FDRL 1892, 155

55: FDRL 59–17(1)

56: Groton School Archives; FDRL MO 1981.13; Groton School Archives

57: Groton School Archives

58: HU olvwork387175; Naval History & Heritage Command 71839-KN

59: HU olvwork444462

60: both SAHI

61: HU olvwork379593

62: LOC LC-USZ62–26060; Getty 50596606

63: Corbis BE037652; HU olvwork375512

64: THRB 3560; THRB 1706

65: HU olvwork448687

66: Dartmouth College Library; Wisconsin Historical Society WHi-9474

67: HU olvwork448871; Oyster Bay Historical Society

68: Groton School Archives

69: FDRL Album 1899–1901 48–22:3618(68)

70: Corbis BE070643

71: Brown Brothers, Sterling, PA; Dartmouth College Libraries

CHAPTER 2

72–73: HU olvwork378128

74: HU olvwork482656; HU olvwork378060

75: HU TRC-PH-1 (9)

76: *Minneapolis Journal* 10/18/1901; LOC LC-USZ62–49568; Old Politicals Auctions/www .oldpoliticals.com; Collection of Tom Peeling

77: HU olvwork538366

78: Corbis IH185271

79: Dartmouth College Library

80: HU olvwork478407

81: HU olvwork478668; HU olvwork478692

82–83: all Berkshire Athenaeum BC Acc2; BC Acc3–3; BC Acc3–5

84: Corbis IH151733

85: Catholic University of America Archives

86: The Granger Collection, New York 0060285

87: LOC LC-USZ62–32674; The Granger Collection, New York 0078320

88: FDRL 48–22:3626(75); FDRL 47–96:174

89: HU olvwork282746; FDRL Family Papers:Harvard/Memorabilia/Undated, Box 19

90: Corbis IH183049

91: Anonymous source; FDRL 48–22:1942

92: HU olvwork482504; Archives of American Art, Smithsonian; HU olvwork482507

93: Getty 79039778

94: HU olvwork378079; University Libraries of Notre Dame

95: SAHI-8064

96–97: Golden Gate National Park Archives GOGA-1766

97: Theodore Roosevelt Association

98: UCR/California Museum of Photography 1996.0009.X68923

99: THRB 1636

100: Dartmouth College Library; UCR/ California Museum of Photography 1996.0009.X68807

101: THRB 3573; Dartmouth College Library

102: FDRL Album 294, PX54–22(64); FDRL 72–158:1

103: FDRL Album 294, PX54–22

104: FDRL 1903 48–22:3619(56)

105: FDRL Family/Business/Personal Papers, Box 3

106: White House Historical Association (White House Collection); LOC LC-D4–17399

107: SAHI/ courtesy The White House Historical Association; LOC LC-USZ62–127875; White House Historical Association (White House Collection)

108: LOC LC-USZ62–4698; HU olvwork490610

109: THRB 823

110: LOC LC-DIG-ppmsca-25853

111: LOC LC-DIG-ppmsca-25881; LOC LC-DIG-ppmsca-25894

112: LOC LC-DIG-ppmsca-25888

113: Ohio State University, Billy Ireland Cartoon Library

114: FDRL 48:22–3619(102)

115: FDRL ER 1904, 47–96:2388

116: Culver Pictures NYC017 CP001 155

117: FDRL 58–271; FDRL MO 1974.375

118–119: Keystone-Mast Collection UCR/ California Museum of Photography WX9913

120: NYT 3/19/1905; FDRL 73–182:51; FDRL Family/Business/Personal Papers, Box 37

121: FDRL MO 1968.25.33; FDRL 62–41

122: FDRL Album 478, 47–96:4927(8); FDRL Family Papers Donated/Children, Box 11 FDRL Honeymoon, folder 3

123: FDRL Album 478 47–97:284; FDRL 47–97:317

124: LOC LC-DIG-jpd-01931

125: HU olvwork533722; THRB 1214

126: HU olvwork586931

127: LOC LC-USZ62–113665; HU olvwork593145

128: HU olvwork376664; HU olvwork593020

129: LOC LC-USZ62–93742; HU MS Am 1454.48 (29)

130: Museum of the City of New York 16868

131: HU olvwork590018

132: HU TRC-PH-1 (89)

133: LOC LC-USZ62–94240

134: Dartmouth College Libraries

135: HU TRC-PH-1 (9); LOC LC-DIG-ppmsca-26061

136: Special Collections, UMass Amherst Libraries

137: Florentine Films

138: HU olvwork538723; HU olvwork538714

139: HU olvwork539199

140: Hunter College, Roosevelt House; FDRL 66–66(7); FDRL Family Papers Donated/ Children, Box 8

141: FDRL 47–96:88; 143.2 : FDRL ER 1908, 77–55(103)7

142: FDRL 73–135:1

143: FDRL MO 2005.1.2

144: Bill Stewart—Great White Fleet Collection; THRB 1186

145–147:(except br) Bill Stewart—Great White Fleet Collection

147: (br) HU TRC-PH-1(53)560.52:1908–1909

148: LOC LC-USZC4–6430

149: HU olvwork547481; LOC LC-USZ62–7757

150: HU olvwork577965

151: HU olvwork642270

152: HU olvwork592835; LOC LC-USZ62–106033

153: HU olvwork576760

154: HU TRC-PH-1 (61); HU TRC-PH-1 (62)

155: HU TRC-PH-1 (64)

156: SAHI 6595 Album-Kaiser Prints

157: LOC Lot 13455; THRB 426

159: Culver Pictures PRE034 CP005 130

CHAPTER 3

160–161: HU TRC-PH-1(67) 560.7

162: FDRL Cars driven by FDR; FDRL MO 1981.17.1

163: FDRL 48–22:4014(24); FDRL 48–22:4014(22)

164: THRB; HU olvwork382711

165: HU olvwork382650; THRB 3016

166: LOC LC-DIG-ppmsca-27830

167: Theodore Roosevelt Association

168: (b) *NY Herald* 1/19/1911

169: LOC LC-DIG-ggbain-14182; Albany Inst. of History & Art 1993.010.2256.1P

170: Corbis BE056400

171: LOC LC-DIG-hec-02215

172: Dartmouth College Library; LOC LC-DIG-ppmsca-27889

173: Dartmouth College Library; LOC LC-DIG-ppmsca-27821

174: Chicago History Museum DN-0059369; THRB 290; THRB 303

175: Corbis IH169081; Hake's Americana Auctions/www.hakes.com

176: FDRL

177: FDRL 1913, 47–96:514; *Poughkeepsie Eagle* 11/7/1910

178–179: HU TRC-PH-1(67)

180: HU TRC-PH-1(67); HU TRC-PH-1(67); THRB

181: Getty 56226093; Chicago History Museum DN058838; HU TRC PH-1(82); HU TRC-PH-1(67)

182: FDRL; FDRL 47–96:736

183: FDRL 1913, 48–22:3868(700)

184: NARA RG 181, F644 N150

185: FDRL 47–96:511

186: LOC LC-DIG-ggbain-14436; HU TRC-PH-1(73)

187: HU TRC-PH-1(73); HU TRC-PH-1(72); HU TRC-PH-2(560.81)

188: SAHI 7642 Album-Amazon

189: American Museum of Natural History Library 342099; HU TRC-PH-1(73)

190: Corbis SF13595

190–191: HU TRC-PH-1(69)

192: HU TRC-PH-1(70); HU TRC-PH-1(70); Onondaga Historical Association

193: Theodore Roosevelt Association; LOC LC-USZC4–1129

194: Hunter College, Roosevelt House

195: Getty 50870781; Florentine Films/Dan White

196: FDRL Halsted, AR Childhood w/brothers

197: FDRL Halsted, AR Childhood w/ brothers 47–97:120; FDRL FDR Jr.(1); FDRL Halsted, AR Childhood w/brothers 47–96:2344

198: HU TRC-PH-1(80); LOC LC-USZ62–84134

199: LOC LC-DIG-acd-2a05491

200: The Image Works ESVB0220162

201: THRB

202: LOC LC-DIG-hec-11935; THRB 2919

203: HU TRC-PH-1(81)

204: Unknown; FDRL 1917, 56–301(40)

205: R-VNHS 1220

206: Corbis BE003047; Corbis BE003089

207: Ball State University Libraries SPEC054–0066–0010; FDRL 1917 56–301(22)

208: HU olvwork378825; Colonel Robert R. McCormick Research Ctr.

209: HU olvwork378759; Theodore Roosevelt Association; LOC LC-USZ62–66285

210: THRB 278

211: LOC LC-DIG-ppmsca-35745

212: FDRL 1918, 48–22:3690(2)

213: FDRL 1918, 47–96:4802(66); FDRL 1918, 47–96:4802(191)

214–215: Lucy M. Knowles and Alice R. Knowles

216: HU TRC-PH-1(82)

217: THRB 884

CHAPTER 4

218–219: FDRL 1924, 48–22:3868(726)

220: Corbis SF32886

221: FDRL 1919, 47–96:681; Corbis U9821cINP

222: FDRL 48–22:3868(71)a

223: Corbis BE003065

224: Corbis BE003102

225: FDRL 42–22:3696(7); Florentine Films

226: Corbis BE002927; LOC, Recorded Sound

227: HU olvwork594514; FDRL MO 1976.43

228: Corbis BE003098

229: FDRL Album 175 77–94(126); FDRL Album 175 77–94(159); FDRL Album 175 77–94(129); FDRL Album 175 77–94(146)

230: Culver Pictures PRE033 CP003 071

231: Getty 52782481

232: FDRL 1917, 47–96:3618

233: FDRL 1927, 76–69(94); Library of Virginia Special Coll. #20022

234: FDRL Album 258, 48–22:3619(48); Hunter College, Roosevelt House; FDRL Album 207 47–96:4804(190); FDRL 1904, 48–22:3668(725)

235: FDRL 47–96:884

236: FDRL 47–96:822

237: FDRL PX54–21(89); (bottom) Roosevelt Campobello International Park

238: Museum of the City of New York X2010.7.1.6080; FDRL Alone/Childhood 81–106(1)

239: FDRL 1920–1929, 63–28(1); FDRL MO 1998.1

240: Wilderstein Historic Site; FDRL 47–96:895

241: FDRL 72–199:4

242: FDRL 72–170; LOC LC-USZ62–85394

243: FDRL 81–91(493); The Granger Collection, New York 0069304

244: Museum of the City of New York

245: Boston Medical Library, Countway Library of Medicine; R-VNHS

246: FDRL 1924, 48–22:3983(7)

247: FDRL 1924, 48–22:3983(4)

248: (tl and bottom) Boston Medical Library, Countway Library of Medicine; FDRL 48–65:1

249: FDRL 1924, 48–22:3983(3)

250: Corbis U247132INP

251: Corbis BE060249

252: FDRL 74–20 (499); *Syracuse Herald* 6/27/1924

253: LWH; FDRL 1924, 77–55(590)

254: Florentine Films; FDRL 58–348

255: Evan Cowles & Brie Quinby

256: LWH

257: Roosevelt Warm Springs Institute for Rehabilitation; LWH

258: FDRL 48–22:3700(5); FDRL 77–55(565)

259: FDRL 1927, 82–71(35); FDRL Moving Picture MP 52–3:1–2

260: FDRL Exterior(1), 58–246; R-VNHS 0803

261: R-VNHS 722; R-VNHS 843

262: Florentine Films

263: Corbis BE003323

264: (all) FDRL Moving Picture MP 73–19

265: Corbis BE003005

266: FDRL 1928, 48–22:3700(5); AP 281106045

267: AP 281106036

268: FDRL 1931, January-April 60–38(18)

269: R-VNHS 1191

270: FDRL 1934, 48–22:4185(68); Getty 3240342

271: (all) R-VNHS Home Movies, Marion Dickerman Collection

272: Corbis U640179INP

273: Corbis BE030406

274: FDRL 1930, August

275: FDRL 1930, Oct-Dec 72–7

276: © 2014 Liberty Library Corporation. All rights reserved; FDRL Papers, Gov. Not Politics, Box 39

277: FDRL 1932, June 48–22:3868(644)

278: Getty 73953610

279: FDRL MO 1947–93–190; Corbis U192981ACME

280: FDRL 1932, Sept. 24–27, 48–22:3704(254)

281: FDRL 1932, Sept. 24–27, 56–303(24); Corbis BE041202; Corbis BE003458

282: AP 321031049; LOC LC-DIG-npcc-15936

283: Theodore Roosevelt Association

284: (b) FDRL 1933, Jan 53–146

285: FDRL 1933, Aug.-Sept.

286: Corbis U643123INP

287: AP 330128035

288: Corbis U215066ACME

289: Corbis BE002788; Corbis U215493ACME; Corbis U215135ACME

290: Corbis BE039618

291: LOC LC-DIG-ppmsca-19179; Arno/*The New Yorker*: © Condé Nast

CHAPTER 5

292–293: FDRL 1933, Ap.-May Px 52–218

294: Corbis U647740INP

295: LWH; Wilderstein Historic Site

296: Corbis BE003055; FDRL MO 2009.19.2

297: Corbis BE003465; FDRL

298: Corbis BE002763

299: Getty 97284168

300: LOC LC-USZ62–93597

301: LOC LC-DIG-ppmsca-12896; Corbis BE084178; FDRL Basil O'Connor Papers, Box 6

302: Tamiment Library, New York University, *The Worker* Aug. 1933; 304: AP 330713018

303: Corbis U670008INP

304: Corbis VV6759

305: FDRL MO 1999.30

306: Getty 71186312

307: CSU Archives/Everett Collection CSUA000
CS072

308: FDRL 55–405; FDRL Hickok Papers 1932-
June 1934, Box 1

309: FDRL 1933, July 48–22: 3724(33); FDRL
1933, July 59–163(2)

310: FDRL LOC LC-USF331–030180-M2

311: West Virginia & Regional History
Collection, WVU Libraries; NARA
69-RP-1

312: West Virginia & Regional History
Collection, WVU Libraries; FDRL Alb
453 Broken Up (2) 65–585(33); FDRL WV,
Arthurdale 49–182:2(5)

313: West Virginia & Regional History
Collection, WVU Libraries

314: FDRL 1934, January 47–96:1756

315: AP aphs 52504–1; FDRL MO 2006.22.1;
FDRL MO 2011.14a,b

316: NMAH/Smithsonian, Scurlock
AC0618.001.0000029; Corbis BE052824

317: Getty 90001398; LOC LC-USZ62–139542

318: Corbis U 19720INP; Amsterdam News,
1/12/1935; AP 350719038

319: Reginald Marsh/The New Yorker: © Condé
Nast

320: LWH

321: Florentine Films; FDRL 1939, April 1–14
67–111(1)

322: U.S. Department of the Interior; LOC
LC-USZC2–1018

323: LOC LC-USZC2–922; LOC LC-
USZC4–515; LOC LC-USZC4–6179;
FDRL; Corbis AAED002605

324: Dartmouth College Library March 1936/
Gregor Duncan; AP 0902150

325: Corbis U332860ACME; Corbis
42–16646424 © 1935, The Picture Collection
Inc. Used with permission; FDRL BK 58–293

327: Corbis U315637AACME; Getty 50443121;
LOC LC-DIG-ppmsca-07216

328: (both) Wildenstein Historic Site

329: FDRL 1938, Aug. 16–31 54–300; FDRL
1940, August 73–113(53); FDRL President's
Secretary's File 139/140

330: (clockwise from tl) FDRL 1935, Jan-Feb
47–96: 1687, 1689, 1693, Px 74–20(859),
1690, 1694, 1691, 1688

331: LOC LC-DIG-ppmsca-12876; LOC LC-
USF34–046442-D; © 1934, The Picture
Collection Inc. Used with permission

332: FDRL MO 1947.93.74; FDRL 1933, July

333: Getty 53106002

334: Boston Public Library, Leslie Jones Coll.
08 06 027090; Getty 50556724; FDRL
Bankhead, William

335: Getty 50868442; The Amarillo Globe News
7/11/1938

336: Corbis BE003313; FDRL 1933, July 62–53;
FDRL L 1971.43

337: AP 350921014; FDRL 1933, June
57–247(21); Corbis U486767ACME

338: Getty 174288937; FDRL NY, NY (1)
56–131(538); American Museum of Natural
History Library PPC A45.P57, box 1

339: AP 3404170189; American Museum of
Natural History Library 286258

340: NARA Moving Picture 200 UN 1820 X 3
MPSA; FDRL MO 1947.93.405,1–2

341: FDRL 1936, May-June 56–534; Corbis
U353547ACME

342: FDRL 1936, Sept. 56–131(609); Ron Wade/
ronwadebuttons@aol.com; FDRL MO
1985–8

343: FDRL MO 1992.3; Corbis U369216ACME;
Corbis BE002611

344: AP 370120020

345: Supreme Court Historical Society; Brooklyn
Eagle 2/9/1937

346: Corbis U203276ACME; Chicago History
Museum DN-C-8769

347: Corbis BE003052; LOC LC-DIG-hec-25688

348: FDRL 48–22:3711(14); FDRL 74–20:537

349: FDRL 74–20(8); FDRL 74–20(9); FDRL
74–20(10)

350: Corbis U224713ACME

351: FDRL 74–70:904; LOC LC-
USZ62–116159; Getty 50713203

352: AP 380528036; NARA 306-NT-969–41

353: U.S. Holocaust Memorial Museum 87449;
FDRL Significant Docs. 11/15/1938; FDRL
Official File 76c, Church/Jewish:1938 box 6

354: FDRL 47–96:1886

355: Corbis U507590ACME; FDRL 56–131(185);
AP 3906190149

CHAPTER 6

356–357: NARA 306-NT-341D-2869V

358: FDRL 1941, June

359: FDRL 58–585(1)

360: FDRL MO 1941.12.40

361: FDRL MO 1971–49–16

362: NARA 200-SFF-52.

363: Getty 3232592; FDRL Significant
Documents

364: © 1942, The Picture Collection Inc. Used
with permission

365: AP 400401025; Solo Syndication/Associated
Newspapers Ltd., David Low

366: Getty 50688441

367: Corbis HU030970

368: FDRL MO 1967.10.67.1; Corbis IH179010;
FDRL 1976.46.124; FDRL MO 1976.46.181

369: FDRL MO 1967.10.8.2; Corbis BE003417

370–371: Corbis BE002965; Getty 50503200

372: Corbis U569955ACME; FDRL 1940, Oct.
43–151–3

373: Getty 51303661

374: AP 401008011; LOC
LC-DIG-ppmsca-19004

375: Getty 50618645; Corbis 42–36912127

376: FDRL 1940, Nov. 56–384; Corbis
U577123ACME

377: AP 4011051101

378: Corbis BE027915; © 1943 The Norman
Rockwell Family Entities

379: Magnum Photos PAR48475; Corbis
BE047974–1

380: Corbis BE028303

381: LOC LC-USZ62–94870

382: Corbis BE047504; LOC Mss Division, A.
Philip Randolph Papers Reel 22

383: LOC LC-USW3–024141-C

384: FDRL; Lucy M. Knowles and Alice R.
Knowles

385: Somerville Public Library

386–387: (both) FDRL Atlantic Charter
48–22:3616(17), 48–22:3616(37)

388: George Eastman house 1977:0116:1293

389: FDRL 73–113:217

390: FDRL 55–495; FDRL 47–96:3334; Eleanor
Roosevelt II

391: Corbis IH189629; Florentine Films; UC San
Diego Library Special Collections

392: Getty 50691197; AP 410707016

393: Culver Pictures PEO127 CP005 019

394: FDRL Significant Documents; Corbis
BE004216

395: Corbis BE002869

396: Corbis U631982ACME

397: FDRL 74–20(492)

398: Corbis U942531INP

399: NARA 208-PU-172I-23; Corbis BE041267

400: AP 420330074

401: LOC LC-USF3301–013289-M5; UC San
Diego Library Special Collections

402: FDRL Significant Documents

403: NARA 242-GAV-43B

404: Corbis U992203INP

405: FDRL; FDRL 62–383

406: Corbis BE002829; AP 4206261390;
Wisconsin Historical Society WHi-64627

407: Corbis U676289AACME; Getty 50598573;
Getty 106889551; Getty 53370200

408: R-VNHS 1214; Getty 3096698

409: FDRL 48–22:3832(159); FDRL
48–22:3832(156); 1942 Herblock/The Herb
Block Foundation

410: Air Force Historical Research Agency

411: Museum of History & Industry
1986.5.40746; Corbis U988936INP; Corbis
U972923XINP

412: NARA 208-PU-119JJ-10

413: BPK, Berlin/Art Resource, NY 30.003.980

414: Corbis BE046795

415: FDRL 1943 Casablanca 51–115:121

416: Argenta Images EDS 1352322488SCPIGU

417: SAHI; Alaska State Library, Army Signal Corps ASL-P175–146

418: FDRL 51–115:169(311; Corbis BE003288; FDRL 51–115:169(128)

419: FDRL 48–22:3852(127); FDRL; FDRL 1943, September

420: NARA 111-SC-188692

421: FDRL 1943 Teheran 48–22:3715(107); FDRL 1943, Oct-Dec (Not Teheran) 68–146

422: *New York Times* 3/31/1944; FDRL Bruenn Papers—FDR Medical Information

423: FDRL 72–18:330

CHAPTER 7

424–425: Collection of Edna P. Gurewitsch

426: Belle W. Baruch Foundation, Hobcaw Barony

427: FDRL Motion Picture MP71–8:68; FDRL MO 1948.22.3917.11–14

428: Corbis BE003491; FDRL 56–297

429: FDRL 64–269

430: Wilderstein Historic Site; Colonel Robert R. McCormick Research Center

431: Corbis BE001074; NARA 111-SC-189923

432: *Berkshire Evening Eagle* 7/24/1944; Corbis SF37562

433: Getty 50492763; Corbis U1132016A

434: Getty 50492950

435: FDRL Quebec Conference 58–270(1)

436: Getty 50488070; FDRL MO 76-5-8

437: Getty 50493387; FDRL MO 1969–13

438: WPA Film Library WPA 7838 (185503–1)

439: Corbis U740631ACME; FDRL MO 1945.58.20

440: FDRL 1944, November 7; NARA 111-SC-198534

441: FDRL 1944 Undated 72–53(16); FDRL Tully: Memorabilia/Christmas Cards, Box 8

442: Getty 807204

443: (all) Fox Movie Tone MTA02082B 16 053–932

444: FDRL 48–22:3659(66)

445: Getty 50693270; Corbis UKD122INP

446: FDRL 61–558(2)

447: FDRL 53–227(1a)

448: (all) FDRL 03–49, 03–47(a), 03–46, 03–51

449: FDRL Warm Springs 48–22:3659(66)

450: Wilderstein Historic Site

451: FDRL 03–48

452: Getty 92926408; FDRL Stephen Early Scrapbook

453: FDRL 61–205(17); Corbis NA002221; Corbis U1015631INP

454: Corbis BE002700

455: LWH; Corbis U756871ACME

456: FDRL ER,1948

457: Culver Pictures PEO127 CP005 096

458: Corbis BE003062

459: FDRL 1946, January; Getty 3321406

460: FDRL 1948, Dec 63–214

461: FDRL 1947, July 63–338

462: Collection of Edna P. Gurewitsch

463: FDRL 2001.8.7a,b; Collection of Edna P. Gurewitsch

464 to 465 (top): Dr. A. David Gurewitsch, © 1945–1962 Edna P. Gurewitsch

465: (b) FDRL MO 1976.302

466: Dr. A. David Gurewitsch, © 1945–1962 Edna P. Gurewitsch; FDRL MO 2010.1; FDRL MO 1972.24.14

467: Corbis RZ001307

468: Dr. A. David Gurewitsch, © 1945–1962 Edna P. Gurewitsch

469: Jules Alexander, Photographer

470: AP 600713078; Dr. A. David Gurewitsch, © 1945–1962 Edna P. Gurewitsch

471: Corbis IH154863

472: Getty 53466804

473: (both) Dr. A. David Gurewitsch, © 1945–1962 Edna P. Gurewitsch

474: Corbis BE003495

475: FDRL 65–14

476: Oyster Bay Historical Society

BACKMATTER

479–501: all photographs Daniel J. White, fugitiveblue.com

Film Credits

A FILM BY
Ken Burns

WRITTEN BY
Geoffrey C. Ward

PRODUCED BY
Paul Barnes
Pam Tubridy Baucom
Ken Burns

EPISODE EDITORS
Paul Barnes, A.C.E.
Tricia Reidy
Erik Ewers
Daniel J. White

ASSOCIATE PRODUCERS
Susanna Steisel
Daniel J. White

NARRATED BY
Peter Coyote

VOICES
Paul Giamatti
Theodore Roosevelt

Edward Herrmann
Franklin Roosevelt

Meryl Streep
Eleanor Roosevelt

Adam Arkin
Keith Carradine
Patricia Clarkson
Kevin Conway
Ed Harris
Michael Klug
Jason Lambert
John Lithgow
Josh Lucas
Carl Lumbly
Amy Madigan
Carolyn McCormick
Massimiliano Pala
Pamela Reed
Billy Bob Thornton
Joanne Tucker
Eli Wallach

CINEMATOGRAPHY
Buddy Squires
Allen Moore

ORIGINAL MUSIC
Written and Performed by
David Cieri
Piano and Accordion

ASSISTANT EDITORS
Daniel J. White
Margaret Shepardson-Legere
Ted Raviv

TECHNICAL DIRECTOR
Dave Mast

APPRENTICE EDITORS
Bryant Naro
David P. Schmidt

SENIOR ADVISOR
Geoffrey C. Ward

PROGRAM ADVISORS
Sarah Botstein
H.W. Brands
Alan Brinkley
John Milton Cooper, Jr.
Dayton Duncan
Julie Dunfey
Gerald Early
Doris Kearns Goodwin
Clay Jenkinson
William E. Leuchtenburg
Jon Margolis
Lynn Novick
Bernard A. Weisberger
Beau Willimon
David Woolner

CHIEF FINANCIAL OFFICER
Brenda Heath

ASSOCIATE FINANCIAL OFFICER
Patty Lawlor

COORDINATING PRODUCER
Elle Carriere

ASSISTANT TO THE DIRECTOR
Christopher Darling

ABOVE The view from Dowdell's Knob that FDR recommended to any Warm Springs patient who felt momentarily discouraged—the view Roosevelt himself shared with Lucy Mercer Rutherfurd three days before he died

501

THE BETTER ANGELS SOCIETY
Kim Klein, Executive Director

LIGHTING BY
Ned Hallick

ADDITIONAL CINEMATOGRAPHY
Anthony Savini
Daniel J. White
Bryant Naro

ASSISTANT CAMERA
Anthony Savini
John Romeo
Patrick Kelly
Kurt Parlow
David L. Blackburn
Linda Slater

GAFFERS
John Roche
Bryant Naro
Kevin Hunt

SOUND RECORDING
Mark Roy
John Osborne
Bob Silverthorne
Linda Spears

PRODUCTION ASSISTANT
Brandy Spear

SUPERVISING SOUND EDITOR
Erik Ewers

DIALOGUE EDITORS
Meagan Frappiea
Marlena Grzaslewicz
Ryan Gifford
Margaret Shepardson-Legere

SOUND EFFECTS EDITORS
Erik Ewers
Ryan Gifford
Mariusz Glabinski
Dave Mast
Margaret Shepardson-Legere
Ira Spiegel
Dominick Tavella

MUSIC EDITOR
Jacob Ribicoff

ASSISTANT SOUND EDITORS
Ted Raviv
Bryant Naro
Matt Rigby

SOUND POST PRODUCTION
Soundtrack New York

RE-RECORDING MIXER
Dominick Tavella

VOICE-OVER RECORDING
Lou Verrico
CityVox, New York, NY
Rob Dickson
Command Productions,
    Sausalito, CA
Stephen Dickson
POP Sound, Santa Monica, CA

DIGITAL IMAGE RESTORATION AND
ANIMATION
Richard Rubin
Evan Barlow

ANIMATED MAPS
Evan Barlow

ADDITIONAL RESEARCH
Martha Davidson
Michael Dolan
F. Kennon Moody
Polly Pettit

MAKEUP ARTISTS
Jean Carney
Roxanne Manzano

HD FINISHING SERVICES
Goldcrest Post

HD COLORIST
John J. Dowdell III

HD FINISHING ARTIST
Peter Heady

ADDITIONAL HD FINISHING ARTIST
Katie Hinsen

HD FINISHING SUPERVISOR
Tim Spitzer

FILM DAILIES
DuArt Film Labs
Deluxe New York
Movette Film Transfer
Film & Video Transfers, Inc.

ARCHIVAL FILM TRANSFER
Colorlab
Henninger Media Services

LEGAL SERVICES
Drew Patrick
Valerie Marcus
Robert N. Gold

MUSIC CONSULTANT
Peter Miller

ADDITIONAL MUSICIANS
Jonathan Barnes—trumpet and
    flugelhorn
Dan Brantigan—trumpet and
    flugelhorn
Jay Frederick—drums and
    percussion
Rubin Kodheli—cello
Putnam Murdock—guitar and
    banjo
Jordan "Jorscan" Scanella—bass
Chris Speed—clarinet
Doug Wieselman—clarinet and
    bass clarinet

MUSIC PRODUCED BY
Erik Ewers
Paul Barnes

MUSIC RECORDED AT
Mission Sound, Brooklyn, NY
Avatar Studios, New York, NY

MUSIC ENGINEER
Bryan Pugh

GRAPHIC DESIGN CONSULTANT
Mac Talmadge

INTERNS
Daehyun An
Johnny Bassett
Garrett Beltis
Marley R. Brown IV
R. Tyler Buckingham
Daniel Callahan
Robert Collins
Marci Cooke
J. Alex Cucchi
Brittany Debelis
Máximo Dell' Oliver
Monae Dewitt
Mathew Evans
Justin Foreman
Emma Frankel
Kristin Greco
Christopher Green
Erin Heinert
Caroline Heydinger
Jeff Holmes

Laura Hopkins
Stephanie Houle
Lindsay Taylor Jackson
Rebecca Branson Jones
Ethan Kamer
John Kelly
Ryker J. Kelvin
Carlene Kucharzcyk
Meredith Helene Lackey
Ian Lewis-Slammon
Fernando D. Maldonado
Adnelly Marichal
Charlie Mars-Mahlau
Emily Maysilles
Stephen R. Miceli, PhD
Julia Miville
Anne Munger
Hunter Nichols
Nicole J. Perry
Cauley Powell
Tina Rapp
Benjamin Savard
Emily Searles
Laura Shepard
David P. Schmidt
Eliza Smiley
Nathaniel Smith
Chris Snyder
Matthew A. Stanley
Natalie Thomson
Taylor Nagel

FUNDING PROVIDED BY
Bank of America
Corporation for Public
    Broadcasting
Public Broadcasting Service
Mr. Jack C. Taylor
National Endowment for the
    Humanities
The Arthur Vining Davis
    Foundations
Rosalind P. Walter

AND BY
Members of The Better Angels
    Sociey
Bernstein Family Foundation,
    Washington, DC
Ray and Barbara Dalio
The Lynch Foundation,
    Boston, MA
Mauree Jane and Mark Perry
Robert and Gillian Steel

A NOTE ABOUT THE AUTHORS

Geoffrey C. Ward is the author of seventeen books, including three focused on FDR: *Before the Trumpet: Young Franklin Roosevelt, 1882–1905; A First-Class Temperament: The Emergence of Franklin Roosevelt, 1905–1928* (which won the Los Angeles Times Book Prize for Biography, the National Book Critics Circle Award, and the Francis Parkman Prize of the Society of American Historians, and was a finalist for the Pulitzer Prize); and *Closest Companion: The Unknown Story of the Intimate Friendship Between Franklin Roosevelt and Margaret Suckley.* A longtime collaborator with Ken Burns, he has also won seven Emmys and written twenty-seven historical documentaries for PBS, either on his own or in collaboration with others, including *The Roosevelts: An Intimate History.*

Ken Burns, director and producer of *The Roosevelts: An Intimate History,* has been making documentary films for more than thirty-five years. Since the Academy Award nominated *Brooklyn Bridge* in 1981, Burns has gone on to direct and produce some of the most acclaimed historical documentaries ever made, including *The Civil War, Baseball, Jazz, The War,* and *The National Parks: America's Best Idea.* Burns's films have been honored with dozens of major awards, including thirteen Emmy Awards, two Grammy Awards, and two Oscar nominations; and in September 2008, at the News & Documentary Emmy Awards, Burns was honored by the Academy of Television Arts & Sciences with a Lifetime Achievement Award.

A NOTE ON THE TYPE

This book was set in Adobe Garamond. Designed for the Adobe Corporation by Robert Slimbach, the fonts are based on types first cut by Claude Garamond (c. 1480–1561). Garamond was a pupil of Geoffroy Tory and is believed to have followed the Venetian models, although he introduced a number of important differences, and it is to him that we owe the letter we now know as "old style." He gave to his letters a certain elegance and feeling of movement that won their creator an immediate reputation and the patronage of Francis I of France.

Composed by North Market Street Graphics, Lancaster, Pennsylvania

Printed and bound by Courier, Kendallville, Indiana